Christianese

The Language of Those Who Believe in Jesus

By: Dan Lemaire

*Restoring the soul
Making wise the simple
Rejoicing the heart
Enlightening the eyes
More desirable than gold
Sweeter also than honey
Giving warning
and granting reward.*
(Psalm19:7-14 paraphrased)

© Copyright 2017 – Dan Lemaire
All rights reserved. This book is protected by the copyright laws of the United States of America. This book may not be copied or reprinted for commercial gain or profit. The use of short quotations for personal or group study is permitted and encouraged.

For permission requests in regard to commercial use of this book or portions thereof, or for any communication with the author, use email address: christianesethebook@gmail.com

Unless otherwise noted, Bible quotations (Scripture) is taken from the New American Standard Bible, copyright © 1960, 1962, 1963, 1968, 1971, 1972, 1973, 1975, 1977, 1995 by the Lockman Foundation. Used by permission. (www.Lockman.org)

Scripture quotations marked NLT are taken from the *Holy Bible*, New Living Translation, copyright © 1996, 2004, 2007 by Tyndale House Foundation. Used by permission of Tydale House Publishers, Inc., Carol Stream, Illinois 60188. All rights reserved.

Cover
Cover design by Jena Molina Graphic Designer:
jenamolinadesign@gmail.com

Endorsement

"Words have meaning" we are told, yet the same word can have a different meaning, depending on the context or the group using it. Such it is with trying to communicate within our world. Communications are not difficult, they are impossible, particularly when what we say is not what is heard.

Every group, culture, profession or club has its own language. It is a phenomenon that develops with time and the history of the group. But that leaves misunderstandings when the meanings of words change within a subculture and between groups who use the same words to mean different things.

Finding a solution to that problem may be an impossibility overall, but my friend Dan Lemaire has tackled that impossibility. The result is an amazing list and description of words used by Christians within our church world. I congratulate Dan, not only for attempting the impossible, but for the huge work that went into this definitive work of linguistic definitions.

I've known Dan Lemaire for many years and think highly of his ethics, intellect and ability to persevere. It is those qualities that have gained for the Christian world, this work on Christianese.

Dan has a broad base of experience in the Christian world and has studied under a number of high profile teachers. His grasp of things Christian is both amazing and rewarding to those who use this work.

I highly recommend this work for those new to the Christian faith or those who are trying to understand the concepts, phrases and meanings of conversations concerning Christian concepts.

The work is arranged alphabetically so it is easy to use. Please enjoy the end result of years of work by Dan Lemaire.

Pastor David Fritsche Th.D.

[Pastor Fritsche is himself a prolific author, and he has also produced new editions of several out-of-print Christian classics. All are available at **www.dynamixworx.com**.]

These explanations of Christian words make up a unique and practical book. Looking something like a dictionary, it presents a brief but detailed overview of Christianity. Much is in these words about the God of Christianity, its church, its people, its book, its worship, its history, its opponents, its toolbox, and its struggles, all in a readable form that leads from one discovery to the next.

More than a reference book to be brought out in order to look up one word at a time, it is meant to be a door of entrance into the mysteries of faith in Jesus Christ. It is an examination of who He is, what it means to believe in Him, what He will do in response to a believing heart, where the power of Jesus is today, and how the love of God is expressed to mankind through Jesus.

It is my fervent hope that it will be read cover to cover. You could read a word a day as a daily meditation. Or take the challenge with a group of friends to examine a few words a week. You will make discoveries no matter what your background might be. You will move into a deeper understanding of the view of life as seen by Christians, those who believe in Jesus. This book is for the curious, truth-seekers, or the devoted.

Dedication

This book must be dedicated to all from whom I have learned over the last forty years. I am still learning and my only apology is that, in another twenty years, I will be able to write a better book. Constantly learning is part of the process of understanding God. It will never be a completed task.

Many of my past teachers are cited in the book for the pearls of wisdom that they have imparted. So many others are not mentioned, but are definitely part of the fabric of the belief systems presented in this writing. I will not try to list them all, but allow me to mention a few. Charlie Moore and Herb Brasher were the president and vice president of Bodenseehof Bible School where I spent five months as a brand-new Christian hearing the truths that have entirely shaped all the years to follow. They invited other stellar men to come teach for a week at a time, among them were Ken Needham teaching from the book of Matthew, George Murray a missionary from Italy who made it crystal clear that Jesus is God. Christian Bastke, whom I remember as my first Christian mystic, enthralling in the way his speaking went far beyond the meanings of words. Alan Redpath, who at almost ninety, still emanated a fierce excitement about all of Jesus. Fred Wright now leading a network of churches called Partners in Harvest. Roger Forster, now head of Ichthus Fellowship in England, who was the first Christian I heard from who was also an intellectual, deeply analyzing the study of God and making sense.

There have been several Pastor/teachers, most notably David Fritsche, who pastored for 27 years and I was able to benefit from the last half of that. So much world-view, so much encouragement, so much perspective and wisdom flowed from his ministry to all whose lives he touched.

Elim Bible School was led by H. David Edwards, and theology was taught by Mike Webster, now leading Spirit and Word Ministries. Stacy Cline, Ruth Rodriguez, Palmer Johnson, Paul Johansson, Mike Cavanaugh are just a few of the intrepid teachers whom I admire for their tenacity and passion to teach, lead, and model.

There are many others whom I have never met personally, but from whom I have learned by their books, recorded messages, and by visiting their churches. Among them are; Rick Howard, Jack Hayford, Bill Johnson, Beni Johnson, Graham Cooke, Kris Vallotton, Shawn Bolz, Mike Bickle, John Wimber, and far too many more to list. I also must include my wife Georgann whose partnership I so value. She kept me going, reviewed words, talked over ideas, edited, corrected, and came alongside in this venture all along.

Any one of the people mentioned above could have written *Christianese* and probably could have done a better job, but for some reason I was asked to do it (see the story on the back cover). And, with God's oversight, and by listening to these men and women, and by decades of daily studying the Bible, this book has emerged. I am so very thankful to all those who have been a part of conceiving and writing these brief explanations. Those who have spoken into my life spoke not only the words, but the life imparted through them. May they impart life to you also, dear reader.

Foreword

Christians have their own language which some call "Christianese." Words that mean one thing in every-day use can have a very different meaning when used by Christians. This book is about learning that language of Christians. Christianese is the language used to talk about and understand God's love. Christianese is also the language of Christians as a social group, and it can be a foreign language to everyone else. Christians talk about the "Lamb" and "sin" and the "saints," but what do they really mean? Christianese definitions in this book are intended to help the reader discover, in some depth, what many common Christian words mean.

Understanding the meanings of words makes all the difference. Since the same word can have different meanings to different people, it is essential that each word is understood in the way it is meant. For a simple example, consider a four-year-old who learns the word "fun" because Mommy says, "You are having fun with that toy!" As the child grows up, she builds broader understanding of the word based on her experiences, and the word "fun" becomes the tag for a rich and deeply meaningful part of life. By the time she is nineteen, she knows what fun is, who to have fun with, and where to have fun. Since each person grows up exposed to different things, for one young adult, "fun" could mean reading and talking about good books over coffee. For another, "fun" could mean working on the engine of a friend's car. When a friend says, "Let's do something fun," it is important to know what is meant by fun. When a Christian says something about his "walk," his "faith," or his "devotions'" what is he talking about?

How to use this book

Christianese is organized as a simple alphabetical listing of words.

Each word is followed by a brief Christianese definition, similar to a dictionary. That definition applies only to Christian society. That definition is followed by further explanation of the Christian word including a few Bible passages since the Bible is the source of most of the words and their definitions. Many of these words have had entire books written about them, and often those books are listed. Most of these definitions are a half-page or less, but they are an overview.

Bible quotes: Christians are known around the world as "Bible people" or "people of the book." Christians rely on the Bible as the handbook for life as it establishes their values and belief systems. One cannot explain Christianese without constant reference to the Bible. A few Bible verses are suggested in most of the entries for further reading. These Bible suggestions are only samples. In most cases there are many more verses that could apply to the subject. Notes in the margin of the Bible will usually lead the reader to other verses.

He and **she:** Rather than use the cumbersome "he/she" or "him/her," the reader is to understand that "she" applies to both genders, as does "he."

Asterisk: Any word that appears with an *(asterisk) before it is a word that has a full definition elsewhere in this book. Christianese words are not used to define Christianese words as much as possible, however occasionally a Christianese word will be used for a full understanding of the word being studied at the moment. An *(asterisk) tells the reader to look that word up if interested.

There are a few exceptions to the asterisk rule on the following page:

Christian and **believer:** These two words are Christianese, but appear so commonly in the explanations that they will not usually be preceded by an asterisk. Both of these words mean one who trusts in and depends upon Jesus Christ. These two words are synonyms. A full definition of each of them is in the book as a Christianese word.

Sin: This is another Christianese word with its own definition in the book. The word "sin" appears so often in the explanations that an asterisk would just be annoying. Let the reader understand that sin means wrong-doing in the Christian understanding. Sin is wrong because God defines it as wrong. Christians call some things sin that the rest of the population does not see as wrong. See the definition for a better understanding. There is no list of sins in this book. That would be a separate point of study for the reader who wants to know if something is a sin.

Bible reference system When quoting from the Bible, Christians have a system to help find every part of the Bible.
- The **address** for a part of the Bible has three parts:
- First, the **Book** is the name of that section of the Bible. There are 66 books.
- Second, the **Chapter** is a number. Each book is divided into chapters.
- Then the **Colon** (:) is a punctuation mark that divides the chapter number from the verse number.
- Last, the **Verse** is another number. Each chapter has many numbered verses.

Example: Genesis 12:3. This **address** says it is in the **book** of Genesis; it is in **chapter** 12, and it is **verse** number 3.

Some of the books in the last section of the Bible were originally written as letters to various people. Some of those letters have a number in front of them, for example 1 Timothy, and 2 Timothy. (There were two letters written to Timothy. Most people say "First Timothy" and "Second Timothy"). There is also "John," popularly known as the "Gospel of John," and near the end of the Bible, there are 1 John, 2 John, and 3 John which are short letters that John wrote also ("First John," "Second John," etc.).

Unless noted otherwise, all of the Bible quotes in this book are from the version of the Bible known as the *New American Standard*. It is used because it is the most literal translation, meaning that it translates as clearly as possible what the original writing said rather than trying to make it more readable, or more poetic.

Hopefully these word-explanations will open up a greater understanding of Christianity and the God of Christianity.

List of words, alphabetically:
Abide
Accept Jesus
Adopted
Adultery
Agnostic
Altar
Amen
Angels
Anointing
Antichrist
Apostle
Ark (Noah's)
Ark (of the Presence)
Atheist
Atonement
Babylon
Baptism of the Holy Spirit
Baptize
Beast
Believer
Bible
Bishop
Blasphemy
Bless/blessing/blessed
Blood
Body
Born again
Bride of Christ
Called/calling/call
Calvary
Canon
Carnal
Cast out a demon
Catholic
Charismatic

Children of Israel
Christ
Christian
Christianity
Christmas
Church
Circumcision
Commandments
Communion
Condemnation
Confession (of sin or wrongdoing)
Confession (of faith)
Conscience
Convicted/conviction
Covenant
Covet
Creation
Cross
Crown
Crucified
Cult
Curse
Day of the Lord
Deacon
Death
Death to self
Deity
Deliverance
Demon
Demon possessed
Denomination
Depraved
Destiny
Devil
Devotions
Discernment of spirits

Disciple
Divination
Divine
Doctrine
Dogma
Easter
Eden
Edify/edification
Egypt
Elder
Elect
End times
Enemy
Eternal
Eternal life
Eternal security
Eucharist
Evangelical
Evangelist/evangelize/evangelism
Evil one
Evil spirit
Exodus
Exorcism
Faith
Fallen/the fall
Fate
Father
Fear
Fear of the Lord
Fellowship
Firstborn
First fruits
Fish
Flesh
Forgive/forgiveness
Fornication

Free
Free will
Fruit
Fundamentalist
Garden
Gentile
Gift (spiritual gift)
Glory
God
Godhead
Gospel
Grace
Grace (prayer before a meal)
Great Commission
Great Tribulation
Hades
Hallelujah
Healing
Heart
Heathen
Heaven
Hebrew
Hell
Holy/holiness
Holy Spirit
Homosexuality
Hope
Humble
Hypocrite/hypocrisy
Idol
Inerrancy
Iniquity
Intercede
Israel
Jacob
Jerusalem

Jesus
Jesus' name
Jew
Judge
Judgment
Justified
King James Version
Kingdom of God
Lake of fire
Lamb
Law
Legalism
Lion of Judah
Lord
Lord's Prayer
Lord's Supper
Lost
Love
Manna
Mantle
Martyr
Mercy seat
Messiah
Millennium
Minister
Miracle
Missionary
Mount Sinai
Mount Zion
Natural man
New Age
New man
New Testament
Occult
Old man
Old Testament

Ordain
Original sin
Orthodox
Overcomer
Pagan
Parable
Passover
Pastor
Peace
Pentecostal
Persecution
Pharisee
Praise
Prayer
Preach
Predestination
Pride
Priest
Principality
Prodigal son
Promised Land
Prophet
Propitiation
Proselytize
Protestant
Quiet time
Rapture
Reconcile
Redeemed
Reformation
Religion
Remission
Remnant
Repent
Resurrection
Revelation (the book)

Revelation (the experience)
Revival
Righteous
Rock
Sabbath
Saint
Salt
Salvation
Sanctified
Satan
Saved
Savior
Scepter
Scripture
Second coming
Second death
Self
Seminary
Shechinah glory
Sheol
Sin
Sin nature
Sinai
Soul
Spirit
Spiritual
Spiritual gift
Spiritual warfare
Stronghold
Tabernacle
Tabernacle (or tent) of David
Temple
Temptation
Ten Commandments
Testimony
Thanksgiving

Theology
Thorn
Tithe
Tongues
Transgression
Tribulation
Trinity
Unbeliever
Unforgivable sin
Unforgiveness
Vanity
Veil
Victory
Vine
Virgin
Vow
Walk
Warfare
Will
Will of God
Witness
Word
Word of knowledge
Word of wisdom
Works
World
Worldly
Worship
Wrath
Yahweh
Yoke
Zion

Abide: old English, meaning to remain, or to dwell. Christians believe that Christ *abides* (dwells, lives) in them and that they *abide* (dwell) in Christ. This concept of living in Christ is a spiritual activity. It is an invisible form of living together, a spiritual idea, not a material one. The word *abide* is used to talk about the way in which this happens. *Abide* is an old-fashioned word for "lives," as in, "He lives with me." This is a word that gets used in the Bible, even in the modern language versions, because it has a deeper meaning than just "lives." Christians are to *abide* in Christ and He *abides* in them. (In John 15:4, Jesus instructs His followers to *abide* in Him and states that He will *abide* in them.) Furthermore, Jesus tells His followers to have His words *abiding* in them and promises to answer their prayers. The words that Jesus has said are to take up residence in believers, and it changes everything. Compare *abiding* with visiting. Abiding Christians do not occasionally visit God or spend a few minutes in the Bible now and then. *Abide* means something more like they live there.

Abide also carries a deeper meaning than just being roommates. *Abide* has more to do with relationship than with location. In other words, it does not matter where a Christian is, he believes that he is *abiding* with Jesus. The Greek word used in the Bible for *"abide"* is *"meno"* and it means a deep, loving and long-lasting relationship.

Abide is also used in the Bible to mean "permanent," or "unchanging." Christ *abides* in the Christian in an unchanging way. Jesus' love does not change; Jesus' commitment does not change. There are places in the Bible where the word *abide* is also used to mean, "It remains; it is consistent, predictable, always there." 1 Corinthians 13:13 says, "but now faith hope, love *abide*, these three…" This passage means that faith hope and love are not going to disappear. There will always be faith hope and love; they *abide*, that's just the way it is with God.

Abiding in Christ is an important principle of Christian life. Pastor/teacher Graham Cooke says that *abiding* is a key New Testament principle.

Books have been written about how to *abide* in Christ and how Christians can let Him *abide* in them. The most well known is titled, "Abide in Christ," by Andrew Murray. It covers topics such as how wisdom comes to Christians by this *abiding* presence of Christ, how one finds rest, how joy, love, and strength are found in that habit of *abiding*. A newer and very refreshing book about *abiding* in Christ is *Christ in You*, by Eric B. Johnson.

Here are a couple of additional mentions of the word: Psalm 91:1 says, "He who dwells in the shelter of the Most High will *abide* in the shadow of the Almighty." 1 John 4:12 says, "if we love one another, God *abides* in us."

Accept Jesus: to become a Christian. Christians will ask, "Did you ever *accept Jesus*?" They are asking if you are a Christian. The reason they ask it that way is because in order to become a Christian, one must *accept* that Jesus is who the Bible says He is. This is similar to the terms of agreement that one has to click on to download a new program. If that "*accept*" box is not checked, there is no download, yet very few people read through the whole "Terms of Agreement" page. In *accepting Jesus* few people read through the whole story and *accept Jesus* with a full knowledge of all the things about Him that are important to *accept* and understand. People come to God with a need, or a crisis; they *accept* what they do know about Jesus up to that point, then He meets them, and later on they gradually learn the details. God has a reputation among Christians as One whose terms and conditions are always good: there is no "catch" later on. So what is it that has to be *accepted*? This is not an exact science; there are no pat answers. Each individual comes to Jesus at first for very personal reasons.

Many come crushed with guilt, and He is the forgiver. Some come empty and hopeless and He fills and gives hope. Some come confused looking for God, and He reveals Himself as God fully. Some come full of pain and find Him to be Comfort.

Most who *accept Jesus* find themselves suddenly, curiously able to surrender their lives to Him, to be able to trust Him, to be convinced that He is the answer. Then as that surrender happens, a relationship begins to emerge, a relationship in which Jesus is totally trustworthy, totally loving, forgiving, accepting of the seeker, and powerful on his or her behalf. And so it begins. Christians call this, "*accepting Jesus* as personal Savior." It is personal because one *accepts Jesus* as an individual, one-on-one. And He is Savior because He saves people from guilt, emptiness, confusion, pain, and, ultimately, from *hell, the place where there is no Jesus, no love, no life, no joy.

People come to that place of trust and surrender in a variety of ways. Sometimes it is through reading the Bible or some other Jesus-centered literature; often it is through the conversation and encouragement of friends who happen to be followers of Christ, sometimes it is through a crisis in which the person cries out in desperation (not even necessarily out loud) and asks God to reveal Himself, or to help. And sometimes Jesus just shows up, especially to children.

Eventually, actually *accepting Jesus'* love is the key. *Accepting Jesus* to be who the Bible says He is often takes place over time; *accepting* all the truths about Him: believing He is the Son of God, that He died on a cross to forgive the sin of anyone who will believe, and that He rose from the dead to live forever. Christians find that the facts, those truths about Jesus, are a never-ending journey of discovery and transformation into becoming a person who lives in the world we know, but lives by the truths of the life of Jesus.

Accepting Jesus is a matter of faith, a matter of believing, and faith is a gift from God. (Ephesians 2:8 says, "For by *grace you have been saved through faith; and that not of yourselves, it is the gift of God.") So God calls people to faith and He also somehow makes it possible to believe. God draws; people come near; God becomes lovely and attractive to the seeker.

As the seeker engages in this process of *accepting Jesus*, the seeker becomes a child of God, *saved, with a new destiny. It is not a matter of just learning some new facts, or carrying out a ritual. Every believer will acknowledge that it was God's influence that brought them to Him, and they are keenly aware that they could have refused to accept the invitation; anyone can *accept Jesus*.

Adopted: to become an actual member of a family that one was not born into, and just as entitled as any natural born children of the family. The Bible talks about being *adopted* into God's family (Romans 8: 15-17). Christians believe that they have been *adopted* into the family of God. They do not believe the common notion that all people are children of God. The Biblical view comes in part from John 1:12 which says, "But as many as received Him [Jesus], to them He gave the right to become children of God, even to those who believe in His name." In addition, Galatians 3:26 says, "For you are all sons [or daughters] of God through faith in Christ Jesus." This is so important to God that, in the Bible, He is actually called a "Spirit of adoption." Romans 8:15-16 says, "you have received a Spirit of adoption… The Spirit Himself [God] testifies with our spirit that we are children of God."

Christians believe that they start out as children of the world, and in fact, actually opposed to the things of God. They become a part of God's family only by *adoption* because they believe in Jesus. When one does become a part of God's family, God doesn't just become the legal guardian; He is not a foster dad; He is not babysitting; it is not a symbolic formality. He becomes the "Heavenly Father," and the believers are His children. He says, "You are my son/daughter; come and receive all the benefits and privileges of being in My family." Nothing is held back. And Christians don't call Him, "Mr. so-and-so," like a child visiting from the neighborhood might. Christians call Him, "Heavenly Father, Daddy, or Abba." "Abba" means "Daddy" in the Hebrew language (one of the original languages of the Bible).

Children get in trouble sometimes, but parents don't say, "That's it! You are not my child anymore!" (At least parents shouldn't say that.) In the same way, God doesn't kick people out of the family, once *adopted*. When His children do some wrong things; even a lot of wrong things, they are not removed from the family. Christians didn't get into the family by doing everything right. They got in by faith, by believing in Jesus. So they don't get kicked out of the family by doing wrong things.

That is the beauty of *adoption*: it is settled in God's mind. A Christian is God's child. Now, she can relax and begin to function as a permanent, loved, accepted, forgiven, and empowered member of the family.

Did you know that when a child is *adopted* in the U.S.A., she gets a new birth certificate? On that certificate, the parents named are the *adoptive* parents, and there is no mention of the biological parents, or that the child was *adopted*! In the same way, when one is *adopted* into God's family, it doesn't matter what one's past was. That past life as a child of the world is irrelevant now; the one who believes in Jesus has come into God's family and receives the destiny of the only natural born child of the family (Jesus) which includes *eternal life (eternity in heaven with God) and holiness.

Adultery: being married and having sexual relations with someone other than one's own husband or wife. One of the *Ten Commandments (basic Bible guidelines for behavior) specifically prohibits *adultery*, so Christians view this much more seriously than popular culture, which tends to think of it as humorous and good material for jokes. However, *adultery* hurts people's hearts, destroys marriages, causes hatred and even murders because of the betrayal and abandonment.

When two people trust each other enough to commit to one another for life (get married), nothing can be more crushing than for one or the other to break that commitment through *adultery*.

Christians do not call it a "fling," or "an affair," or make light of it. Christians are distressed by this whenever it happens, particularly in Christian circles of friends because of the damage it does. Christians also see adultery as a bad thing simply because it destroys the beauty and the goodness that is inherent in a faithful marriage that is full of love, commitment, mutual sacrifice and partnership.

Now, beyond the literal definition of the physical act, Jesus challenges believers to think about *adultery* in a new way. He says in Matthew 5:28, "everyone who looks at a woman with lust for her has already committed *adultery* with her in his heart." In other words, the same devastation that literal physical *adultery* causes is also beginning to happen when a man or woman allows lust to run away with his or her eyes, thoughts and emotions.

Also, on the spiritual side of things, *adultery* is the term used when God's people in Biblical times pursued and worshiped other gods, (small "g") gods represented by idols. There is a reason for that: all of the people who have believed in Jesus for all history (that entire group of people, also known as the Church) are called the "*Bride of Christ" in the Bible. Jesus has loved her, wooed her, sacrificed much for her and He will marry her. Revelation 19:7-9 gives the story of the marriage of Jesus to the Church (all believers). Consequently, when believers run off with some other god, it is just like *adultery*, only spiritual rather than physical.

Here are some Bible passages that give rise to the general Christian mindset in regard to *adultery*: Proverbs 6:24-35 (a warning to the young man), Proverbs 7:5-27 (a story of what can happen as a result of *adultery*), 1Thessalonians 4:3-8 (guidelines for sexual behavior), and 1 Corinthians 6:13-20 (an explanation of why *adultery* is so seriously damaging). Jeremiah 5:7-9, Ezekiel 23:37 (places in which worshiping idols is referred to as *adultery*). See "*fornication" also.

Agnostic: a person who has concluded that God, if He exists, is unknowable. This word is the label given to a certain type of belief that some people have about God. *Agnostics* have a major question about the existence of God. They think there may indeed be a god but that one can never know for sure. "God, if such a thing exists, is unknowable," is the conclusion of the *Agnostic*. Many of today's Christians started out as *agnostics*, which indicates that there is clearly a way to move from a rigid belief that God is unknowable, to discovering Him to be personal and known.

Altar: the place where one makes a sacrifice. In the first part of the Bible, the *Old Testament, before Jesus, the *altar* was a large square pan of fire where animal sacrifices were given to God by burning them (Exodus 38). This *altar* was used until the *Temple was destroyed in AD 70. The word *altar* is still used symbolically in modern-day Christianity meaning a place to go to give something up to God. Many Churches call the front of the church the *altar*, and people go up there to pray and lay things down before God (things like a bad habit, a tormenting situation, or a life of sin that is laid down before God at the *altar*, and new life is given by God). Sometimes the leader of a church will say something like, "Come to the *altar* and give it to God." Christians by faith are able to give things up to God on that *altar*, and see them completely gone, as if burned up and reduced to ashes, and the smoke goes up to God as a soothing aroma (Numbers 29:8, 13, 36).

Amen: "yes," "truly," or "I agree." Since this is used mostly at the end of a prayer, it would be easy to think that "*amen*" means, "This is the end of the prayer." However, if someone says, "*amen*" at the end of a prayer, it means, "Truly, this is my heartfelt communication to God." If one says it in response to the end of someone else's prayer, it means, "Yes, I agree." ("Those are my heartfelt words to God too.") In normal conversation outside of times of prayer, Christians will also just use the word to mean "I agree."

And in the Bible, it's not just used at the end of the prayer, but also sometimes at the beginning of something that is said, and it is used to add emphasis. In some churches, the preacher will say, "Amen" at the beginning of a sentence. Jesus did this too, but it's usually translated "verily" (or, "truly") in the Bible.

Jesus is also called "the Amen," in Revelation 3:14. It becomes one of His names, and it seems to mean that Jesus is the true One; He only speaks the truth, or that He represents the agreement of the heavens.

For some examples of *amen* at the end of a prayer or a statement: Ephesians 3:20- 21, and Revelation 22:21 (the last word in the Bible). For examples of *"amen,"* ("truly" or "verily") at the beginning of a sentence, see Matthew 5:18-26, Matthew 18:3.

Angels: powerful spirit beings from God sent to help people on earth. *Angels* are spoken of in many places in the Bible and it is apparent that they are beings who are superior to man (superior because: *angels* are not going to die, not in opposition to God, and they are "Mighty in strength, who perform His word, obeying the voice of His word" Psalm 103:20). *Angels* are engaged in service to God, and are seen in the Bible as beings who protect people and sometimes assist people or bring messages, encouragement, and help. Hebrews 1:13-14 states that *angels* are sent out to help "those who will inherit salvation." Luke 15:10 says that, "there is joy in the presence of the *angels* of God over one sinner who repents." (The *angels* get happy when someone accepts God's love and decides to begin to worship Him only.)

Angel means messenger. One of the most famous *angels*, Gabriel, came to Mary the mother of Jesus (Luke 1:26 begins the story). Gabriel also came to Daniel with a message (Daniel 9:20-21). Often in the Bible the "*Angel* of the Lord" appears, and sometimes it is clear that the *angelic* being is actually God. (Judges 6:11-24 is the beginning of a story in which the Angel of the Lord appears and sets a plan in motion.)

Some *angels* (about one third of them, most Bible scholars agree) are fallen from following God and follow Satan as their leader (see the definition of *demons). They are no longer called *angels*, but are evil spirits.

Contrary to popular belief, Christians do not believe that people become *angels* when they go to heaven. *Angels* are an entirely different kind of being than humans. Angels are sinless and immortal, and though they worship Jesus, they do not know Him as Savior (since they never have done wrong things, they do not need to have a Savior to save them from a wayward life and the subsequent judgment). They do not have material human bodies, but are spirits. Consequently, they are usually invisible, although they may appear as physical men or women when necessary, and often with wings, like all the classical paintings of *angels*.

For some other examples of *angelic* appearances and activities read: Matthew 4:11 (ministering to Jesus after 40 days of fasting), Acts 12:6-11 (coming to Peter in prison), Psalm 91:11-12 (promise of *angels'* help), Matthew 18:10 (the guardian *angels* of children), Hebrews 1:13-14 (sent out by God to help).

Anointing: to apply oil on someone ceremonially, and it symbolizes power or capability being given to that person. You will hear Christians say, "That was *anointed*," or, "The Pastor really had the *anointing* today." They mean that the power of God was working through the Pastor (or whoever) beyond his or her natural ability. There was an empowering from God. *Anointing* is power that is imparted to the Christian by God, also known as "unction," that gives Christians capability beyond what they can accomplish in their natural strength. Pastor Shawn Bolz writes that the anointing is about a relationship with God, not just a connection to His power. *Anointing* means supernatural capability, and it can be used to signify a supernatural assignment, usually to be a king or priest, but always yielded to God in relationship.

When a believer is called upon by God to do something, if he attempts it without *anointing*, it will be of little effect. Usually God calls His people to do things they cannot do; things that are beyond their capability or things that they are naturally fearful to do (in their own strength). Thus, Christians are driven to depend upon God in their obedience to serve God, and He sends the *anointing* to get the work done in a powerful way that surprises everyone and is very effective. Any Christian can be amazingly *anointed* and serve God powerfully; the only requirement is for the Christian to be yielded to God, admitting that he cannot do, in his own strength, what God wants him to do, and then do it anyway, depending upon God's help through His *anointing*. Christians most appreciate leaders that have the *anointing* and they desire to become people who function under the *anointing*.

Anointed Christian leaders can sense God's empowering, and they expect miracles, and those leaders know how to live in the *anointing*. It is not some mysterious power that God drops randomly here and there; it is available from God when it is sought after and depended upon by mature Christian leaders submitted to God. Jesus was *anointed*; Luke 4:18 says that Jesus said, "The Spirit of the Lord is upon Me, because He *anointed* Me to preach the gospel to the poor."

Some other famous historical figures that were *anointed*: David, when he fought Goliath (1 Samuel 17), displayed supernatural ability from the *anointing* he had received in 1 Samuel 16:13. Daniel in the lion's den (Daniel 6), Peter healing the cripple (Acts 3), Paul and Silas arrested, singing in prison and miracles occurred (Acts 16:19-34). *Anointing* in the Bible is often symbolized by pouring oil on the person to be *anointed* (oil represents the Holy Spirit of God). Saul becomes king (1 Samuel 10:1), David becomes king (1 Samuel 16:13), Aaron and his sons become priests (Leviticus 8:10-12).

Antichrist: one who is either a false christ, or opposed to Christ. John the apostle is the only one who used this word in the Bible (1 and 2 John). He used it when writing to people around 90 AD. He was pointing out certain people who were teaching things that diminished the clear definition of Jesus Christ as the Son of God who came in the flesh, that is, born as a real human being and yet fully God. In those early days of Christianity John, who knew Jesus very well, wanted Christians to know that there were some very wrong things being taught about Jesus. Some were teaching that Jesus was not fully human, replacing Jesus with a mysterious god-man figure, and those teachers John called *antichrists*.

He also used this word to refer to people who taught wrong things about Christ by teaching that He was not born of a virgin (see *Jesus and *Virgin), since this is an important part of Christian understanding of Jesus. He was born by natural childbirth, so fully human, however His Father was not Joseph, the husband of Mary. His Father was God; He was conceived miraculously. Therefore He did not inherit the sin nature that every other person was born with since the *fall, and He was able to live sinlessly.

In his writing, John also seemed to imply that there was yet coming a certain person who was the *Antichrist*, and most scholars believe that the *Antichrist* is a person who will arise as a famous and powerful influence in the world. He will be empowered by demonic powers from the devil, and he will be in clear opposition to Jesus Christ and His people.

John only used the word in 1 and 2 John, but it is believed that the *Antichrist* was also predicted by some of Daniel's visions (Daniel 7 and 8); that he is the same as the "man of lawlessness" in Paul's writing (2 Thessalonians 2:3); that he fits the prediction Jesus made about false christs in Matthew 24:24, and that he is the same as the *beast in Revelation 13:8. Opposition to the *Antichrist* by Christians will result in being persecuted or killed, but the *Antichrist* himself will be destroyed by Jesus (Revelation 20:10).

Apostle: one who goes out as a representative may be called an *apostle*, meaning an ambassador or a delegate. Usually the 12 men whom Jesus chose to be with Him and carry on His work are the ones called His *apostles*. They are: Simon (later renamed Peter), Andrew, James and John (the sons of Zebedee), Philip, Bartholomew, Thomas, Matthew, Simon the Zealot, James (the son of Alphaeus), Thaddaeus (elsewhere known as Judas the son of James) and Judas Iscariot (the one who betrayed Jesus). However, there are others in the Bible, who are also called *apostles*: Paul and Barnabas are *apostles* (Acts 14:4-14) Andronicus and Junias (or Junia which would be feminine) (Romans 16:7), and there are many others who are not specifically named. *Apostle* means "delegate" or "one sent forth." The Bible speaks of Jesus Himself as an *apostle* sent from God (Hebrews 3:1).

Today there is disagreement among Christians whether there are modern day *apostles* or not. Some Bible scholars insist that there are no longer any *apostles*. Other scholars say that the gift of *apostles* to the church according to Ephesians 4:11 is still ongoing, and that the Church still needs *apostles* as much as it still needs the other ministries listed there (*prophets, *evangelists, *pastors, and *teachers). The *Catholics believe they hold the only authentic succession to the *apostolic* office (in the person of the Pope). Others have various criteria that must be fulfilled in order to be an apostle.

In churches that are comfortable with the idea of *apostles* for today, there are those who are recognized as *apostles* without any definite requirements or credentials other than a long history of faithful and inspired leadership. These people carry a gift of being able to help believers move forward into new understanding for this season of time, something that can be validated in the Bible. Apostles usually have the ability to function with supernatural capability in a wide range of the supernatural, and they are people of integrity.

Since *apostle* means "one sent forth," these modern day *apostles* tend to carry a message that has an emphasis that is so clear and powerful, that it is evident that they were indeed sent forth to break new ground, bring new understanding and build up believers as chosen delegates of God and His Kingdom.

Ark (Noah's): the most famous boat in all history; the one that carried all the animals and eight people through the biblical flood. (The whole story is in Genesis chapters 6 through 8.) God was grieved that mankind had become so wicked, and sent a great flood to destroy all the earth, but He gave favor to Noah and told him to build a big boat to survive the flood and to take along his family and some of all the varieties of the animals. When the boat was completed and loaded, it rained until everything was under water. Months later, when the water subsided, Noah, his family, and the animals went out to live and populate the earth again.

A great mystery surrounds what happened to the ark after it ran aground on Mt. Ararat (in present-day Turkey). Christians would love to find concrete archaeological evidence of the ark. Many claim to have such evidence, but the skeptics are not convinced.

Perhaps more importantly, Christians see the story of Noah's Ark as a parallel to their own story. Christians, like Noah, are among the few who believed that God was providing a way to be saved (from the flood, in Noah's case, and from hell and death, for the Christian). Christians see themselves, like Noah and his family, as among those who were carried miraculously to safety and a new life (by the ark for Noah, and by faith in Jesus, for the Christian). Noah and his family entered the ark believing what God had told them. They were saved from the flood and taken to start life anew. Those who refused to believe in the ark, as Noah told them what God had said would happen, died in that time of judgment.

Christians believe that those who ignore the invitation of Jesus to be saved will experience death and separation from God's love forever. This is one of the reasons that John 3:16 is so commonly quoted by Christians: "For God so loved the world, that He gave His only begotten Son, that whoever believes in Him shall not perish, but have eternal life." Believing in Jesus is like getting on the Ark. One must believe it is the only way out of predicted judgment.

Ark (of the Presence): a special piece of furniture in the earliest place of worship for the Jewish people, the place where God was present. It was made famous by the Indiana Jones movie, "Raiders of the Lost Ark." The *"Ark of the Presence,"* or the, *"Ark of the Covenant,"* is an actual historical item described in great detail in the Bible (Exodus 25, beginning in verse 10). Briefly, it was a wooden box (*"ark"* is an old English word for "box") completely overlaid with gold. It was about four feet long, two feet wide and two feet high, standing on short legs or carried by long poles like a stretcher. On the top, which was a removable lid, were two figures of gold angels, one at each end, facing each other with wings outspread. Inside were a few sacred items. There were stone tablets upon which the *Ten Commandments were written. There was a jar of the *manna (the miraculous food that God supplied in the wilderness), and a few other things of spiritual and historical significance. The lid of the *ark* was also called the "*Mercy Seat," and that was where the cloud of God's glory (also known as the *Shekina glory) rested. The *ark* was kept in the most holy place of the *Tabernacle of God, at first, and later in the *Temple. Numbers 7:89 says that Moses would go into the place where the *ark* was and God's audible voice would speak to him from just above the *ark*. After the time of Moses, it was usually only seen by a human being once a year when a priest would enter that place and ask for forgiveness for the people on a holy day called the Day of Atonement, or Yom Kippur.

The very existence of the *ark*, which God directed them to build, makes a statement that God desires to be recognized and present among His people, and He desires to make a way for man and God to meet. He says in Exodus 25:8, "Let them construct a sanctuary for Me, that I may dwell among them." God will eventually accomplish His desire to dwell among His people. Revelation 21:2-3 describes God's very real presence among those who get to heaven, and 22:3-5 says that His people will see His face, and His presence will be so brilliant that there will be no more night.

Originally built at the start of the 40 years in which God's people traveled in the desert, (about 1500 BC) the *ark* was carried along as they moved from place to place. When they reached the *Promised Land (the territory that God promised to give them, now the country of Israel), it remained in the *Tabernacle (the tent that they built for it) in a city called Shiloh, but eventually it was captured by enemies, forgotten for about 20 years and finally returned to Jerusalem by David the King. He put up a tent for it and organized worship leaders to worship continually before the *ark* (1 Chronicles 16:37). The *ark* was eventually put into Solomon's Temple (1 Kings 8:1-11) where it remained until the destruction of the Temple in about 586 BC. It is never mentioned again in the Bible and presumed destroyed, but folk tales keep alive the possibility that it is being kept secretly somewhere. Some historical writing, not in the Bible, says the *ark* was hidden in a cave by Jeremiah before the temple was destroyed. (Maccabees 2:4-8). But it has never been discovered or reappeared.

Atheist: a person who believes that there is no god. *Atheists* have concluded that God does not exist. Both believers and *atheists* are operating by faith. There is no concrete proof for the existence or non-existence of God. Even to be anti-God is to acknowledge the possibility of God, just as the person of faith must admit he could be wrong about God.

Lee Strobel was an *atheist* and the legal editor of the Chicago Tribune. He set out to investigate the evidence for the claims of Jesus. He wrote the book, *The Case for Christ* which documents his journey during that time, and how he changed from *atheism* to being a believer. This is not an uncommon journey among people who are sincerely seeking the truth.

Atonement: that which removes any uncleanness or erases any wrong doing so that relationship may be restored. *Atonement* means making up for things that have broken a relationship. Christians believe that Jesus is their *atonement*. There was originally an unstained love relationship between man and God. The first disobedience of Adam and Eve, the first people created, broke that relationship. Christians believe that because of that, mankind is by nature more prone to do wrong than right. Every person has done wrong things that have broken the relationship with God, so mankind's natural position, instead of in love with God, is to be an enemy of God. That is how seriously Christians view the breakup between man and God. So there is a need for the wrong to be made up for, or *atoned* for, in order to heal the relationship, in order to be close to God.

Because the broken relationship is with God, and not just another human being, the compensation, or the *atonement* to make up for the wrongs has to be a perfect act by a perfect life. Before the time of Jesus, *atonement* would be made by a priest through the sacrifice of a perfect animal (Numbers 15:27-28). Christians believe that Jesus is perfect, lived a perfect life as a man, and through His own death, He worked a perfect *atonement* for mankind so that God and man can be friends, but <u>only if</u> a person believes in the perfect *atonement* of Jesus. The *atonement* is there for everyone, but each person must come to believe in it individually in order to receive it and be restored into relationship with God.

In the human realm, making up for wrongs is usually done by making an apology, giving a gift, or doing something nice. In mankind's relationship with God, the wrongs that have been done by man will result in death. This is much more serious than *atonement* for a personal insult or offense. In the first parts of the Bible, blood is seen to represent life, and only blood is the acceptable *atonement* for the forgiveness of the wrongs done against God. The blood of an animal was used to *atone* for sin. *Atonement* required that a substitute would shed blood (die) in the place of the offenders. Therefore to <u>be</u> the *atonement*, Jesus died on the *cross, and shed His blood. Hebrews 9:26 says, "He [Jesus] has been manifested to put away sin by the sacrifice of Himself." His *atonement* makes it possible for those who desire closeness with God to draw near. Anyone who wants to know and love God may have the opportunity to freely enter into that mended relationship with God by accepting Jesus as the *atonement*. Jesus suffered a painful and shameful death in order to <u>be</u> the *atonement*, which demonstrates how important it was to God to provide the opportunity for people to come back to Him. It was worth an incredible cost to Him in pain and suffering.

Jesus is the only *atonement*, Christians believe. A person cannot be good enough to *atone* for his or her own wrongs, because to be reconciled to God, one must be perfect, not just nicer for a little while, and not just apologetic. Without Jesus' perfect *atonement*, the Christian believes he or she is impossibly separated from God, but Jesus' *atonement* is complete, bringing full restoration of the love relationship between man and God.

Babylon: the name of the ancient city where the Tower of *Babel* was built. (To read the full story, see Genesis 11:1-9). The people of Babel decided to build a tower that would reach to heaven and perhaps make them famous. Christians see the story of the tower of *Babel* as a city's misguided attempt to reach heaven without God's help.

The name Babel means "The Gate of the Gods," and it was built in the Plain of Shinar, which means "strange power." It is seen that they tried to get all the benefits of Heaven by human effort and by accessing alternative spiritual forces (the devil), instead of by seeking God's ways. George Otis Jr., in his book *The Twilight Labyrinth,* states that God was not opposed to the tower as such, but He was not willing to allow the *Babylonians* to succeed in creating a connection to deceptive and misleading devilish spiritual forces. God did not allow that. He confused the languages of the people, and the project stopped, and the people were scattered. In the Biblical record of history, the city or kingdom of *Babylon* shows up several thousand years later as the enemy of the people of God, the Jews. Armies from Babylon destroyed *Jerusalem (the Jews' most important city), destroyed the *Temple (their place of worship), and took much of the general population captive back to *Babylon* as slaves.

Babylon is seen in the Bible as opposed to God and God's people. In the parts of the Bible that were written after Jesus (the New Testament), *Babylon* came to represent a spiritual kingdom that is a counterfeit of the Kingdom of God. For today's Christian, *Babylon* represents the present-day self-centered world system that now enslaves many people to materialism, fame, sex, drugs, and alcohol.

Babylon, in Christianese, represents any other system of belief that draws people away from Jesus. Christians commonly quote Revelation 18:4 "Come out of [Babylon], my people, that you may not participate in her sins and that you may not receive of her plagues." Many of today's serious Christians reject the materialism and media-hype in American culture as a way to come out of *Babylon.*

Christians use the term *Babylon* to mean virtually anything in the system of the world that can become a distraction from knowing and pursuing God.

"*Babylon,*" in Christianese, includes unrestricted seeking of pleasure and money, adoration of famous people or fame itself, seeking non-Christian spiritual powers (see *Occult), and worship of idols. *Babylon* is about rejecting God's guidelines for life and it leads to immoral passions, witchcraft, deception, pride and arrogance, murders, slavery and the selling of human lives. Judgment is predicted for all of this in the book of Revelation, chapters 17 and 18.

Baptism of the Holy Spirit: an encounter with God that is part of becoming a Christian. The Bible says that "by one Spirit [the *Holy Spirit] we [Christians] were all baptized into one body…we were all made to drink of one Spirit." (1 Corinthians 12:13). This is the basis of the idea of the *baptism of the Holy Spirit*. Some Christians see this as automatically part of coming to faith in Jesus. Other Christians believe that it is a separate second experience with God that launches the believer into a whole new level of relationship with God. All Christians believe that the power of the Holy Spirit is necessary to be a Christian, on the basis of the above verse. Those who study how God works among men attempt to clearly define whether this *baptism of the Holy Spirit* is a second experience or an initial experience of faith, but they are unable to agree. There are Bible stories about people being filled with the Holy Spirit at the same time they came to believe in Jesus (Acts 10:44-48), and there are stories of believers receiving the baptism of the Holy Spirit later, after coming to believe in Jesus (Acts 19:1-7).

Many believers today do have a second (or third, fourth) experience with God, a strong sense of His presence in power, that dramatically amplifies their enthusiasm about God and their partnership with His purposes, including *gifts of the Holy Spirit that enable powerful things to be done in the name of Jesus. These experiences are often labeled as the *baptism of the Holy Spirit*.

Another Bible verse that contributes to this conversation is Ephesians 5:18 which says, "be filled with the Holy Spirit," which in the original language indicates that this filling is to be continuous and on-going, not a one-time experience, or a second experience. Jesus is the baptizer in the Holy Spirit, as it was predicted by John the Baptist when he said, "I baptized you with water; but He will baptize you with the Holy Spirit." (Mark 1:8). Christians need the *baptism of the Holy Spirit*, no matter what form it takes or when it happens. (See *Holy Spirit.)

Baptize: to dip or to wash. *Baptism* is a ritual in which one personally and publicly declares faith in Jesus; that he or she has become a Christian. A person who wants to be *baptized* as a Christian, is usually submerged under the water by another Christian and then lifted out (some churches just sprinkle a little water). *Baptism's* meaning is clear: it represents a washing away of sin, a cleansing. The cleansing has already happened because believing in Jesus brings about the forgiveness of all wrong; it is all washed away, but the *baptism* provides a public, visual image for what has happened already in the invisible spiritual realm.

Another clear meaning of *baptism* is that it represents death and resurrection. Going under the water symbolizes death, and the believer's death to the old selfish ways is a central idea in Christian thinking. Coming up out of the water of *baptism* symbolizes being raised from the dead, to a new life, a new beginning. When someone is *baptized*, it is a statement of identification with Jesus' death and His resurrection. This is a central idea to Christians, clearly written about in Romans 6:3-11: the Christian who has been *baptized* has been "united with Him in the likeness of His death [and]...in the likeness of His resurrection."

One thing that *baptism* says when one chooses to be publicly *baptized* is, "I am serious; I am becoming a Christian." However, people become Christians by faith and not by *baptism*.

Baptism is not necessary to become a Christian. Christians get *baptized* <u>after</u> the fact of coming to believe in Jesus, partly in obedience to Jesus' command to *baptize* those who believe in Him. A person who is a Christian, but did not ever get to be *baptized* is still heaven-bound if he or she dies. Many put it this way; "*Baptism* is the outward sign of the inward transformation."

Interestingly, Jesus got *baptized*. For Jesus, His *baptism* was not because He was becoming a Christian (someone whose sins are washed away) because He did not have any sin that needed to be washed away. It was because He was symbolizing that He was going to eventually accept the sin of the world upon Himself (which He did when He was nailed to the cross) and <u>that</u> sin, mankind's sin, was going to be washed away by His own submission to literal death, symbolized by His water baptism. This event was so important that all of God's presence was there to participate in it. A dove representing the Holy Spirit was there, and a voice form God the father spoke, and Jesus of course was there. So another statement made by a *baptized* Christian is, "I receive Jesus' taking my sin within Himself when He was on the cross for me, and dying for me so that I don't have to die in my sin."

There is some controversy among Christians surrounding *baptism*, some insisting that the person should be immersed under the water, some saying it serves the purpose just to sprinkle the new believer. It seems that the more relevant question is whether the person being *baptized* has a heart-felt and faith-filled understanding of what he or she is doing.

Another debate centers around whether it is proper to *baptize* infants. In this, the more relevant question is to consider what the statement of the parents is regarding this child. If it is, "We will raise this child up to know Christ's salvation," then later the young person must make his or her own profession of faith and choose to get *baptized*.

Infant baptism does not make babies into Christians; it is at best, just a statement by parents of the intention to bring a child up to know Jesus.

Here are some Bible passages about *baptism*: 1 Peter 3:21-22 (as an appeal to God), Romans 6:3-11 (a detailed explanation of identifying with Jesus), Colossians 2:9-14 (what happens spiritually when one is *baptized*). Mark 1:9-11 is the account of Jesus' *baptism*.

Beast: a scary looking creature described in Revelation 13 that is involved in ever-increasing opposition to Christians. Most scholars think the *beast* represents a politically powerful individual, a world leader. The early church believed that the *beast* was Emperor Nero of Rome, who certainly met the biblical descriptions of the beast. Modern teaching about the *beast* usually presents it as a thing of the future.

It gets confusing because there is more than one *beast* written about in Revelation. The first *beast* is given power by a dragon (clearly representing the devil) and then there is a second *beast* who deceives people into worshiping the first *beast* and a statue of the *beast*. And then they together set up a one-world government system of controlling food so that no one gets food unless they worship the *beast* or the statue of the *beast*. Those who do worship the *beast* will get a mark on their right hand or forehead.

So when today's Christians talk about the *beast*, they are referring to future events, a time in which there will be widespread persecution, deception and confusion. Revelation says that the *beast* has a number and it is 666, and some people get very nervous about that number for that reason. (Interestingly, Emperor Nero's name can come out 666 using numerology). It is understood that the intention of the *beasts* and the dragon is to keep people from worshiping Jesus. The devil, represented by the dragon, is clearly in opposition to God, to Jesus, and to the people of God, the Christians and Jews.

There is a bumper sticker that says, "I have read the end of the Book, and God wins." In the end of Revelation (19:19-20, and 20:10) it states that the *beast* and the devil are to be thrown into the lake of fire. In the big picture then, it is important to the Christian to be a person who is not deceived, to be prepared for difficulty and severe opposition during this life on earth, and to be strong, able to resist the powerful influence of the *beast*, however that really looks. Christians are destined to end up in heaven rather than follow the lead of the *beast*, whoever he is. Those closing chapters of Revelation equip the Christian to face the adversaries that will come. Harold Eberle's book, *Victorious Eschatology* has more information on Nero as the *beast*.

Believer: a Christian. *Believer* is one of the words meaning any person who has accepted that Jesus has forgiven her of all wrong doing and has been given newness of life. Of course the word *believe* came to be used as synonymous with "Christian," because the basis of Christianity is *belief* (*faith). Christians have moved from being doubters to being *believers*. One does not become a Christian by obeying the commandments of God (as important as that is), or Christians would be called "obey-ors," or "the obedient ones." Christians are not called "achievers," or "workers," or "the good," or "the perfect," they are just called *believers*. Anyone can *believe*. Not everyone can carry out all those other things.

Believing, as a Christian is more than agreeing with the historical facts about Jesus. That alone does not make one a *believer*. Christian *belief* includes trust in Jesus and dependence upon Jesus. Well known Pastor Charles Stanley says that a person who will jump from a burning building into a net held by the firemen below is required to *believe* in this profoundly important way. The net is offered by the firemen and the plan is clear. She can stay and die, or she can become willing to *believe* in the alternative offered by the firemen, an equally frightening choice.

The decision to jump is *belief,* trust and dependence. To be saved she must *believe* in that way. The *believer* depends on the alternative plan of God that is offered for life itself.

What do Christians *believe?* They *believe* that Jesus loves them in a very personal way, one-on-one. They *believe* that Jesus and God the Father (who are one, see *trinity) have completely forgiven them of all wrong doing because of Jesus' death on the cross. In 1 Corinthians 15:3, "Christ died for our sins," is a Christian statement which does not make any logical sense to the natural mind, but Christians have come to understand that statement enough to *believe* it is true. They also *believe* that they have received a new life and a new desire to be good. These are some of the most basic *beliefs* of the *believer*. The Bible is full of other truths that Christians learn over a lifetime and come to *believe*. 1 Corinthians 15:1-8 gives a brief summary of what Christians are taught and come to *believe:* that "Christ died for our sins according to the Scriptures, and that He was buried, and that He was raised on the third day according to the Scriptures, and that He appeared [to many after His resurrection]." Romans 10:9-10 gives a summary of what it takes to be a *believer:* "If you confess with your mouth Jesus as Lord, and *believe* in your heart that God raised Him from the dead, you shall be saved; for with the heart man *believes*, resulting in righteousness, and with the mouth he *confesses, resulting in salvation." This passage makes it clear that one must *believe* with enough conviction to be eager or excited to <u>say</u> something about it.

Bible: the Christians' book. Most religions have a book or books which followers of that religion read, and that book presents the inspiration and the explanation of the religion, and usually a set of rules or guidelines. Christians look to the *Bible* for all of that and much more. Well-known Women's Minister Carrie Sandom presents the idea that the *Bible* is a Book of promises and their fulfillment.

God makes promises throughout the *Bible* and then fulfills those promises. And even though some of those promises are yet to be fulfilled, Christians hold dearly to those promises, such as the promise of *eternal life in heaven, or the promise of Jesus' *second coming. Other scholars see the Bible as God's love letter to mankind. Well-known professor George Grant of the King's Meadow Study Center says the Bible is about *creation, the *fall, *redemption and *restoration; everything in the Bible is involved with one of these themes.

Christians regard what the *Bible* says as God's message to mankind, directly inspired by God. God wrote the Book using the minds and pens of many different people over a period of about two thousand years. Over all that time and through all those different authors, the Bible presents an interrelated narrative and a progressive revealing of God and His love and His plan for mankind.

Christians believe that there is spiritual power in the Bible. It is power to change lives, to reveal mysteries, and to find connection with God. Serious Christians call the Bible the Bread of Life, and they need it every day for the sustaining of Christian life. There is genuine excitement among Bible people about the book. It is loved; it is found to be exciting; it is the source of answers to life's questions; they carry it around with them, refer to it often, and tell others what it says because they find it to be so full of life.

There are two parts to the Bible: the Old Testament and the New Testament. The Old Testament (O.T.) is almost three times as long as the second part, the New Testament (N.T.). The O.T. was written entirely before the birth of Jesus, and the N.T. was all written after the death and resurrection of Jesus. "Testament" means covenant, or agreement. The O.T. is the old agreement between God and man (actually there were several agreements in sequence recorded there) and the N.T. is the new agreement which was made possible by the life, death and resurrection of Jesus.

The N.T. is viewed as final and complete: no further revelation is needed, and the Bible is all that any person needs for spiritual life and eternity.

There are 66 separate books in the Bible, and they are somewhat arranged in the order they were written, but it gets mixed up, because some books overlap, and some are just out of order historically, so it takes a little study to figure out how it all fits together. There are 39 books in the Old Testament and 27 in the New Testament. There is much about Jesus in the Old Testament that foretold that He was coming, who He was, and what He was to accomplish. (Much of that was not understood until He fulfilled it.) So Christians have a poetic little slogan: "The New is in the Old contained and the Old is in the New explained."

Clear evidence exists that shows that the Bible has not been revised over the thousands of years that it has existed. In that respect, it stands alone among the other religious books. (Most other religious books differ greatly between today's version and those from hundreds or thousands of years ago.) Strict rules have guided all copying of the Bible from the earliest times to ensure that absolutely nothing was changed from one copy to the next, especially back when all that was done by hand. So Christians believe that what they have today as the Bible is pretty much the same as what people were reading in the first century and even earlier.

Christians believe the Bible to be without errors in the original writing. See *inerrancy for more on that. (Inerrancy means that, since God wrote it, of course it has no mistakes.) So there is nothing written in the Bible that is a mistaken idea about who God is, about history, or about what God intended. There is no second-guessing with Christians reading the Bible; they just read it and believe it.

There are many different versions of the English Bible. English versions of the Bible are not significantly different from one another in meaning, but differ in style. For example, the King James Bible, (KJV) is written in 17th century English, and the New King James Version (NKJV) seeks to update the language. Other popular modern versions include New American Standard (NAS, a very literal translation). The New International Version (NIV), the English Standard Version (ESV), and the New Living Translation (NLT) are in styles for easier reading. Some other versions are paraphrases, which means that they are not translated word for word, but just loosely carry the same meaning, like the Living Bible (TLB) and The Message (Msg). *Catholic Bibles do include a few extra books called the Apocrypha which *Protestants didn't think belonged in the Bible, but otherwise it is the same.

Also, there are many study Bibles, which means they include a lot of notes and comments which can really be helpful. A few well respected study Bibles are: The Spirit Filled Life Bible, the Thompson Chain Reference, Ryries Study Bible, the New Living Translation Study Bible, and the New Inductive Study Bible.

There <u>are</u> some versions of the Bible which have been altered to change the meaning in order to promote the ideas of certain *cults (groups that are not really Christian, though they <u>claim</u> to be Christians, and claim to be the only ones who got it right). These are, most notably, the Mormon Bible (the *Joseph Smith Translation* or *Inspired Version*, portions of which are included in other books by him even though they usually read the King James Version of the Bible) and the *New World Translation*, which is from the Jehovah's Witnesses. Both of these versions present a non-biblical altered and inaccurate picture of Jesus, and have clearly been altered to fit the goals of those groups.

There are about 7000 languages in the world, and it is the goal of many Christian groups to translate the Bible, or parts of the Bible, into every language.

According to Wycliffe Bible Translators, only 531 languages have the whole Bible. Another 1329 have just the New Testament, and another 1023 have at least one book. 2195 are in process, and 1860 languages, so far, have no one translating the Bible into those languages.

Bishop: a person with authority in the concerns of the church, a leader. Some churches call their Pastor, *Bishop*. Some churches use the term *Bishop* to mean someone who has leadership over a large territory, or over a number of churches, over a number of Pastors. Many churches do not use the term at all. It comes from a Bible word written in the in the original Greek: *episcopos*. This is translated into *bishop* in the *King James Version of the Bible, but also translated as *overseer* or *elder* in other versions. It means superintendent, or officer in charge. Very clear guidelines are given in 1 Timothy 3:1-7 as to the qualifications necessary to become a *bishop*. This is an appointed position. In various ways, the organization of the church appoints the *Bishop* to that position because the *Bishop* is recognized to be old enough and wise enough to be a good leader and a good example.

In the Army, there are firm titles given to the leaders: Captain, Major, Lieutenant-Colonel, etc. In the Christian church, unlike the army, there is no standardized ranking of authority in the churches. There are levels of authority, yes, but the names of the titles given to those various leaders differ from one church to another.

There is a generally recognized set of leaders called the "five-fold ministry." These are found in Ephesians 4:11, and they are *apostles,*prophets, *evangelists, *pastors, and teachers. This is not necessarily a ranking of these leaders in order of authority, but identifies a team (each one is necessary) given to the church to fill out all of the necessary operations of the living church that Jesus is building (1 Peter 2:4-5).

The *bishop*, as a member of that team, could have outstanding ability in any one of those roles, or could have a mix of several, but he would be recognized as an example to all, in his overall personal conduct, in his marriage, with his family, and even in his reputation outside the church. When the church calls someone a *bishop*, that person is a highly respected leader.

Blasphemy: to speak evil of God or to deny the goodness of God, <u>or</u> to claim to be God. *Blasphemy* means either talking about God, who is truly sacred as if He were not, <u>or</u> calling something equal with God that is not sacred, not God. For example, it is *blasphemy* to say things about God that are not true, things like: "God is dead," or, "He is a liar." It is also *blasphemy* to talk about things that are <u>not</u> of God as if they were actually from God. People who claim to <u>be</u> God are *blaspheming*. (Oddly enough, when Jesus stated that He was God, people then accused Him of *blasphemy* because they did not recognize that He was telling the truth. John 10:33.)

Blasphemy was a big deal in Jesus' time, but now, at least in American culture, people *blaspheme* commonly and are not even aware that they are doing it. For example, just saying, "Oh my God!" Is technically *blasphemy*, because it is really just an exclamation, but the words spoken are those of a sacred prayer. Any use of the names of God as a figure of speech, or as a swear word, is *blasphemy*. In the 10 *Commandments (God's guidelines for human life) the third commandment is about *blasphemy*: Exodus 20:7, "You shall not take the name of the Lord your God in vain." It apparently has always been a problem that people tend to use God's name in some meaningless or inappropriate way.

Why is it a problem? *Blasphemers* are not big enough, in the grand scheme of things, to offend God. However, it is a problem because believers use the name of God to call on Him for help, for comfort, for peace, for blessing etc., and using that name when one doesn't really want to contact God disrespects that God is available to intervene and give help.

Similarly, in Exodus 20:7 "...the Lord will not hold him guiltless who takes His name in vain." God keeps that Name reserved for those times when a person intends to seek God's intervention, wisdom, healing encouragement, or help.

Bless / blessing / blessed: something good that flows from God to a person, from one person to another, or from a person to God. (Yes, people can bless God.) To be *blessed* is to feel good or to receive good things. To *bless* others is to help them feel good or to be generous with them. *Blessing* flows from God to His people (those who believe in Him), and *blessing* flows from His people to God, and from God's people to others who may not even know God or the source of the *blessing*.

Another very specific meaning of *blessing* is to receive the approval and affirmation of a parent or a leader. Having the *blessing* of the most important people who care, gives a Christian the assurance of being well supported by those who mean the most in life, and ultimately, by God's *blessing*. Gary Smalley and John Trent PhD. wrote a book called *The Blessing* that explains this important idea very well, especially the importance of receiving the *blessing* of parents.

God's *blessing* to His people is simply the way He most likes to be toward them. He loves to *bless* His people: to prosper them; to make them happy, secure, loved, full of joy, freedom and peace. But then Jesus takes believers beyond the normal view of *blessing*. Jesus says, "*Blessed* are the poor, *Blessed* are the meek," (the famous "Sermon on the Mount," beginning with Matthew 5:2-11). He is declaring that these things are the highest good, and are ultimately good for those who are in those conditions. *Blessing* goes far beyond the material world that tends to be the center of attention in most people's lives.

A prayer at meal time is also called a *blessing*. When Christians give thanks for the food and receive it as a *blessing* from God, they agree with God's intention to *bless* them by giving them food.

God gives food according to Acts 14:17; "He did good and gave you rains from heaven and fruitful seasons, satisfying your hearts with food and gladness." They also are agreeing with God's promise to *bless* the food and keep them from sickness, which is in Exodus 23:25.

Blood: Jesus' blood. When Christians talk about "the *blood*," they are always talking about the *blood* of Jesus. Here is the significance of Jesus' *blood*. When Jesus was killed, first, there was a whipping, which was always a very severe and bloody punishment. There were the nails driven into hands and feet, big nails tearing *blood* vessels open. There was also the crown of thorns shoved down over His head, so He did bleed a lot on the cross; and finally after He was dead, the soldiers made sure He was dead by piercing His heart with a spear, which let out a lot of *blood* and water (water, because when a person dies, a sac of clear liquid forms around the heart.)

Prior to the coming of Jesus, if a person was feeling guilty for something he or she had done wrong (sin), God's forgiveness was gained by bringing a lamb, a goat, a bull, or even a pigeon if the guilty person was poor, and then draining of the *blood* from the animal; sacrificing it, and ceremonially sprinkling the *blood* around in certain ways. In this way the wrong (sin) was ritually forgiven. When Jesus arrived on the scene, He was called, "the Lamb of God who takes away the sin of the world," by John the Baptist (John 1:29). What John the Baptist meant was that the *blood* of Jesus would take away sin like the *blood* of sacrificial lambs had. The difference was that Jesus would take away the sins of the <u>whole</u> world, <u>once</u>, for all time, not just the sin of the one individual who brought a lamb, and not just temporarily until the next sins needed to be forgiven, but even sins which had not yet been committed were to be forgiven by Jesus' *blood*.

Jesus was the Lamb of God provided by God to fulfill the forgiveness that had been seen only temporarily in the sacrificial lamb.

The importance of *blood* and its role in granting forgiveness is very clearly explained in Hebrews 9:13-14. The *blood* of Jesus accomplished the eradication of sin, guilt and shame, which had only been hinted at in the thousands of years before His appearance. God's heart has always been to provide a way for total forgiveness to be granted.

For those who are not culturally accustomed to compensating for any wrongdoing, the idea of pouring out *blood* to compensate for sin, or to forgive sin just seems strange. However, for many cultures and religions around the world, killing a goat, a chicken, or a cow, and doing things with the *blood* as a forgiveness ritual is quite common. There seems to be a primitive understanding that *blood* is required to make the guilt of sin go away. Jesus' *blood* comes in to finally make all the chicken and goat killing unnecessary. He's got it covered for all mankind forever. No more man-made rituals. Every person who has become a Christian is forgiven through faith in Jesus because of His *blood*.

Body: "The *body*" is usually short for "the *body* of Christ," and "*body* of Christ" means the church. Christians will say, for example, "Yeah I am part of the *Body* that meets over on Main Street." This term can mean a local church, but it also can be used to mean the whole church world-wide, or citywide. If everything that prevents churches from being united was removed, the result would be the Body of Christ. Christians have been divided up into different camps, called *denominations (for example, Presbyterians, Episcopalians, Catholics, Methodists, Assembly of God, etc.) However, one denomination will say of another, "We are all part of the *Body*." There is a longing among Christians to be united, and the idea of "*body*" expresses the unity.

This use of the word *body* also comes from the idea that Christians now living in bodies continue the work of the Gospel which Jesus began when He was here, in His body. So Christians are the on-going, still-working *body* of Christ, doing what He did: healing, teaching, and glorifying God the Father.

Christians are His arms helping, His feet going, His mouth speaking, His heart loving and caring, His eyes seeing, and His ears hearing. An ear is different from an eye, and in the same way, Christians are different from one-another, yet all those parts are needed working properly together to be a *body* (1Corinthians 12:18-27, Ephesians 1:23, Colossians 1:18).

Another meaning of *body* in Christian speaking is the literal human *body*, as in "*body*, soul, and spirit." It is used to literally mean flesh and bones, the material of the human *body* apart from the spiritual side of human life. Christians are to use self control in dealing with the appetites of the *body*, and they are to present their *bodies* as useful to God, as instruments of doing good, bringing recognition to God, helping others to come to know God. (1 Corinthians 6:13-20, Romans 6:12-13.)

Born again: to have a new life, a new start, through believing in Jesus. *Born-again* has become a favorite term used by American Christians to mean a genuine Christian, as opposed to someone who just goes to church and practices religion in a shallow way, or thinks he's a Christian because he was born in America. *Born again* means a real, total, complete "new start." There is no more basic new start than to experience a new birth, just as a new baby starts out with new life, unstained, no bad reputation, no guilt, no shame. This is what Jesus means when He says. "Unless one is *born again* he cannot see the kingdom of God" (John 3:3). Being *born again* is a spiritual experience; it happens in the spirit or in the heart. It is not a mental experience; understanding only comes later. It is not an experience in the body, although it eventually affects the body powerfully. The kingdom of God that Jesus talks about begins when one is *born again*, when one gets saved. Well-known pastor Bill Johnson says that the kingdom of God is simply the place of the dominion or rulership of the King. That means each person who is *born again* has become a place of God's rulership, because that person is submitted to Him, and that life is profoundly influenced by the Kingdom of God all around.

This new start or new birth is from the Spirit of God. It's not like a New Year's resolution that will succeed or fail only on the strength of one's will-power. Being *born again* is empowered by God. Jesus calls it being "born of the Spirit," which is very different from being born in a natural birth. When one believes in Jesus, it doesn't mean that one just accepts a new set of strict rules for life. It means that a person is given new spiritual power to change and to want to do better; power to desire to do God's will. *Born-again* Christians have an unnatural excitement about God that shallow religious people do not have, and nonreligious people really can't understand it at all. *Born-again* Christians aren't perfect, but they are forgiven and "*reconciled" with God, that is, friends with God again, no longer under His condemnation, no longer opposed to His ways. Being *born again* doesn't mean a person has accomplished something to please God. It really means that person has decided to receive, by trusting God, the forgiveness and cleansing that God offers to anyone who will believe. Born of the Spirit means that new believer is spiritually alive rather than either spiritually dead, or spiritually deceived. Until one is born of the Spirit of God, a person's spiritual life is either subject to all manner of deceptive fake spiritual ideas, or there is no interest in any of it. *Born-again* Christians are really the only kind of Christians there are. According to Jesus (John 3:3-8), "You must be *born again*." For further study: Romans 10:9-10 is about how to get *saved; "saved" in that passage, means the same thing as "*born again*." Ephesians 2:8-9, says that faith by which one gets saved is a gift of God (people are *born again* by faith).

Bride of Christ: the bride of Christ is the church. It is true that Jesus never got married, however, there are several obvious parallels between marriage, as we know it, and Jesus' relationship to the Church. Jesus, the Groom has "fallen in love" with the Church, and she loves Him. All who believe in Him get to be His *bride,* and He longs to spend all of eternity with the believers of the church.

The grandest expression of love for all time is that Jesus literally died for the spiritual enrichment of His *bride*. He courts them, drawing them to Himself. The *bride of Christ* is the church: the whole church, worldwide, all believers, everywhere.

Several places in the Bible it is clear that Jesus intends to marry, not thousands of brides, but the one *bride*, the church. (Revelation 19:7-9, 21:9-11, Ephesians 5:25-32)

Some men get nervous about being called the *bride of Christ*, but it is nowhere even suggested that it is a sexual union. (Similarly, some women get uncomfortable being called "sons of God.") It is all figurative language, descriptive of the type of relationship Christians have with God, and not specific to one's gender.

Jesus made great sacrifices to open the way through which people might be able to become His *bride*. One way to think about it is that, although Jesus loves common people, He is Royalty, so special provisions had to be made to make it possible for Him to be together with the common people. The church had to be made as Royal (holy), and as wealthy (spiritually), as He is. Believers are made Royalty (they are adopted into His family). Believers are made holy (believers are in Christ, and holy because He is holy). And believers are made to be as wealthy as He is (believers are joint-heirs with Christ, Romans 8:17) that is, they get the same inheritance for God that He does.

It may also be helpful to observe this: God the Son, Jesus, has asked the Church to accept His pledge of love forever, as one does in a wedding. Believers enter into a forever love relationship with Jesus when they say, "I do." (I do take You to be my love forever.) That's what it means to become the *Bride of Christ*. 1 Peter 2:9 says that the Church is royal and holy. Revelation.19:9, describes the great dinner that will be held in honor of the marriage of Jesus to the church, all of the believers for all of time.

Additionally, in the prophecies of Hosea and Jeremiah, the idea of the people of God being a *bride* to God was first introduced. (in the book of Hosea, the entire theme of the prophecy is that God's *bride* has been unfaithful, see Hosea 1:2, 2:2, 3:1). And Jeremiah 2:2 speaks of God's people as betrothed to Him, His *bride*, at the time that they followed God through the wilderness to the Promised Land, their new home.)

Called / calling / call: a God-given role; that which God is directing a believer to be or do in this life. These words about the *call*, when spoken by Christians, mean something about being chosen by God for a specific purpose or task. "He's got a *call* on his life." Or, "He is *called* to preach." Or, "She's following a *calling*." One who is *called* of God knows that she is being asked to spend her life in serving God. Often this is a realization that God is able to impress upon a believer as she grows up or matures in the knowledge of God. God often *calls* an individual to do life so very differently from how she would spend her life if left to herself, consequently it is often difficult for a believer to discover her *calling*. Christians pray, "God confirm this to me if it is Your *calling*, and help me to be willing." One may be *called* to *preach or to *evangelize, (see definitions), to counsel or to give mercy (like medical help, financial help, help with food, etc.) or to pray for people (*intercession); there is obviously an infinite variety of *callings*. With each *calling* are many *gifts that empower the *called* one to carry out the work effectively.

In one sense, all Christians are *called*. Romans 8:28 says that God is working all things together for good for those who are *called* according to His purpose. It is clear that this applies to all believers. Not all believers obey the *calling* of God, because it requires one to step out of the comfort zone and represent Christ. All Christians are *called* to help others to know God, and to be the kind of influence in daily living that broadcasts the goodness of God.

Romans 11:29 says that the *calling* of God is never to be withdrawn. (That passage is about how the Jewish people were *called* to represent God to the world, which many Christians believe is still true.) 2 Timothy 1:8-12 talks about how Timothy and Paul were *called*. Hebrews 3:1 says that all Christians are, "partakers of a heavenly *calling*." Philippians 3:14 says that the *call* of God is always upward. Romans 8:28-30 is kind of a general explanation of what the *calling* of God leads to in a believer's life.

Calvary: the name of the place where Jesus died on the cross. It is a little hill outside of the city of Jerusalem where crucifixions took place. (Crucifixion, nailing a convicted criminal to a wooden cross, was the standard means of execution used by the Romans in those days.) The place's name translated is, "the skull," and in the Latin language it is "Calvarius," which the King James Bible writes as "*Calvary.*"

When Christians speak of *Calvary*, it is usually with reverence as the sacred place where Jesus changed everything (see the *cross). "The way of *Calvary*" is spoken of as the way that Christians need to walk as they follow Jesus. The way of *Calvary* is the way to lay down all selfish interests, learn to love sacrificially, and become authentically humble. There is a classic book called "The Calvary Road," by Roy Hession that explains the idea of *Calvary* as applied to the Christian's life. Another book is by Amy Carmichael, titled "If." It is about what she calls "Calvary love," the love expressed by Jesus, the One who would die for those He loves.

Calvary to the Christian is loaded with sacred implications about Jesus' atoning sacrifice, about the true life of humility that Jesus lived and Christians are to follow, and about the scandalous injustice which took place that day and the way God turned it all around to work the greatest act of liberation from injustice ever accomplished.

Canon: the collection of letters and books which are included in the Bible. This word *Canon* speaks about the way in which certain writings were chosen to be included in the "*Canon* of Scripture," the Bible. Since the Bible is a collection of books and letters written by many different people over thousands of years, the decision about what to include and what to leave out was obviously an important one. Whether to include something or not was always based on whether what was written seemed to be inspired by God, or "God breathed." In 2 Peter 1:20-21, Peter says that, "...no prophecy of Scripture is a matter of one's own interpretation, for no prophecy was ever made by an act of human will, but men moved by the Holy Spirit spoke from God." Peter makes it clear that the Bible he knew, which was only the Old Testament (all written before Jesus) was really written or inspired by God. Later, as the New Testament (written after the time of Jesus) was compiled, the same standard was used to determine whether to include various selections or not. That standard is called the *Canon*.

Decisions were made over the centuries, and by many different groups of individuals and a general agreement as to what was really the Bible did not emerge until almost four hundred years after Christ. It is amazing, actually, that there could be such an agreement about which writings to choose from a wide collection. (Christians believe that God's Spirit was overseeing the process, bringing unity and agreement.) Certain selections apparently just stood out as inspired by God and the rest paled in comparison, and were not recognized. Christians trust that what they have as the Bible today has been divinely verified by the best minds with the most sincere hearts for God. These people examined and compared the various things that had been written. And with the help of God, these men (and probably women too) agreed, "This is the Bible," and other writings about similar topics were excluded.

It is accepted in Christianity, that the *Canon* was ultimately determined by God; there are no mistakes, no books were included that shouldn't have been, and none were left out that should have been included. Nobody brings up that sort of question in mainstream Christianity. It has been settled for over 1500 years. For Christians, the Bible is untouchable. B.B. Warfield writes about this in his classic book, "The Inspiration and Authority of the Bible."

Carnal: of the physical body without concern for spirit or soul. Someone who is *carnal* runs his life on the basis of his physical pleasures and comforts. Appetites of the body such as hunger, lust, greed, and ambition are the controlling factors of the *carnal* life. The *carnal* person doesn't think about what God's commands are, or take into consideration the needs of others. He doesn't even think about what is best for his own long-term wellness, and will sometimes do things that are damaging to himself, for example binge-drinking and drug abuse. "*Flesh, fleshly, and *natural man" are other terms used by Christians to apply to the same phenomenon, *carnal* living. This is the manner in which most non-Christians live. It is very natural.

Carnal living, or living according to the desires of the physical body, the flesh, is always opposed to how God would lead one to live. Romans 8:5-8 says, "For those who are according to the flesh set their minds on the things of the flesh, but those who are according to the Spirit, the things of the Spirit. For the mind set on the flesh is death, but the mind set on the Spirit is life and peace, because the mind set on the flesh is hostile toward God; for it does not subject itself to the law of God, for it is not even able to do so; and those who are in the flesh cannot please God."

Often, *carnal* living involves doing things that the *carnal* man knows to be wrong, but he does them anyway. So there is a problem in the *carnal* man, that he is constantly doing things he knows he shouldn't. In fact, he's often doing what he really wishes he could stop doing.

This is a problem for many people; wishing they could live a more pure life than they actually do. Christianity addresses this problem in a different way than religions. (Remember that Christians do not consider Christianity to be a religion, but a good relationship with God.) Religions recognize that being a good religious person goes against man's natural, fleshly, or *carnal* desires. It is hard work to be religious, so religions lay down strict rules to get people to turn away from carnal desires; drinking, sex, stealing, etc. in order to become religious or spiritual. (Severe rules and harsh punishments are religion's methods to get people to quit doing those activities.) In contrast, Christianity's solution to the problem is for the believer to <u>die</u> to the natural life by identification with Jesus' death on the cross (see *cross and *crucified.) A Christian has experienced a death when he put Jesus in charge of his life. The *carnal* man died. Then Jesus took over, and the spiritual side of the Christian came alive, was filled with the Spirit of God, and the Spirit became the one in charge instead of the flesh. Flesh could no longer run things the way he used to, in fact the flesh is dead (Romans 6:1-11). Galatians 2:20 says, "I have been crucified with Christ: and it is no longer I who live, but Christ lives in me; and the life which I now live in the flesh I live by faith in the Son of God, who loved me and gave Himself up for me." This passage is a popular verse for Christians to memorize, because it wraps up the whole process of how to give up the old ways and become a new person. If a person chooses to believe in Jesus, he has the opportunity to replace the old man, (fleshly, *carnal*, natural self) with the new self, "which in the likeness of God has been created in righteousness and holiness of the truth," (Ephesians 4:22-24). For further study, 1 Corinthians 2:14-15 compares the *carnal* person to the spiritual person. Spiritual things are foolishness to the *carnal* man.

In contrast to the *carnal* life, the Christian is meant to live spiritually, aware of what is real. He lives in newness of life as a new man, following after the Spirit of God, not by self-effort, but by receiving the power of Jesus' resurrection-life by faith. Galatians 5:19-25 compares the "deeds of the flesh" (what the old self will tend to do naturally) to the "fruit of the Spirit"(what the new self will begin to do supernaturally, by the indwelling life of God in the believer).

Cast out a demon: the procedure used by Christians to remove evil spirits from a person's life. This is also called "*deliverance." Demons are evil spirits, usually invisible, but having definitely observable influence. See "*demon" for a full definition. Christians understand that demons are up to no good; they can torment, lie, and bring oppression to people. Demons can cause illness in a person, addictions, uncharacteristic behaviors, and socially unacceptable behaviors. Often, the afflicted person cannot stop that behavior. There are two levels of demonic influence that Christians talk about. Christians refer to demonic activity as "oppressed or "demonized" when it is less extreme, but when it gets more severe, and there seems to be a power that has taken over a person in some specific ways, then it is referred to as "possessed." Either way, *casting out the demon*, or *deliverance, is the way to get help.

Demonic presence in a person may be *cast out* by a Christian who knows that believers have authority to tell demons to leave. In Luke 10:19 Jesus says "behold, I have given you authority...over all the power of the enemy." It is part of normal Christianity to have that authority, and the demons must do with the Christian says as a representative of Jesus, or face the consequences from God. Demons will often try to bully and frighten Christians into thinking that they are powerless to *cast the demons out*. Strong faith and understanding of the Bible is necessary to stand firm.

Once a demon has been *cast out,* the problem that was caused by the demon will be miraculously gone, and the person who was incapable of change has changed. There is a classic story of Jesus *casting out a demon* in Luke 8:26-36. The man went from being scary, naked, and crazy, to being peaceful, clothed, and in his right mind in an instant. (For more on deliverance read Don Basham's book. *Deliver us from Evil*, or Kenneth Hagin's *The Believer's Authority*.)

Catholic: or Roman Catholic, a large percentage of the Christian Church worldwide, which is distinct because of its organization, its ideas about God, and its worship styles. Some people will say, "I'm a *Catholic*," instead of "I'm a Christian." There are *Catholic* churches, Catholic schools, *Catholic* priests and *Catholic* nuns. A *Catholic* is a certain type of Christian. Catholics had a lot of power and were the only well organized form of Christianity in the 1500's. A deep religious division developed among Christians when some Catholics objected to the standard Catholic beliefs and practices of the time, and the result was two branches of Christianity: *Catholics* and *Protestants. Over the centuries, a lot of blood has been shed, tragically, when one of these groups has attacked the other, and in some places there is still deep division between them.

The *Catholic* Church is led by the Pope; what he says is the final authority. He presides in the Vatican, a small city within the city of Rome, but he travels and has authority worldwide, over the *Catholic* Church. There is a very strict order of authority from the Pope on down through Cardinals, Bishops, Priests, Deacons and so-forth. In their style of worship, Catholics use rituals, robes, candles, and incense smoke. They recite standardized prayers that everyone has memorized, and have a very formal, or what is called "liturgical" style of church service, which they call "Mass." One of the big differences is that Catholics absolutely revere or even worship Mary the mother of Jesus. Protestants do not.

So the *Catholic* Church is distinct in its leadership, and in its worship style from the Protestants, but both have much the same understanding of the essentials of Christian faith, so *Catholics* are not a *cult. (Cults look like Christians, may claim to be Christians, but are <u>not</u>. They usually do not believe that Jesus is God. *Catholics* and Protestants do.) It is generally agreed that *Catholics* are Christians as much as Protestants are *Christians*. There are protestants and *Catholics* that would disagree, but most people from both groups accept their differences and are willing to work together within their communities.

Charismatic: Christians who believe they have received the power of the Holy Spirit as a gift from Jesus. "Charisma" is a Greek word (the language in which parts of the Bible were written). It means a "gift of grace," a gift given by God just because He wants to be generous. A renewal of interest in these spiritual gifts took place in the 1960's and continues to the present, not as a formal division in the Christian church, but in fact infiltrating virtually every sector or denomination of Christianity. There are *charismatic* Catholics, *charismatic* Lutherans, Baptists, Methodists, etc. The *Holy Spirit (the Spirit of God) gives these *spiritual gifts to believers. These are gifts of abilities which are always supernatural, miraculous, beyond the natural, and empowered by the Holy Spirit. These gifts result in renewed fervor for the faith, increased likelihood that a miracle will be prayed for and experienced, and a general enthusiasm about everything within Christianity (Fellowship, prayer, worship, study of the Bible, missionary endeavor, etc.).

Children of Israel: these are the *Jews or *Hebrews, descendants of one man, Abraham. Abraham had one son, Isaac, and his son Jacob was also known as Israel. Jacob (or Israel) had twelve sons who, in time, became twelve tribes and a whole race of people called Jews or Hebrews, or "children of Abraham," but the most common is the "*children of Israel.*"

Abraham was the first person to whom God began to reveal Himself with a plan to bless all mankind. God promised Abraham that his descendants would be a blessing to all the world (Genesis 12:1-3). But Abraham and his wife had only one son, Isaac, but that was the beginning of what eventually became the whole race of the Jews, the *children of Israel*. These people became God's chosen people (not God's favorite people). They were chosen to be representatives of God in the earth and to worship only Him instead of worshiping idols like the rest of the peoples of the earth. They were to be examples of what can happen when God alone is worshipped. God continually worked with this people redirecting them back to Himself when they got distracted. The story of how that all happened fills much of the Bible. Eventually, Jesus, who was also a descendant of Israel, came to make a way for all the *children of Israel* to finally worship Him in Spirit and in truth, and to represent Him in the earth.

Furthermore, Jesus opened the doors for Gentiles (people who are not literally descended from Israel) to become the people of God too. Christians see themselves as spiritually *children of Israel,* or descendants of Abraham. The whole point of the *Children of Israel* was to glorify God and make Him known in the earth, and that is the point of the church as well. Christians have gone out to the remotest parts of the earth in joyful obedience to Jesus' command that they do so. Jesus told the first Christians, "Go therefore and make disciples of all the nations, baptizing them in the name of the Father and the Son and the Holy Spirit, teaching them to observe all that I commanded you; and lo, I am with you always, even to the end of the age" (Matthew 28:19,20). Galatians 3:29 says that all who belong to Christ are Abraham's descendants *(Children of Israel).*

Christ: the Messiah, the anointed one, expected one, savior. *Christ* is Jesus' title, not Jesus' last name. It is what He is. He is the *Christ*. *Christ* is the Greek translation of the Jewish word "*Messiah."

Messiah and *Christ* in two different languages, both mean the anointed one, or the expected one, or Savior; the one who is going to come and set everything right again. See *Messiah for more on that. There is an expectation of a yet-future Messiah among many peoples besides the Jews. Buddhists, Muslims, Hindus, Indonesians, and some American Indians, notably the Hopi and Sioux, and many other peoples around the world have an expectation of a Messiah. Christians believe that Jesus is the Messiah, the *Christ* who has already come and who will come again to finalize the work He began and set up His final Kingdom.

One other thing; there are a lot of religious groups that are not really Christian, but have the Bible and say some things about Jesus in what they believe, and they use the word *Christ*, but in very odd ways, like "the *Christ* principle" or, "*Christ* energy." Not everyone who talks about *Christ* means the same thing as Christians. See *cults.

Christian: one who worships Jesus Christ as God. A *Christian* person believes in Jesus and lives the new life that Jesus promises to give to those who believe in Him. *Christians* are changed people because they believe. *Christians* are not people who have done something for God, they are people whom God has forgiven, transformed, and given newness of life. *Christians* are *disciples of Jesus, that is, they are interested to learn about Him and they want to be like Him. *Christians* believe in Jesus as presented in the Bible: that He is the Son of God; that He provided love, forgiveness and new life to all who believe.

Anything, any group, or any person that is called *Christian* is reflecting the influence of Jesus Christ in some way, or at least attempting to. It has been said that Jesus Christ has had more impact on mankind for good than any other person in history. His influence continues to be a powerful life-changer all over the world. This book exists because there is a whole language that is used by *Christian* people who have come to faith in Jesus Christ.

Christianese is the language that is used among those who are talking about the influence of Jesus. Jesus' influence is many-sided, and most people are influenced first in one way, then, as they get to know Him better, that influence broadens. Perhaps the first change that believers experience is the change from following selfish pursuits to following Jesus and His ways of love and selflessness. Sometimes having the weight of guilt lifted through Jesus' forgiveness is the first influence. Some *Christians* find the discovery of the truth about God quite intoxicating. Some find freedom from confusion. Some are released from the fear of death as they discover Jesus' promise of *eternal life. And the list goes on. Lewis Sperry Chafer, well-known American Bible scholar, says that at least thirty-three simultaneous and instantaneous effects take place upon the believer the moment one exercises faith in Christ (begins to believe).

A *Christian* Church, a gathering of *Christians*, exists to celebrate Jesus' love, mercy, and forgiveness, to worship Him (declare Him to be God), and to organize a variety of ways in which the good news of Jesus may be made known to those who have not yet come to understand Him.

Christians believe that Jesus' death on the cross was not some terrible mistake, but it was the very way in which He took man's sin (wrong-doing) upon Himself and nailed it to the cross, never again to cause guilt or fear to the *Christian*. *Christians* know that Jesus put all that wrong-doing away, because He rose from the dead to live eternally in a supreme state of glory and holiness in which He is King over the Kingdom of God, never to experience death again. These are the basics of what *Christians* believe.

Christians also live a new life, a righteous life, a life that they are empowered to live, by faith (just because they believe). *Christians* experience a new <u>interest</u> in doing the right thing (this does not mean that Christians always <u>do</u> the right thing, but they have a real choice).

God gives them help to choose the right thing, against all temptations. That is why so many drug addicts and alcoholics can't overcome their addictions until they believe in Jesus and receive that new life with that new power. However: can a person who is a Christian still use drugs, or lie, or commit adultery, or do other wrong things? Apparently yes, because the best Christian still does wrong things, and God does not draw a line and say, "You can be a Christian and do this little thing, but you cannot be a Christian and do that big thing." God is very patient with the process of bringing about change. Only God really knows whether a person has become a Christian or not, and it is not on the basis of behavior. Romans 10:9-10 tells how to become a *Christian*; "...if you confess with your mouth Jesus as Lord, and believe in your heart that God raised Him from the dead, you will be saved; for with the heart a person believes, resulting in righteousness, and with the mouth he confesses, resulting in salvation." 1 Corinthians 15:3-4 is a summary of what *Christians* believe. John 20:31says all one has to believe is that Jesus is the Christ, the Son of God.

Christianity: the belief system of those who have accepted the Bible account of Jesus as true. There is a general resistance against calling *Christianity* a religion. Christians say, "*Christianity* is not a religion. It's a relationship." When Christians use the word religion in this way, they mean religion as a man-made system by which one may try to gain acceptability before God. Religions are man-made attempts to connect with God. Christianity is a God-made opportunity for people to enter into relationship with Him. *Christianity* offers a relationship of love with God. Religions offer definite rewards such as status, recognition, or a good life after death, or Nirvana, or whatever, if the religious person performs well. *Christianity* does not work on the basis of performance.

Christianity is based on the work God has done to make it possible for man to know Him. All one has to do is to receive what God offers. 1 John 4:19 says, "He loved us first." People are fully accepted by God, <u>not</u> on the basis of their performance, but because He loves them. "God loves you" is one of the foundations of *Christianity* (1John 4:10-11). The love of God is offered to all who will receive it.

Christianity, like religion, has some codes of behavior, but, unlike religions, if a believer fails to meet that code, he is not rejected or somehow made to make up for the wrongs he did. (There may be the natural consequences of what he has done; God won't usually stop consequences from taking effect.) *Christianity* extends mercy and forgiveness to those who are imperfect in obeying the commands of God. There is no system in *Christianity* that says that if a Christian did some bad thing, then he has to do this many good things to make up for it. Religions typically have that kind of system. *Christianity* does <u>not</u> have a list of things one must do in order to remain in good standing with God, like church attendance, dress in a certain way, eat certain foods, etc. Most Christians do attend church, give money to the church, read their Bibles, and pray. Many also are involved in serving in the community or in serving in the church (the pastor does not do it all himself). However, none of these things are required by God in order to remain a Christian. What is required is faith in Jesus as the Son of God. That faith most often leads to a lifestyle that includes all of the above, not as an obligation, but rather as a joyful offering.

God is love. No other so-called god comes even close to the Christian idea of love. That's the basis of *Christianity*. God is love (1 John 4:8 and 16) God's kind of love is described in 1 John 4:7 through 5:3. This passage starts out saying, "Beloved, let us love one another, for love is from God; and everyone who loves is born of God and knows God."

In 1 Corinthians 13 it says, "Love is patient, love is kind and is not jealous; love does not brag…bears all things, believes all things, hopes all things." In love, Jesus died so that believers don't have to, and He purchased by His own death forgiveness and the opportunity for new life, granting everything needed for life and godliness (2 Peter 1:2-3). Philippians 3:4-10 says, "whatever things were gain to me, those things I have counted as loss for the sake of Christ…that I may know Him." Christians long to know more of the love of God.

Christmas: the Christian celebration of the birth of Jesus. Jesus was born in Bethlehem, a little town in Israel, and the full story is in Mathew 1:18-2:15 and, with some different details, in the first two chapters of Luke. It is important to Christians to celebrate Jesus the Son of God, born as an infant. He did not descend from heaven miraculously as an adult; He was born as a baby who had to be cared for and grow up in a very normal fully human experience. All this is important to the understanding of Jesus' life and work.

A lot of cultural traditions have come to surround *Christmas* that many Christians disagree with, but the holiday remains rather wonderful in that the love of Jesus and the transforming power of His love seem to be present at that time of year as people turn their attention, even slightly, to Jesus. The famous story by Charles Dickens, *The Christmas Carol*, is a favorite of many Christians at that time of year, because it is a story, although fictional, of that transforming power of *Christmas*, the celebration of Jesus grand appearance on earth.

Church: any assembly of people who believe in Jesus as the Son of God. *Church* is people. *Church* buildings are meeting places for people. *Church* buildings get called "*Church*," of course, and there is nothing wrong with that, but in the Bible, "*Church*" <u>always</u> means the people who gather. Pastor David Fritsche teaches that the *Church* is not so much an organization as it is an organism, a living thing, a family.

Literally, *church* means "the called out ones," or "those set apart." Christians are set apart, <u>not</u> as some kind of elite group, nevertheless distinct from the ways of the rest of the world. *Church*, by its very nature is not just like the rest of the world any more than Jesus was just like everybody else. Jesus stood out as being very different. As a man walking the dusty roads of Israel, there were things about Him that were so unique and so good that people flocked to see and hear Him. The *Church* is to be that radically different and attractive in its goodness.

There is really only one *Church* world-wide, and it is often referred to by Christians as the "*Body of Christ." It is through the *Church* that the Gospel has been presented around the world for two thousand years. The truth has been seen, not just through words on Sunday morning or at special events, but in the life and love and deeds of *Church* people all week. God is seen all the time and every place that there are people who know Jesus.

Church is also where those who believe in Jesus gather together to get encouragement, teaching, comfort and direction. Being with people at *Church* has the miraculous effect of solving a lot of petty problems and lifting people above the circumstances of their lives. (See *fellowship.) Talking to other Christians, people of the *Church* get encouraged to deal with life's situations in the right manner, avoiding the traps of violence, revenge, pride, unforgiveness, fear, etc., which are the natural ways in which people without Jesus handle difficult situations. *Church* people stand out the most when, in interaction with others, there is the surprise of love and forgiveness instead of small-minded hurtful ways.

A good church teaches from the Bible, not philosophy or humanism. People there will be genuinely friendly. People will most likely finish a *Church* meeting feeling encouraged or happy. Christians who attend a good *church* generally thrive and have Christian friends.

People who allow themselves to drift from the *Church* tend to lose their purpose, drift from their faith, and lose the freshness of their relationship with God. Attending *Church* does not earn extra credit with God, or do anything to make one more deserving of God's love. *Church* is central to the plan that was established by God in His purpose to bless all of mankind. Church is the community in which His people can thrive and His message of love can be sent worldwide.

Circumcision: ritual surgery, removing the foreskin of the penis of a male. Circumcision was originally a ceremony that permanently marked any male as *Jewish, as a *Hebrew, or as a descendent of Abraham. Jewish boys were required by Biblical law to be *circumcised* eight days after being born. It was meant to be a sign of their relationship with God, a sign of the *covenant, or agreement, between man and God (Genesis 17:9-14). It was always only the outward sign of something much more meaningful than just membership in a group or a religion.

Circumcision in the Bible always represented more than the physical act. It represented a heart attitude towards God. Romans 2:29, says, "*Circumcision* is that which is of the heart by the Spirit." In other words, what circumcision symbolizes as an act on the body, God accomplishes in a person's heart: a permanent change and a commitment to loving God. God the Holy Spirit will do the work of *circumcising* the heart. And this heart change accomplished by God doesn't require the physical act first. There is no mystical, spiritual power in physical *circumcision*, it is only a sign of what is to happen in a person's heart. Deuteronomy 30:6 says that the purpose of *circumcision* is that one should "love the Lord your God with all your heart and all your soul, so that you may live." Colossians 2:11-12 says that believers are "*circumcised* with a *circumcision* made without hands, in the removal of the body of the flesh by the *circumcision* of Christ." In other words, for a Christian, the *flesh is removed; it is no longer in control of a Christians' life. The appetites of the body are cut off.

In the *New Testament (written after Jesus lived) it is written that *circumcision* is not necessary to become a *Christian. Galatians 5:6 says, "for in Christ Jesus, neither *circumcision* nor un*circumcision* means anything, but faith working through love." *Circumcision* was, and is, necessary to become a Jew, because that is what the original agreement between God and man (the *Old Testament) required, but in the New Testament it is clear that *circumcision* is not required to become a Christian. There is a careful explanation of this in Romans 2:25-29.

Commandments: God's directions for how to live right. Usually, the *Ten *Commandments* is what Christians mean when they say, "the *commandments*." This was an ancient law code that was given by God to Moses and to the Jewish people. This code contains instructions about how to relate to God and instructions about how to relate to one another.

The *commandments* are more about freedom and peace of mind than about restricting behavior. Pastor Louie D. Locke says that the *commandments* are not a fence surrounding the believer and restricting life down to a very narrow place, rather they are a "keep out" sign around a small area of certain activities or attitudes that are bad for the believer. Pastor Kristopher Dahir says that obedience to the *commandments* creates a basis of relationship with God. Pastor teacher Graham Cooke says that the *commandments* since the time of Jesus are an invitation to see something new since the believer has the opportunity to live in newness of life (Romans 6:4).

Here are the Ten *Commandments*, briefly paraphrased:
(1) Have no other gods besides Me [the God of the Bible].
(2) Don't make or worship any idol [a statue or picture of a god].
(3) Do not use God's name except to speak to or about Him reverently.
(4) Keep the seventh day of each week holy [rest and worship God].

(5.) Honor your father and mother.
(6) Do not murder.
(7) Do not commit *adultery [have sexual relations with another person's spouse].
(8) Do not steal.
(9) Do not lie.
(10) Do not covet [that is, don't desire for yourself that which belongs to someone else] (Exodus 20:1-17).

    These are often referred to as "the law," although the whole *law actually includes much more detailed requirements for those who worship God in the Old Testament (the first ¾ of the Bible written before Jesus). In the New Testament, or the new agreement that Jesus made between God and man, the *commandments*, although definitely not ignored, were replaced by *grace through *faith. You'll hear Christians say, "We are not under the law, but under grace. "What that means is that keeping the Ten *commandments* perfectly is not what is needed to have a relationship with God. The requirements to enter God's presence or to go to heaven are met by God's love alone, rather than upon obedience to the *commandments* or any of the rest of the law. One gets to heaven by faith in Jesus, rather than by keeping the *commandments*. Does this mean Christians get to ignore the *commandments,* of course not. How God wants people to behave has never changed. What changed was that Jesus came and made forgiveness possible for anyone who believes in Him.

    Jesus simplifies the law down to just <u>two</u> *commandments*. These two *commandments* really carry the overall intention of the Ten *Commandments* and all the rest of the law. These two are: (1) Love the Lord your God with all your heart and with all your soul and with all your mind. (2) Love your neighbor as yourself. (Matthew 22:36-40).

The Bible says that those who are "walking after the Spirit", meet the requirements of the law (Romans 8:4-5). "Walking after the Spirit" is what Christians, who believe in Jesus, do. They have the Spirit of God in their hearts, and the Spirit leads them towards doing what God wants, which is in harmony with the Law rather than being led by their appetites. The *commandments* set the standard, and then Jesus made it possible for believers to meet that standard.

Communion: A ritual meal shared by Christians to remember Jesus. (Also known as the "*Lord's Supper" or "Eucharist") Christians have a ceremony called *communion* in which they eat bread and drink wine or grape juice. Jesus started this ritual on the last evening He had a meal together with His disciples before He was killed. He said the bread was His body which was given for all who believe in Him. He also said the wine was the new covenant (new agreement between God and man) in His blood. He said, "Do this in remembrance of Me" (Luke 22: 19, 20). Some churches do communion weekly, some do it monthly, or only for special occasions. Jesus gave directions for only two rituals: *communion* and *baptism, so, since there are so few, it seems that they must be very important to observe. There is something very real in *communion*; it is not just an empty ritual.

For Christians, *communion's* reality is that in receiving the bread, by faith they receive the full effect of Jesus' death. In His death, He carried all the sorrows, all the pain, sickness and wrongdoing of the whole world in His own body (1 John 2:2, Isaiah 53:4-5), and in trade, He gave believers His wholeness and righteousness and perfection. For Christians who don't feel very righteous, or very strong, *communion* is a reminder that Jesus is their righteousness and their strength, giving hope, health, courage, love, forgiveness, peace, joy, and sound mind, to believers. They eat that bread and receive the nourishment on a spiritual level, very real nourishment to the spirit.

In receiving the wine or juice, believers remind themselves of the new *covenant, or the new agreement which Jesus established, the agreement between God and mankind. The Christian's part in the new covenant is to believe. God's part in the covenant is to grant destiny and ability to serve God's purposes on earth and life forever with Jesus after death. *Communion* is an opportunity to eat and drink the new covenant, let it become flesh and bone in the believer, and remember the promises of life in Christ.

Communion takes many different ritual forms in different churches, but, to all believers who take it, faith in Jesus is restored and refreshed.

Condemnation: to declare a wrong-doer to be guilty and deserving of the punishment to be given. Christians know that God can *condemn* (He can declare people guilty and send people to death and hell) but Christians believe that they are free from that *condemnation* of God. Romans 8:1 says, "There is therefore now no *condemnation* for those who are in Christ Jesus." Mark 16:16 says that believers will be saved, but "he who has disbelieved shall be *condemned*." The act of believing in Jesus is what saves Christians from *condemnation*. Believers know that God does not *condemn* them when they do wrong things. Christians believe that the *devil is full of *condemnation* for them. The devil tempts people to sin (do wrong) and then *condemns* them for doing it. In Revelation 12:10 the devil is called the "accuser of the brethren." The devil is only able to accuse and make people feel guilty. Making people feel guilty and <u>feel</u> *condemned* is about all the devil can do. He can deceive people into believing that they are lost and hopeless, but the truth is that no one takes people from Jesus' hands (John 10:28). In Jesus' hands, the believer has the promise of eternity with Jesus in heaven after death.

Condemnation is the opposite of the promised eternal destiny with Jesus (eternal life). Those who are *condemned* will be put in hell with the devil (Revelation 20:10-15) and will not go to eternal life as promised to believers.

Confession (of sin or wrong-doing): to admit to having done something wrong. To a Christian *confession* is the important first step of getting things right when wrongs have been done. A Christian *confesses* to God and says "I did it; me personally; I am the one, and this is exactly what I did." So *confession* is admission of wrong, exactly as it is seen by God. This word actually means, "speak the same thing," so if a Christian *confesses* lying, he calls it lying, not a fib. And it is admitted as wrong; God calls it wrong so the confessor must call it wrong too. The Christian doesn't try to justify himself or make excuses about why it was not so bad. The Christian agrees that it was the wrong thing to do. That is *confession*.

The other half of *confession* is to *repent (to change direction, to change one's mind). God will grant repentance (2 Timothy 2:25) that is, He will empower the believer to take the new direction. *Confession* brings the Christian into God's help with the problem. Refusal to *confess* keeps the Christian under the heat of God's *conviction and under the heat of the devil's accusation and guilt. *Confessing* to another believer and to God is a powerful cure to the accusation of the devil, and it is the door to healing in whatever way doing wrong has caused damage. 1 John 1:9 says. "If we *confess* our sins, He is faithful and righteous to forgive us our sins and to cleanse us from all unrighteousness." See also Psalm 32:3-7 which says how good it is to *confess*, to acknowledge sin to God, and James 5:16 says, "confess your sins to one another." Psalm 51 is an entire *confession* and repentance written by King David for his wrong-doing.

Confession (of faith): to state one's beliefs in agreement with God. Christians talk about their *confession of faith*, meaning that they agree with Bible truths. Christians believe, or *confess*, a <u>long</u> list of things, so the term *confession* covers all of that. Literally, the word *confession* means to be of one mind (with God), to speak the same, or to affirm, to agree.

Hebrews 10:23 says, "Let us hold fast the *confession* of our hope without wavering." In 1 Timothy 6:12, Paul writes to Timothy, "you made the good *confession* in the presence of many witnesses." Even Jesus is said to have "testified the good *confession* before Pontius Pilate," (1 Timothy 6:13). Romans 10:9-10 says, "if you *confess* with your mouth Jesus as Lord, and believe in your heart that God raised Him from the dead, you will be saved." So this *confession* is a reference to the Christian <u>saying</u> something about what he <u>believes</u> as a Christian. Christians can use this word to mean agreement with any truth from God, for example a Christian might be making the *confession* that he believes that God has healed him or has promised to give him a wife, or any other thing about which he has received a prophecy, found in the Bible, or has been taught by his Pastor. And his Christian friends will say, "He is *confessing* it." Well-known teacher Graham Cooke says that confession guarantees experience. In other words, *confession* is the key to receiving any promise of God. Christians begin to *confess* that they have it before they see or feel anything; they just begin to agree with God about it, and expect the realization of God's promise.

Confession of what a Christian believes is powerful. Humans stand alone in all of creation as creatures that have words, powerful words that bring changes to their lives, and Christians believe that the *confession of faith* changes things, creates a superior reality that is in agreement with God, and replaces inferior ideas about what is real.

<u>Conscience:</u> the combination of moral judgment and emotion that result in a conclusion that something is either right or wrong. A person's *conscience* tells her when she is moving in a bad direction, or about to do a bad thing, or it brings on feelings of guilt when she has done something wrong. A person can sometimes wrestle with her conscience. Sometimes a person doesn't like it when her *conscience* won't let her do something even if she already knows she shouldn't.

Conscience is mentioned several times in the Bible, see the references below. As a Christian, it is of primary importance to keep a clear *conscience*. The Bible teaches that one must pay attention to the *conscience,* or it may become "seared." Conscience can be scorched, no good anymore (1 Timothy 4:2). If a Christian keeps ignoring her *conscience* and doing the things she knows she shouldn't, pretty soon she won't hear from her *conscience* anymore. That warning system that the *conscience* provides is gone.

Christians find also that the longer they live by what they believe about Jesus, their *consciences* get strengthened as they mature. They come to rely on the *conscience* instead of fighting with it.

Conscience is not however, the same as the Holy Spirit. Ultimately a Christian *conscience* is formed by maturity and experience as a believer. Christians learn to listen to the Holy Spirit. He is the higher authority. Christians learn to take guilt, fear, doubt, and worries (all of which may come from an untrained *conscience)* to the Lord, and let Him bring in the truth. That is how one develops a truly Christian *conscience*. 1 Corinthians 8:7-12 talks about the problems caused by a *conscience* that is in error. 1 Timothy 1:5 and 19, and 1 Timothy 3:9 talk about the importance of a clear *conscience* to the believer. 1 Peter 3:16 and 21 gives encouragement to keep a good *conscience*. And in Acts 24:16 the Apostle Paul talks about how important it is for him to have a blameless *conscience* before God and men.

Convicted/conviction: to be convinced that what one is doing is wrong; guilty. A Christian who says that God is *convicting* her is saying, "I realize now that I am doing wrong, I am guilty." *Conviction* from God sometimes comes as a surprise to the believer when she realizes that the behavior she thought was justified is actually very wrong in God's eyes and she needs to change her mind (*repent) and she needs to call it wrong (*confess) and turn away from that activity, or that talk, or that way of thinking.

Pastor Bill Johnson emphasizes that *conviction* is God pointing out, "You are made for more than this. Lift your head and set your sights higher." The purpose of *conviction* is to realize God's best.

Conviction sometimes comes when a Christian has done wrong and knows it, but somehow she thought it could slide, and then, suddenly she realizes God is not going to let it slide. *Conviction* is the realization for the Christian that she <u>has</u> done wrong, and *conviction* includes the understanding of just how serious that is. Corey Russell writes in his book *The Glory Within*, that Christians cannot sin happily, cannot do wrong without experiencing remorse, the painful knowledge of wrong-doing. That is *conviction*.

Conviction however is very different from *condemnation. God is faithful to *convict* Christians of wrong, but He does not condemn believers for doing wrong things. God's work of *conviction* leaves no doubt in the believer's mind that she is in the wrong, the question remains, will she confess and change, or will she strengthen herself to continue in wrongdoing, because she prefers to do the wrong thing. This is always an option, and some Christians take that option to continue in sin. The Bible makes it clear what happens if that kind of behavior persists. In Psalm 32:3-4, King David says that when he kept silent about his wrong-doing, God's hand "was heavy upon me: my vitality was drained away as with the fever heat of summer." Hebrews 10:26-31 describes the downward spiral of what happens if a person sets himself on a course of willful wrong-doing in spite of God's generous forgiveness, and ends with the statement, "It is a terrifying thing to fall into the hands of the living God." The ideal, of course, is for the *conviction* to bring about change of behavior, true wholesomeness, true beauty in love, and the holy covering of being right with God.

<u>Covenant</u>: a permanent, love-based agreement with an emphasis on what is given into the relationship rather than on what is the benefit from it.

God makes covenants, but man makes contracts. These two kinds of agreements are very different from one another. Contracts are temporary, and contracts are agreed upon by two parties because each one is going to get something out of the contract. Contracts protect both parties of an agreement from loss. If one party does not do his agreed-upon part, provisions in a contract protect the other party from loss.

A Covenant is not temporary, it is forever. Furthermore, it is about what each party brings to put into the deal. There is great gain in a covenant, but the gain to each person in the covenant is the result of what each brings in to invest in the covenant. Also, if one member of a covenant fails to keep his end of the deal, the other is to remain committed to the promises made upon initiating the relationship. That is the agreement of the covenant; "I am here for you, no matter what." God does that. He promises to love believers and to do them good (Jeremiah 32: 40-41), and even if believers don't fulfill their side of the covenant (to worship Him alone and obey Him,) He will continue to love the believer. That's just the way God is. There may be consequences to the believer's wayward life, but the Father patiently awaits his or her return. (In Luke 15:11-32, Jesus tells a story that illustrates this principle, the story of the *prodigal son.)

God encourages covenant relationships rather than conditional or contract relationships. Marriage is designed by God to be a covenant. Even if a wife spends money unwisely, the husband is to love her. (That is the best way for the necessary changes in spending to take place.) Families are covenant relationships. Even if the children track mud into the house, Mom is in covenant with them and still will be willing to keep them and love them. In church, Christians are actually to be in covenant relationship with one another, biblically. Christians are to be committed to loving one another even if one misbehaves.

In the Bible, there is the *Old Testament and the *New Testament. "Testament" is the old-fashioned word for covenant. The law (the Ten Commandments etc.) was the old covenant. Mankind kept breaking that covenant. "Grace and truth were realized through Jesus Christ," (John 1:17) which is the new covenant, and is fully empowered by God's love rather than threatened by man's disloyalty.

Covet: to envy. Envy is the desire to have things, money, status or fame that someone else has. One of the *Ten Commandments (God's most basic guidelines for thought and behavior) is, "You shall not *covet* your neighbor's house...or anything that belongs to your neighbor." ("Neighbor," here, is not strictly a literal next-door neighbor, but it means anyone whose stuff one might *covet*.) *Coveting* is a *sin, a wrong. It leads to all kinds of other wrongs, like stealing (obviously), but also to bitterness, hatred, etc.

Christians are aware that *covetous* thinking is not only wrong in God's eyes, but also damaging to one's own life and the life of others if it is allowed to run unchecked. Also in the Bible is the more positive directive: "be content with what you have," (Hebrews 13:5). Christians have the opportunity, with God's help, to relax about the material possessions, money, fame, etc. and find true peace in being thankful for what God has provided.

Creation: God's work of speaking the universe into existence. The first two chapters of the Bible detail the way that God *created* the earth. *Creation* refers to all that God made at that time. Much debate exists even among Christians over the time it took to *create* the universe. The literal account in Genesis says that He did it in six days and rested on the seventh day. Geologists and astronomers say that the universe is billions of years old, but the literal biblical account would say it was about 6000 years old. Most Christians hold firmly to the idea that God created everything, and would not be too concerned about how long it took or when it happened.

The real center of debate comes in comparing *creation* to the teaching of evolution, which says that life itself and all the various species of living things gradually evolved through a process of time plus chance; there was no plan or purpose in the mind of a God; it was an accident. Biblical *creation* says that God purposefully made each type of creature just as the narrative of the Bible states, and that life was breathed into man by God. Most Christians hold basically to this story of *creation*. Scientists and Christians seem to be finding a middle ground in the concept of "intelligent design." Many recent scientific discoveries point to the idea that there must have been purpose, innovation, and intelligence (God's intelligence) for things to have been *created* as they have.

Cross: the *cross* of wooden timber to which Jesus was nailed, and upon which He died. The *cross* became the universal symbol of Christianity. There are many important reasons for this, and many books have been written about the meaning of the *cross*. Central to Christianity is an understanding of what was done on the *cross* by Jesus on that scandalous day.

When Jesus was fastened to that wooden *cross* with spikes through His hands and feet, He was there voluntarily. He was there because "God so loved the world…" (John 3:16). He knew that He was there with a purpose. The purpose was that He would take on all of man's sickness, pain, and wrongdoing. It all became personally His; and it killed Him. Isaiah 53:4-6 predicts (*prophesies) that this would happen. The Bible makes it clear that when Jesus was on the *cross* He actually became sin. Jesus, the pure Son of God became impure like mankind, so that mankind might have the opportunity to become righteous like Jesus. (2 Corinthians 5:21 says that God "made Him [Jesus] who knew no sin to be sin on our behalf, so that we might become the righteousness of God in Him.")

As Jesus died, He cried out, "My God, My God, why have You forsaken Me?" The sin of the world had become Jesus' personal sin, and it separated God the Father from God the Son (not two Gods, see *Trinity) but a heart-wrenching inner conflict in the Person of God (Matthew 27:46). Jesus had never in all eternity been stained with sin, and God the Father cannot be in the presence of sin (Isaiah 59:2). So Jesus felt Him turn away and cried out in anguish, as a man to God, "My God, My God." But He still trusted God, evidenced because a little while later He said, "it is finished," (John 19:30), meaning that the work He was sent to do, (sent by God the Father) including bearing man's sin, pain, and sickness on the *cross*, was finished. And then He said, "Father, into Your hands I commit My spirit." (Luke 23:46). Jesus, as a dying man, His life is over, entrusts His spirit to God the Father.

Through His death on the *cross*, Jesus changed everything about how sin affects the lives of those who will believe in Him. Those who believe will receive forgiveness for all wrong, and the ability to refuse to do wrong. Romans 8:1-4 explains this. Before the *cross*, the principle was, "if you sin, you die." (Not immediately, but sin brings death; that is a clear biblical principle.) After the *cross*, through believing in Jesus (*faith), one may be forgiven (1 John 2:2), and nothing can again separate that believer from the love of God and eternal life (Romans 8:38-39).

The final piece in this complicated puzzle-picture is that Jesus rose from the grave, alive again. Death could not hold Him; He took up His life again, and everything that mankind owed for sin (wrong-doing) remained nailed to the *cross* (Colossians 2:13-14 talks about the certificate of debt that man owes to God for sin). Believers owe no more debt for what they have done wrong, and they receive instead the opportunity to be alive together with Him forever. If one believes in Jesus' death and *resurrection, one can receive new life.

New life begins with forgiveness for all past wrong, the ability to turn away from present temptation and to do right joyfully; and if the believer sometimes does wrong, that sin has no power to put the believer to death anymore.

One other important aspect of the *cross* in the lives of Christians is that Jesus instructs His disciples to take up their *crosses* and follow Him. The *cross* is an instrument of death. Christians are to willingly bear an instrument of death; death to that old selfish way of life. Pastor Bill Johnson says, "Taking up your *cross* means embracing the truth that your life is not about you; [Jesus'] *cross* was about pleasing His Father and redeeming us. Likewise, our *cross* is not about us, but about living our lives for Christ."

Brennan Manning, Christian author, writes that whatever it is in the lives of believers that causes self-centered ways to die, that is their *cross*. It may be tragedy, disability, weakness, or a person they don't like, or it may be any difficult situation that they have to put up with. Christians learn to embrace that experience as a real death of something (whatever it kills in their lives) and they thank God that on the other side is a resurrected, newness of life in the real love of God, with limitless possibilities of partnering with God's love on earth.

Crown: an ornamental head-piece that is a reward for a faithful life lived unto God's purposes. Christians believe that there are rewards from God that will be given to those who worked diligently for the purposes of God.

The Bible says in 1 Corinthians 9:24-27 that there is a *crown* or wreath for those who run the race to win, both in footraces on earth and in the economy of heaven. Christians get an everlasting *crown* when they run to win, called the victor's *crown*.

1 Thessalonians 2:17-20 mentions the *crown* that is called the soul-winner's *crown*, or the *crown* of rejoicing. This reward is given to believers who have helped others to come to understand Jesus and believe in Him.

2 Timothy 4:5-8 is about the watcher's *crown* for those who have loved and longed for Jesus' *second coming. It is also called the *crown* of righteousness.

James 1:12 and Revelation 2:10 say that there is a *crown* of life, or lover's *crown* for those who persevere under trial, those who are faithful unto death. It is a sobering reminder that the real reward is not in this life, but the reward is for how well this life was lived on earth.

1 Peter 5:1-4 makes it clear that a *crown* will be given by Jesus to those who pastor the church, those who "shepherd the flock of God," and do it well. It is the Pastor's *crown*, or the *crown* of glory.

Another mention of *crowns* is in Revelation 4:10 which says that the 24 elders in heaven, who have *crowns* because of their faithful service on earth, will "cast their *crowns* before the throne" of God. Giving their precious, hard-won *crowns* freely to God, they express that anything good that was done by them on earth was done only by the help of God, by the *grace of God. Anything they had, even their reward, was because God had given it to them.

Crucified: a method of execution in which one is nailed to a cross of wood and left to die. Without a lot of explanation, it is easily understood that being *crucified* is a cruel and painful way to die. Jesus was *crucified*. (See *cross to find out what that meant for Christians.)

Christians believe that they are *crucified* with Christ by believing in Him. Romans 6:6 says, "our old self was *crucified* with Him in order that our body of sin might be done a way with." Christians die to the old way of life and are resurrected to a new life through believing in Jesus' *crucifixion* and resurrection. It is a painful *crucifixion* when a Christian has to learn to turn the other cheek instead of hitting back, to forgive instead of taking revenge, or to be kind to those who are unkind. The end result is a supernatural way of doing life that would be entirely impossible if the old self were still alive.

Christians call that *death to self and alive to God (Romans 6:11). Paul writes, "I have been *crucified* with Christ; and it is no longer I who live, but Christ lives in me; and the life which I now live in the flesh I live by faith in the Son of God, who loved me and gave Himself up for me." (Galatians 2:20). It is evident here that Paul considers his old way of life over (dead), and his new way of life completely dependent upon Jesus.

Paul also says, "Now those who belong to Christ have *crucified* the flesh with its passions and desires." (Galatians 5:24). In other words, the old appetites of the believer's body no longer run his life by passion. They are dead, and the Holy Spirit now directs his interests and motivations, and strengthens him to carry out the good work of the *Kingdom of God. A believer's work in the Kingdom is how God would have him live; it is what he was created to do.

One interesting thing about *crucifixion:* a person cannot *crucify* himself. God will use someone else or some situation to *crucify* him (not literally of course). When the old way dies, the new way is far better, more peaceful, joyful, and without regrets. Christians find it helpful to know that this difficult thing that they are experiencing is being used by God to *crucify* or transform them to be more like Jesus (Romans 6:5-7). It is actually an opportunity to adore, thank and praise God in the middle of distress.

Cult: a religious system having some Christian elements, but distinctly deviant from and incompatible with Christianity. In Christian circles, this means a religious group that claims to know Jesus, but has redefined Jesus in ways that are not in agreement with the Bible. Usually, the main point of difference is that *cults* don't think Jesus is God (read about *Jesus if this is puzzling.) The *cults* say Jesus was a special man, or that He was sent from God, or is one of many gods, or that He is just an idea inherent in mankind, but they won't say He is the son of God in the flesh, or God the Son.

One's understanding of that idea is absolutely central to Christianity. If Jesus is not divine (actually God), none of the rest of the story makes any sense to a Christian. Christians know Jesus as God the Son. Jesus has been well known around the world for two millennia as the Son of God, as the Bible makes clear. Anyone who says He is not is clearly deviant from Christianity. See *Jesus, *Messiah, *Trinity, *God.

Another feature of *cults* is that they require people to do certain things, act in certain ways, or perform certain rituals in order to gain the benefits of membership in the *cult*. Christianity, on the other hand, does not require anything but faith in Jesus. Christian groups which do require certain acts are called *legalists, and are close to being *cults* because they are presenting that Jesus <u>plus</u> something else is required to get right with God.

Some common *cults* are: Jehovah's Witnesses, Mormons (LDS, or the Church of Jesus Christ of Latter Day Saints), Moonies (the Unification Church started by Sun Myung Moon), Hare Krishna, Christian Science, and Unitarians. Christians believe that these *cults* are driven by a spirit other than the Spirit of God. They are deceiving spirits and very attractive. They are friendly and loving. The overall goal of these deceiving spirits is to trick people into believing in anything other than Jesus, the true Jesus, who <u>is</u> God, the Son of God, and who died for sins of all mankind and lives to offer life abundantly, as made clear in the Bible. The Bible is the only dependable and accurate book about Jesus.

Curse: a declaration of something bad against a person or people. The possibility of proclaiming evil upon a person and then having that bad thing actually happen is a reality in the spiritual realm. In some religions, *cursing* is a routine way to do harm to enemies. In the Bible, God can proclaim a *curse*, some of which are explained below. However, *cursing* is not part of Christian practice. It does not fit with Jesus' instruction to "love your enemies."

In Luke 6:28, Jesus says, "Bless those who *curse* you, pray for those who mistreat you." Romans 12:14 says, "Bless those who persecute you, bless and do not *curse*."

A *curse* is the opposite of a blessing. In the Bible, in the book of Numbers chapters 22-24 is an interesting story about a man named Balaam who was hired to *curse* the people of God, but he kept discovering that God had blessed them, so he could not *curse* them.

Curses are a part of many non-Christian spiritual paths, most notably, in our culture, *Satan worshipers, Wiccan, or the *occult, voodoo, shamans, and so forth. These non-Christian practices of *cursing* are attempts to bring harm to someone through spiritual avenues. Sometimes there is real power to harm in such a *curse*, and it can bring sickness, injury, confusion, etc. without the victim ever having been touched or confronted in person. Christians rest in faith that a *curse* against them will be ineffective because of the protection of God (as in the story of Balaam in Numbers). Christians declare the power of the evil one to be of no effect because of the favor of Jesus and because of the *blood of Jesus. Psalm 91 speaks clearly of the safety in which the believer dwells when she chooses to depend on God as her protection and live under God's blessing. And Proverbs 26:2 says, "a *curse* without a cause does not alight."

In regard to God speaking a *curse*, Christians talk about "the *curse*" which refers to the story in Genesis 3, the story about when God *cursed* the serpent to go on his belly, and God *cursed* the ground so that it would tend to produce weeds instead of food, and it would require a lot of work to make a living. This is also called the "*fall of man," the event in which Man fell from grace with God and life became difficult instead of easy as it had been in the original creation of God. At that time, God did *curse* the serpent and He *cursed* the ground to grow weeds instead of crops, but He did not *curse* Adam and Eve or mankind, their descendents.

He declared how things were to be as a consequence of their behavior, but he didn't *curse* mankind. Nevertheless, you'll hear some Christians say, "We live under the *curse*." What they mean is the *curse* of the ground, that man has to work hard to live, and that life is difficult, and that so much wrong seems to rule in this life. See *fallen.

Another place in which God *curses* is in Deuteronomy 28:15-68. Here, God presents a long frightening list of the things that will happen to His people if they choose to ignore His commandments. Christians call this the "*curse* of the law." Obey the law and get blessed, or disobey and get this list of *curses*. That was the way of the Old Testament, the part of the Bible that was written before Jesus. Jesus changed all that with the New Testament, the part of the Bible that was written after Jesus came with a new approach to God through faith rather than the law. Galatians 3:13 says that "Christ redeemed us from the *curse* of the law," which means that believers are free from that prediction of a *curse* in the Old Testament, and receive forgiveness instead, by faith in Jesus.

In American culture, there is also the issue of *curse* words. Originally this came from the actual practice of *cursing* someone, as in, "God damn you," clearly a *curse*. Christian people were taught not to *curse*. It became the slang word "cuss," and the social rules against cussing are clear.

Day of the Lord: the day in which God will establish His Kingdom and be done with this era on earth. Both the old and new Testaments contain passages that explain that there will be a final day of judgment by God, and it is called the *day of the Lord*. It will be the end of all things as we know it, and the beginning of a new era. There will be a new heaven and a new earth and a New Jerusalem.

Zephaniah, a prophet in the Bible, predicts the *day of the Lord* which came to pass in the nations of Israel and Judah; they were overcome by enemy armies with great destruction and loss of life. Zephaniah and other prophets also predict a yet future *day of the Lord* for the whole world.

That *great and final day of the Lord* is what today's Christians are talking about when they talk about the *day of the Lord*.

On the *day of the Lord*, there will be a final judgment of all people, the day in which all are either to go to heaven or to hell. Everything that has ever been done, good or bad will be exposed on *that day* (Luke 12:2-5 and Revelation 20:12). God will be finished helping man on earth to be free from the influence of the devil and sin; that task will be completed. People will have either refused or received God's help. The new era will be very good for those who have turned to God, and very bad for those who have rejected Him. This is explained in some detail in Revelation chapters 20 and 21.

In the New Testament (the last quarter of the Bible) Christians understand the *day of the Lord* to be when Jesus returns (the *second coming). Christians also interpret every reference of "Jerusalem" to mean the church, the *bride of Christ, and Revelation 21 explains that there will be a New Jerusalem "made ready as a bride adorned for her husband." It is described as a city coming down out of heaven from God, and it is a city 1500 miles long, 1500 miles wide, and 1500 miles high (an engineering impossibility on this earth), so it is clear how drastically and unimaginably everything will change on *that day*, the beginning of a new era of relationship between man and God.

2 Peter 3:7-13 says that on *that day*, "the heavens will pass away with a roar and the elements will be destroyed with intense heat, and the earth and its works will be burned up." Yet Christians believe that they can stand unafraid on that day, trusting God through faith in Jesus Christ. Passages in 1 John 2:28 and 4:17-18 say (paraphrased) that believers may have confidence and not shrink away in fear on the *day of the Lord*. Revelation 21 goes on to say God will wipe every tear from the eyes of all believers; no more crying, no more reason to cry, no more pain or sorrow, no sickness or disease.

So the *day of the Lord* is a good day for *believers and a terrible day for unbelievers, which is perhaps why God continues to be patient for so long. He desires all men to be saved and come to the knowledge of the truth (I Timothy 2:4). God says, "Do I have any pleasure in the death of the wicked, rather than that he should turn from his ways and live?" (Ezekiel 18:23). Also read Joel 2:28-32, Zephaniah 1:7-18, Ezekiel 30:3, 1 Thessalonians 5:2, about the conditions and what to expect when the *day of the Lord* occurs. Titus 2:11-14 speaks of the longing of believers for that *Day*.

Deacon: a person who is a servant in a church. It is a position of leadership, but Christian leadership is always seen as servant-leadership. Leadership in the way corporations think of it is that the leader is the man in charge, and everyone must obey him. Servant-leadership of the *deacons* is carried out by people who have met the qualifications as listed in Paul's letter, 1 Timothy 3:8-13. He describes the qualifications of leaders. *Deacons* (and *deaconesses*) must be people of dignity, not deceitful, not addicted to wine, or making money in questionable ways, having a clear conscience, beyond reproach, not gossips, faithful, having only one wife or husband, with well behaved children and an orderly household. *Deacons* may be either men or women, as noted. Phoebe was a *deaconess* in the early Church (Romans 16:1).

Deacons and deaconesses serve in all manner of work, either directly with the people (who are the church), or with the building in which the church meets (from custodial work to managing the finances), or out in the community reaching the poor, helping people, ministering to the sick etc. Sometimes *deacons* also teach in the church gatherings, preaching from the Bible or teaching classes. These are people who are good examples to all who know them and are devoted to the work of the Lord. In the role of *deacon* or *deaconess*, they will exhibit *gifts of the Holy Spirit, that is abilities that are given by God that are above and beyond natural capabilities.

See *gift to review the wide range of abilities that may be a part of the role of *deacon* or *deaconess*.

Death: the end of physical life on earth, but not the end of the spirit. *Death* is a sobering word; death is mostly viewed with fear in our society. When one comes to know Jesus, all of that changes. A Christian will explain that when a believer dies, the spirit of that person, that is, her full consciousness, her central core of being, her soul, goes directly into Jesus' presence. 2 Corinthians 5:8 says that for Christians, to be absent from the body (physically dead) is to be present with the Lord (Jesus). To be present with the Lord is the same meaning for the Christian as to be in heaven.

In Christian understanding, when an <u>un</u>believer dies, she does <u>not</u> go to be with Jesus, but to a place called Hades to wait for the *Day of the Lord which is the final judgment. It is not actually biblical that, upon *death*, unbelievers go straight to *hell, a place of eternal torment, although many Christians believe that. Revelation 20 makes it clear that in the end, *death* and Hades will give up the dead and all of them will be judged. Anyone's name not found in Jesus' Book of Life will then be thrown into the Lake of Fire [hell]. There are Christian books about people who have visited hell. What they are telling of are experiences that apparently are still in the future. God is not limited by time as man is. If He wants to show people something in the future, He can. People who have been allowed to see hell populated with suffering souls have seen a future situation.

Christians believe that *death* was not in the original design of creation. *Death* was the result of sin coming into the world. To summarize the story: Adam and Eve, the first people created by God, were told that they would only die if they ate from a certain tree, the tree of the knowledge of good and evil. They <u>did</u> eat the forbidden fruit from that tree. That was the first sin, disobeying God, and obeying Satan, and it resulted in *death* eventually for Adam and Eve, and for all mankind ever since.

Death became the domain of Satan, and the keys of *death* were his. But Jesus, after He died on the cross (as a man without sin and therefore not able to be held by death) Jesus took the keys of *death* from Satan (Revelation 1:18) and *death* is no longer master over Him (Romans 6:9). Jesus has promised *eternal life to His believers. Christians believe that they will go to heaven eternally, and ultimately *death* will be abolished in God's new Kingdom (1 Corinthians 15:26).

For Christians, the idea of going to heaven turns *death* from a frightening enemy into a hope for ongoing love and light instead of some dark unknown. Furthermore, *death* to Christians on this earth is not necessarily viewed as the final end of life. Ever since the time when Jesus brought Lazarus and others back to life after *death* (John 11:43-44, Luke 7:11-16, Mark 5:35-42) Christians have prayed over dead bodies, and have seen some come back to life, because not all people who die have ended this life in God's timing. Jonathan Welton's book on the Normal Christian Life has a whole chapter of accounts of people brought back from the dead, recently, not hundreds of years ago, and simply because some Christians prayed.

Jesus states that He has the keys of *death* (Revelation 1:18). He commands His disciples to raise the dead (Matthew 10:8). That changes everything about the understanding of *death*. *Death* is not final. It is not to be feared. Hebrews 2:14-15 says. "[Jesus] also partook of [flesh and blood] that through *death* He might render powerless him who had the power of *death*, that is, the devil, and might free those who through fear of *death* were subject to slavery all their lives." So the devil can't even scare people about *death* anymore if they put their lives and eternity in the hands of Jesus.

Death to self: the end of selfishness as a lifestyle. Jesus instructs His disciples, "If anyone wishes to come after Me, he must deny himself, and take up his cross and follow Me" (Matthew 16:24). That is His description of *death to self*.

Believers must deny themselves, that is, step away from being self-absorbed, "taking care of number one," and step towards regarding others as more important than themselves (Philippians 2:3). Furthermore, the cross is an instrument of death. Christians are to willingly bear an instrument of death to execute that old selfish way of life. Whatever it is in the lives of believers that causes selfish ways to die, that is their cross. It may be the direct confrontation of God, or it may be any difficult situation that they have to bear. Christians learn to embrace that experience of *death to self* (and whatever it kills in their lives) and thank God that on the other side of the cross, just like it was for Jesus, there is a resurrected new life in the real love of God, with amazing new potential.

Selfishness insists on, "me first." Selfishness requires revenge when hurt. Selfishness will easily ignore any of God's commandments for the sake of convenience. Selfishness justifies all manner of behavior that is not in harmony with Jesus' lifestyle. Christians want to see all that selfishness die, and Christians believe that they are *crucified* with Christ by believing in Him. Christians are dead to the old way of life and are resurrected to a new life through believing in Jesus' *crucifixion* and resurrection. The end result is a supernatural way of doing life that would be entirely impossible if the old self were still alive. Paul writes, "I have been *crucified* with Christ; and it is no longer I who live, but Christ lives in me and the life which I now live in the flesh I live by faith in the son of God" (Galatians 2:20). Paul also says, "Now those who belong to Christ have *crucified* the flesh with its passions and desires" (Galatians 5:24). Christians call that *death to self*. Only through *death to self* can the life of Christ be manifest through the believer.

Deity: a god. This word is not used very often by Christians, perhaps because they have so many names to refer to God, but it is actually used in the Bible to explain that Jesus is *deity*." (That means He is God.) Colossians 2:9 says, "For in Him [Jesus] all the fullness of *Deity* dwells in bodily form."

Jesus as *deity* has the qualities of God: unlimited power, He has always existed, He is unchanging, knowing everything, and present everywhere all the time. Read about *Jesus if that is puzzling.

Kings, hundreds of years ago, were usually thought to be *deity*. Idols, usually statues or carvings of a being or creature which is worshiped, are thought to be *deity* by those who worship them. Mankind is hungry to know *deity*. If there is no *deity*, mankind is desperately alone, unloved, lost, and without provision or protection. Christians believe in Jesus as *deity*, fully God, who loves, frees, gives joy, provision and protection to all who will trust Him.

Deliverance: the procedure used to remove the influence of demons from someone's life. (It is also called *casting out demons.) Mary Magdalene, a person in the Bible, needed *deliverance*, and Jesus cast seven demons out of her (Mark 16:9). There are many other stories about Jesus and His followers' *deliverance* ministry (Matthew 9:32-33, Mark 5:1-20). Demons are called an unclean spirit, or (small 's'). These spirits can impart special powers like fortune-telling, or they can do harm, cause muteness, deafness, or crippling, etc. If someone needs *deliverance*, that means that he has a demon which he needs to have cast out (from which he needs to be *delivered*.) To *deliver* someone from an evil spirit, the authority of Jesus needs to be brought to bear against that evil spirit, by prayer, commanding the spirit to leave. (When Jesus tells a spirit to leave it always does, because He is the highest authority). Christians today still may receive a gift from God for this kind of ministry. This ministry includes of course, discerning whether the problem is really one brought on by an evil spirit or by something else. (See *discernment of spirits.)

Christian teacher Dr. Mike Webster of Spirit and Word ministries points out that *deliverance* is not the same as exorcism. *Deliverance* means to throw out the spirit by authority, not by enticing it out, not by making a deal, but just because Jesus commanded it to leave.

Exorcism means more the enticing, deal-making approach, which is not biblical. (Acts 16:16-18 is an example of the authority of Jesus in *deliverance*, and Acts 19:13-16 compares it with exorcism.)

It is easy to get a little nervous about *deliverance*, but really it's a normal part of Christian living; bringing the authority of Jesus as Lord into a life that may have been submitted to other authorities. (For example, there may be areas of someone's life that came under the rulership of sexual perversion, or hatred, or addictions, etc.) As Jesus takes authority, these things must depart, even though sometimes it takes a fairly serious praying with a group of Christians to make that happen. There are some key things that give demonic power a foothold in someone's life: unforgiveness, disobedience to Jesus' words; a refusal to *repent in some area, or just plain not wanting to give up that way of life that is demonic in some way. The one who needs deliverance must agree with the wholeness and purity into which he is being delivered.

Deliverance doesn't require certain formulas, certain words, hand motions, wands, or anything like that; it just requires faith, and the understanding of authority. The combined faith and prayer of a group of believers is the best approach. In other words, praying for someone who needs *deliverance* with a team is most effective. Books for more on this: "Deliver us from Evil," by Don Basham, and "The Believer's Authority," by Kenneth Hagin, and "How to Cast Out Demons," by Doris Wagner.

Demon: an evil spirit. Christians believe that *demons* are the *Devil's co-workers. *Demons* constantly work to deceive, tempt, torment, and generally ruin people's lives, whether Christian or not, but it seems that Christians are particularly subject to their attacks. Strong Christians are a tremendous threat to Satan's kingdom. So he will try to tear them down through various *demonic* attacks.

Here are a few of the basics about *demons* in Christian thinking. Most important is the knowledge that Christians have authority over *demons*. Jesus has given Christians authority over all the power of Satan (Luke 10:19). Jesus has all authority to tell *demons* to leave people alone (Matthew 9:32-33). He can stop their activity and tell them to leave, and He gives Christians the same authority by using His name. Christians don't have to submit to deception, temptation, or torment from *demons*. There are no certain words to use, no arm-waving or yelling required to overcome *demons*, but the believer must know (have faith) that he or she has the authority of Jesus. That kind of faith comes from reading or hearing God's Word, the Bible. Some recommended passages are below, and the first five books of the New Testament would be recommended reading. Knowing God is the key. Studying *demons* or Satan will not help.

Demons are apparently fallen angels who were originally created to love and serve God, but somehow were deceived to think that they should side with Satan when Satan decided he should be worshipped instead of God. The central target of *demonic* attack is to destroy anyone's faith in Jesus. *Demons* are not all-knowing, they don't really know the future, although one of their favorite methods is to trick people with so-called "fortune telling." One especially attractive tactic of these deceiving spirits is to promote the false belief that there can be communication with the dead. This is called "channeling" or a "seance," or using a "medium." *Demonic* spirits use that platform to tell people what to do, but it is all deception. Dr. Mike Webster (Spirit and Word Ministries) says that the spirit of the deceased person is not there, only a lying *demon* impersonating the one who is dead.

Demons are not all-powerful, but do have the power to deceive, to cause confusion, discouragement, loss of faith in God, distraction, addictions, and they are believed to be able to bring sickness and death, and they are part of the power of temptation. (Temptation may be *demonically* amplified.)

Insane people are not necessarily *demonized* (influenced by a *demon*), but people who are *demonized* will look quite crazy sometimes in a variety of ways, and often end up in mental treatment programs.

"Resist the devil, and he will flee from you" (James 4:7). Also see *cast out a *demon*, Mark 3:20-27, Mark 16:17-18. One of the things Jesus most often did was to cast out demons, and it caused great amazement because no one had ever seen that kind of authority until then, and He gave that authority to His followers (Luke 10:19).

Demon possessed: controlled by a demon. This term is used to describe a person whose ability to function in a normal way is taken over in certain areas of life by an evil power, that is, a *demon or demons, (aspects such as speech, dress, sexual behavior, thought-life, violence, addictions, etc. can be influenced by this evil power). For that *demon possessed* person, it is a helpless position, with little or no ability to resist the power of evil within. In fact, these people will sometimes appear to reject help from well-meaning Christians, or from God. That rejection of help that is offered may actually be part of the *demon possession*. In other words, deep inside, there is a God-created person who wants to cry out, "Help!" But the demonically empowered words coming out of that person's mouth say, "Go away!" However, God can overrule all demonic power and free that person. (Mark 5:1-20 is the story of Jesus encountering just such a person.)

The exception to God's effectiveness against demons is when an individual has exercised his *free will, that is, he is determined to live against God's direction, for example, in unforgiveness, or lying, or sexual perversion, or envying others for what they have, or in pride. Not everyone who does these things will become *demon possessed*, but these things and any other stubborn disobedience can give the devil and his demons an opportunity and foothold to move in, to begin to oppress, and eventually *possess* a person, because that person has chosen to live in Satan's kingdom, not God's.

(See *deliverance to see how one gets out of this problem.)

Denomination: a named and defined association of Christian churches. A *denomination* is a group of churches who agree on certain points of Christian thinking, and they associate together as a group, like the Baptists, or the Methodists (these are *denominations*). Between the *denominations* there are points of disagreement which are viewed as serious enough to separate them. Some churches are "*non-denominational*," usually meaning that they are mainline Christians who are willing to associate with just about any *denomination*, and they refuse to give importance to some of the issues that separate the *denominations*. Most of these *denominations* were formed hundreds of years ago, and, at the time those *denominations* were formed, the differences were considered important enough to fight and die for, but these days most of them get along fairly well. Most Christians have the attitude, "As long as we can agree on the *cross and the *blood, we can get along with any Christian." (What happened on the *cross and the meaning of the *blood of Jesus are the basics, for the believer.) It is tragic that Christianity has such a history of deep divisions between the *denominations*. Jesus has the vision that believers should be one in unity, as He and the *Father are one. In the Gospel of John 17:20-23, Jesus prays for all believers to be unified. His intent is that people from every race and every background become one undivided group. He prays, "that they may all be one; even as You, Father, are in Me and I in You, that they also may be in Us, so that the world may believe that You sent Me." When Christians love one another, it sends a message to the world that Jesus is the savior of mankind, sent by God.

Depraved: the human condition without Jesus; completely unable to please God, to choose to do good, or even to turn to God. In fact, *depravity* means to be always prone to evil rather than good. It is generally accepted in Christianity that mankind is lost, or *depraved*, unable to find his way and only able to get right with God through believing in Jesus. Getting right with God is possible when one's offenses have been forgiven by faith in Jesus. By faith in Jesus, one is given a new nature, no longer *depraved*, but able to choose good and able to love God and long for more of God. Romans 3:23-28 says that even though one begins as a *depraved* person, full of wrong and selfishness, God can completely turn that around when that one has faith in Jesus. Christians are no longer *depraved*; they have the choice to do good, rather than being slaves to sin. They are now saints (*sanctified and being sanctified) no longer sinners, though they may still choose sin.

Destiny: a pre-determined plan for a person. Christians will say, "God has a wonderful plan for your life." That is a basic Christian spiritual truth and the Christian idea of *destiny*. However, another elementary truth is that God does not force anyone to carry out His plans. One always has the choice to refuse to obey or to cooperate with God's plan. (Christians call that "*free will.") In fact, it also possible for a believer to miss God's wonderful plan completely by just having his focus on the wrong things. The *destiny* of those who remember God is different from that of those who forget God.

Destiny to a Christian is very different from fatalism, a common non-Christian belief. Fatalism is belief in an unchangeable future that is rigid and unbending. It is going to happen no matter one's efforts to avoid it. God's destiny for a believer takes into account that person's creativity, talents, input, and ideas. It is not so narrowly defined that any mistakes along the way will cancel it out. Christians believe that if a person falls out of God's wonderful plan, it can still be worked out. God gives second chances (and third, and etc).

It is a common fear, thinking that, "If I miss it, my life will be wasted." Christians can read the book of Ruth or Esther, or read about Joseph and Jacob in Genesis or many other Bible characters and recognize the amazing patience and creativity of God's plan and how He works things out in spite of predictable human mistakes.

Christian destiny is centered on two things: (1) how God desires to bless the believer (He always has blessing for the believer) (2) how the believer will be a blessing to others, which is always about helping people see God. *Destiny* is not focused on the exact how, or when, or where. Well known Pastor and author Bill Johnson says that God will glorify Himself through the creativity of His people. (His book is *Dreaming with God*.) God's will is that He may be known in the earth, and that can be accomplished through the life of a lawyer, a pastor, an artist, or a full-time mom. If God has a destiny for anyone that is more specific than that, then God can be trusted to make that abundantly clear to the believer who is eager to hear and do what He asks.

Christians understand that even a believer <u>can</u> set himself against God's plan, and he may miss it. Alan Redpath, famous Christian author, refers to that as a "saved soul and a wasted life." Resisting or avoiding God's directions down the road of life does not mean the loss of one's salvation, it just means that the believer will accomplish little or nothing of eternal value. Alan Redpath also says that there are only two things that are eternal in this world: the souls of men and the Word of God. A life spent laboring to help the souls of men receive the Word of God will not be a wasted life.

In Jeremiah 29:11, God says: "for I know the plans I have for you, declares the Lord, plans for welfare and not for calamity to give you a future and a hope." Colossians 4:17: "take heed to the ministry which you have received, that you may fulfill it."Christians see God's *destiny* for them as always worth discovering, guarding, and living.

Devil: a spiritual being who is in opposition to God. He is also known as Satan, Lucifer, the evil one, the accuser of the brethren (Revelation 12:10), the "father of lies" (John 8:44), and "the ruler of this world" (John 12:31), as explained in the next paragraph. The *devil's* background and what he is all about is in detail in Isaiah 14:12-15 and Ezekiel 28:11-19. Although these two passages are also about the king of Babylon and the king of Tyre, Bible scholars agree these passages have an obvious application to Satan, the *devil*. From these passages, it is generally accepted that Satan was a created being, (originally created by God for good). He was an angelic being of incredible glory (some even teach that he was a worship leader in heaven, but that is not clearly written), but at some point, he turned to pride and ambition and arrogance, eventually stating that he would rise above God to be worshipped as God. He was thrown out of heaven, and apparently took one third of the angels with him (Revelation 12:3-4) who became his co-workers, the *demons. His goal ever since that time has been to gain people's worship, and his purpose is to destroy mankind, especially those who worship God instead of him. (Some people <u>do</u> worship Satan.) True Christians pose a threat to him, because God has made it clear He will use mankind to defeat the *devil* over the world and to establish the kingdom of God (Revelation 12: 10-11).

Satan has had authority over the world since Adam and Eve believed his lies that they could be like God (Genesis 3). When they submitted to his lies, Adam and Eve gave to the *devil* the authority that God had given to them to oversee the world, so now he is called the "god of this world," (2 Corinthians 4:4) or "the ruler of this world" (John 12:31). Look around, and it's not too hard to believe that the *devil's* ways of greed, power, meanness, and selfishness define much of what goes on among mankind all over the world. But Jesus has taken the keys of authority <u>back</u> from the *devil* (Revelation 1:18 and Matthew 28:18) and has made that authority available to Christians by faith.

Therefore, Christians are the *devil's* enemy. He will try to discourage, defeat, disease, derail, distract, disturb, and depress the believer. He is sly and subtle, but the Christians' instruction from God is "resist the *devil* and he will flee from you" (James 4:7). Believers resist him by first recognizing his activity, and his influence. Doubts, fears, and rebellions that Christians wrestle with don't just come from human nature, they are often from the various influences of Satan, but recognizing that, believers can silence him and send him away by the authority of Jesus. Christians also resist Satan by putting on the armor of God. Ephesians 6:11-18 says that God has armor that He gives to praying Christians to help them win against the schemes of the *devil*. That armor helps Christians to stand firm against the attacks, to have faith, think clearly, to remember the truth, to live righteously, and to tell others about Jesus.

Satan is not a little red man with a tail and a pitchfork, as in the cartoons. He is actually quite beautiful, according to the Ezekiel passage, and according to those who have visibly encountered him. He is not all-knowing, not all-powerful, and not present everywhere at once (but God is all of those things). Satan is finite, limited. God is infinite in all his attributes. Satan is powerful, for sure, much more powerful than humans, but Christ plus one believer are infinitely more powerful than Satan.

The *devil* is defeated by Jesus (Colossians 2:15). He is defeated by the believing Christians (James 4:7, Revelation 12:10-11). He will ultimately be thrown into the Lake of Fire (Revelation 20:10). Stacey Cline, teacher at Elim Bible Institute says that the *devil* is a serpent (Genesis 3) with his head crushed, and if you know anything about snakes, that means he is still dangerous, but there is no mistaking it, he is dead.

Devotions: regular time (usually daily) spent by believers to remember who God is towards them and who they are to be in relationship with Him. Christians talk about their *devotions*, or quiet time.

That means time spent reading the Bible, worshipping, and praying, usually in the morning, although anytime is good for *devotions*. (Morning is just the time most people are alert and less distracted.)

Devotions are the Christian's way of staying in touch with God, hearing from Him on a daily basis, being encouraged by Him, strengthened by Him, and learning more about Him. Without *devotions*, believers are unavoidably more in touch with the world, hearing more about the world on a daily basis, just because it is there, very loudly. Without *devotions*, the influence of the world is automatically greater through the media and the attitudes of surrounding unbelievers.

Some Christians pick a book of the Bible and read it, a little each day; that is simple *devotions*. There are varieties of Bible-reading schedules. Most Christians will also spend some time in prayer, responding to anything the Word has spoken, laying all anxieties before God (Philippians 4:6-7), complaining to Him if necessary; God is not offended by that (Psalm 55:17 and 142:1-2), and giving thanks to Him always (1 Thessalonians 5:18).

Regular *devotions* help the Christian either to be blessed or to be a blessing. Pastor Bill Johnson, of Bethel Church in Redding California, has a simple plan: he says to just "read until you hear from God." Many Christians use *devotional* materials that are either published or available on line. These are short, thought-provoking writings from Christian authors that inspire and promote Bible reading, Bible study, and a closer life-relationship with God.

If a day gets missed, it does not mean God is going to be angry, it just means that God and the believer missed getting together that day, both missed out on the potential benefit. God loves to spend time with the believer, and that is one of the main reasons for *devotions*, loving times with God.

Discernment of spirits: a God-given ability to tell what kind of spirit is involved in any situation (also called distinguishing of spirits). This *discernment* is one of the *gifts of the Holy Spirit, a supernatural enabling from God to do something beyond a person's natural ability (1 Corinthians 12:1-11).

Spirits are invisible, but their influence upon people and situations is real and much more widespread than most people realize. This gift of *discernment* allows a believer to be able to tell what kind of spirit is at work. Dr. Mike Webster of Spirit and Word Ministries states that it will be one of three possibilities: the Spirit of God, of the human spirit, or of an evil spirit. It is not always obvious which. A Christian who has this gift of *discernment* will be able to tell what spiritual influence is present. Pastor Shawn Bolz writes that Christians are called to discern most importantly God's heart in any situation. What does God want to do about it? Especially when something negative is discerned, it is vital for Christians who want to bring in the power of God for good to be able to *discern* what kind of spirit is at work. Christians ask in prayer and God usually gives that gift of *discernment* for that situation and at that moment. Without *discernment,* a lot of energy may be spent trying to fix a situation humanly that actually needs to be understood from the perspective of God.

Disciple: one who wishes to learn from Jesus. It just means a student, but also indicates someone who wants to imitate or become like Jesus. In the Bible are lots of stories about Jesus' *disciples;* they were not a special category of people, except that they were people who had chosen to follow as close to Jesus as they could. Anyone who wants to learn from Jesus today is also a *disciple*.

Disciple is also used as a verb, as in, "I want someone to *disciple* me." *Discipleship* is the situation in which a relatively mature Christian links up with new Christians in spending time together in Bible study, usually on a regular basis.

Disciples look to the Bible, and also confess their weaknesses to one another, find God's strength, help one another understand God's ways, encourage one another, and pray for one another. One of the core values of *disciples* is to love one another. Home groups (small church groups) or cell groups, are usually geared to accomplish *discipleship* to one degree or another.

Christians usually come to a point where they seek out *discipleship* because just church attendance alone will not usually accomplish a deep personal examination of character, an understanding and healing of the past, an excited hope for the future, and a maximizing of God's influence upon all of one's life. *Disciples* long for all of that.

Divination: the practice of ritual procedures to uncover secrets or to know the future. These practices includes palm-reading, Tarot cards, the I-Ching, fortune-telling, crystal balls, seances, channeling, necromancy (talking to the dead), reading tea leaves, Ouija boards, and so forth. These are all in the category of the *occult (originating from the devil). All of these activities are prohibited in the Bible according to Deuteronomy 18:9-14. God desires to protect His people from the deception that is built into these practices. *Divination* is an activity that is given power by evil spirits. Evil spirits, also known as *demons, have spiritual power, power to fool the innocent, or power to attract interest, or power to inspire a counterfeit of faith so that otherwise-sensible people will come to believe in quite preposterous ideas that come out of *divination*. Many lives have been ruined by listening to lies of *divination*. It promises a good future and for happy wishes to be granted, but results in disaster, in defeat, and the end of hope, or at best, a false hope that does not stand the test of eternity. Christians stay away from *divination* in every form.

Divine: from God, holy, made excellent by God's influence. God is *divine*. If someone says something like, "That sounds *divine*," she means it sounds like it came from God.

A "*divine* opportunity" is one that is believed to have been arranged by God, and is therefore assumed to be good. Circumstances are sometimes *divine* set-ups (things that God has set up) to get people in the right place at the right time or in connection with the right people. Angels are *divine;* they come from heaven, from God's presence, doing God's work, and their intentions are only good. Christians long for *divine* encounters (encounters with God, or angels, or His people), and they will talk about those *divine* encounters with excitement because they are usually meaningful, God-arranged experiences.

Additionally, people who have gone to a Christian college or seminary and studied the Bible and the knowledge of God can obtain a degree in *divinity* (Masters of *Divinity*, or a Doctorate of *Divinity*.) So *divinity* is an area of study of the things *divine*, the things of God.

Doctrine: standard beliefs and principles taught by the church. They tend to be "set in stone" so to speak, pretty inflexible. Similar to how a government has laws, churches have *doctrines*. *Doctrines* are intended to define the rules of conduct and requirements agreed upon by any church group. Some *doctrines* come straight out of the Bible, and are therefore a necessary part of a Christian group's belief system. Some other church *doctrines* are the thoughts of men used to outline basic ideas that are deemed to be important by that particular group. Either way, the members of the group have agreed to uphold those *doctrines* and they gather together under the guidelines thus provided. *Doctrines* vary from one group of churches to another. Christians are usually careful to examine the *doctrines* of a church they have just begun to attend, to make sure that they are in agreement with them.

Dogma: codes of behavior put forward by the church that are to be accepted without question. Most churches, these days, do not use the term *dogma* because people do not accept things without question any more.

A few hundred years ago, when people did not have the Bible, or were illiterate, *dogma* got the job done, but sometimes churches enforced *dogma* in a very heavy-handed manner that was not entirely healthy for the church or the believer. So the idea of *dogma* generally has a bad reputation in the church community of modern cultures.

Easter: the Christian celebration of Jesus' resurrection (His coming back to life) after He died. On Easter, Christians remember that Jesus really was killed, dead, and was put in a tomb on a Friday night (known as Good Friday). He was in the grave Saturday and then He came alive again the following Sunday morning (Easter). Books have been written on the significance of this, but the basic Christian belief is that His resurrected life means that Jesus overcame death, accomplished complete removal of every record of sin for the believer, and that He provides a new life to all who are willing to believe in His death and resurrection. Romans 6:3-11 says that Christians have been *baptized into His death and are therefore able also to walk in newness of life because of His resurrection. Well-known Pastor Jack Hayford often uses the term "resurrection life," to mean the kind of Christian newness of life that is no longer overshadowed by death, but eternal, no longer guilty from wrongs done, no longer subject to the nature of evil. Jesus said "because I live you shall live also," (John 14:19). In that statement, He is offering to believers the fullness of life He promised, full of confidence, hope, love, strength of heart, and just having good things happening. Pastor Jack writes, "all in Christ are continually made alive...every moment in which you and I live." That is resurrection life.

Because of the message of Easter, this holiday is a joyous one for believers. Many churches have a special outdoor celebration on Sunday morning at sunrise because it was in the early morning that the women discovered that Jesus' body was no longer in the tomb.

An angel spoke to them at the tomb, saying, "Why do you seek the living One among the dead? He is not here, but He has risen." (Luke 24:5-6). Christians greet one another on Easter with the declaration, "He is risen!" and the reply is, "He is risen indeed!"

Eden: the Garden of *Eden,* a place of perfect communication with God. Christians believe the story of *creation (how God made the earth and the universe) in the first three chapters of the Bible. God created a garden in a place called *Eden*, and put people in it (Adam and Eve) to live there and take care of it. It was a place of perfect harmony between all the creatures of creation, and between God and man. A summary of the story is that even though everything was good in *Eden*, Adam and Eve disobeyed God in the garden and ate from a tree which was the only thing in the garden they were told by God <u>not</u> to eat. They ate the forbidden fruit and fell from God's blessing and were forced to leave the garden. (See *fall).

So *Eden* refers to that innocent, unstained time of clear harmony with God and all of creation that existed in the beginning. It refers to the time when man could eat from the tree of life in the garden and never die. Death was not in the picture then. Indeed, there was no evil, not even the idea of evil, no trouble, no pain, no tears, no worries, no fear, no striving.

All of that was lost because Adam and Eve disobeyed God. Christians believe that disobeying God always destroys harmony and beauty, and puts distance between man and God. On the other hand, obeying God maintains or continues the good plans God has, and keeps believers close to Him.

Now, regarding *Eden* and the future, God's long-range plan is to restore the unstained relationship between man and God. This is to be accomplished through faith in Jesus. Those who believe in Jesus will be restored to an *Eden*-like state; perfect unhindered communication and friendship with God and one another. (Hell, or complete separation from God and His love is the only other alternative.)

The final condition of all Christians will be in heaven, in perfect relationship with God, in a place of no evil, no trouble, and no pain. In fact, not even any darkness will be there, because Jesus himself will be the light of heaven.

The difference between what was in *Eden* originally and the final condition of Christians is that Christians will have known evil, but Adam and Eve in *Eden* had not known evil. Christians will understand the destruction that happened because of disobedience, and will have experienced God's mercy. Adam and Eve in *Eden*, however, were curious about what God forbade them, and the devil deceived them, so they disobeyed. Christians will not be curious; they will not believe the lies, they will never again want to disobey because they will never want to go back to the misery they lived in because of disobedience, but will want to remain eternally in the perfect presence of God's love and forgiveness. The story of *Eden* teaches Christians what it is that God wants, and Jesus makes it possible to be restored to that *Eden*-like unstained relationship of mutual love and trust again.

Edify / edification: an influence that has an uplifting effect on others, to build them up. *Edification* happens when people speak compassionate, helpful, teaching, encouraging words to one another. *Edification* is the opposite of cutting comments, gossip, unfounded accusations, mockery, or rough joking. God *edifies*. The Bible *edifies*. Jesus *edified* the crowds as He spoke to those who came to hear Him. Christians are to *edify* one another. It's sort of the Christian version of, "if you can't say something nice, don't say anything at all." 1 Corinthians 14:12 says, "seek to abound for the *edification* of the church." Romans 14:19 says, "pursue the things which make for peace and the building up [*edification*] of one another."

Egypt: symbolic of the world-system that provides food, shelter, and safety in return for enslavement to wrongdoing (sin). "*Egypt*" on the lips of Christians, means the world in which the Christians lived before Jesus came into their lives.

The background for this is in the Biblical book of Exodus. The people of God, the Jews, were being held in the nation of *Egypt* as slaves. *Egypt* was the place where the children of Israel, the Jews, had lived for many generations with plenty to eat, nice houses, and relative security, but they were slaves to the Egyptians. Then God delivered them from slavery through His servant Moses and they went to the *Promised Land (their own good land that God had promised to them). Christians interpret the exodus (coming out of *Egypt*) as the picture of God setting people free today from the old way of life, to give them a new place to live, free from enslavement. Christians through the ages have identified with coming out of slavery in *Egypt* as a parallel to their own coming out of sin (wrongdoing, and enslavement to it, in the form of sex, drugs and alcohol, as well as greed, ambition, and pride).

However, several times on the way out of *Egypt*, on the way to the *Promised Land, the people complained in times of hardship, that they would rather have stayed in *Egypt*. They remembered the food, and the plenty, but they were forgetting the whip of enslavement (Exodus 16:3, Numbers 11:4-6). Christians see this as parallel to their own temptation to return to sin. Christians don't want to "go back to *Egypt*." They remember the enslavement to things of which they are now ashamed. But in times of temptation, remembering how it used to be can be very deceiving. So Christians encourage one another with the words, "Don't go back to *Egypt!*"

Elder: a leader in the Christian church. The word *elder* in the original language of Greek is *presbuteros*, which simply means an older person, but in Christianese it is a title, a position of leadership in the church. Paul appointed *elders* as he traveled around starting new churches (Acts 14:23), and Paul instructed Titus to appoint *elders* in the new churches. These *elders* were the appointed leaders of the churches, doing all the work that would now be called "pastoring," the work of the pastor.

Today, many churches have *elders* as part of the leadership of the church, but usually as assistants to the pastor. At the time that the New Testament was written, the words *elder* and pastor were used as similar in meaning. *Pastor means to shepherd, to lead a flock, or a church, with the care that a shepherd does his flock of sheep. Jesus instructed Peter to "shepherd [pastor] My sheep." (John 21:16). Later on, in his writing, Peter tells the *elders* to shepherd (pastor) the flock of God with eagerness. Some churches do not officially have a pastor, but only have *elders*. Many scholars use the terms *bishop, *elder* and *pastor as interchangeable, as basically the same, even though there are three different Greek words in the original writing of the Bible. These differences between churches and terms of leadership can be confusing, but in any given church, the members there use the titles that indicate who is leading and at what level.

The clearest outline of the positions of leadership in the church is perhaps in Ephesians 4:11-16 which gives five key roles in the church: *apostles, *prophets, *evangelists, *pastors, and teachers. This is referred to as the five-fold ministry of the church. These five places of ministry are held to be essential for the healthy functioning of any church. Notice that *elder* is not in that list, but is apparently the same as pastor, according to Peter's usage of those words.

Elders are given Biblical instruction on how to "shepherd the flock of God among you" in 1 Peter 5:1-4. Peter writes that *elders* should care for the people, "voluntarily, according to the will of God; and not for sordid gain [money], but with eagerness; nor yet as lording it over those allotted to your charge, but proving to be examples to the flock."

There are clear sets of standards in the Bible so that all levels of leadership will be good leaders (1 Timothy 3:1-13). If they are being unrighteous, they don't get to have a lead position in the church.

Christians usually are very careful about who they allow into these positions of leadership in the church and over the life, spiritual growth, and well-being of everyone in the church.

Elect: the chosen ones, selected by God, or Christians in general. Some Christians talk about "the *elect*," meaning generally those who are believers, but exactly what is meant by the word is a point of controversy among Christians. The word shows up several times in the New Testament (the part of the Bible written after Jesus lived on earth), most notably, Matthew 24:22-24, Mark 13:20-27, and 2 Thessalonians 2:13. Exactly <u>how</u> God chooses the *elect* is the point of disagreement. One group of Bible scholars says that God only selected some people (and not all) and also entirely provided the faith for the *elect* (the chosen ones) to believe. In other words, becoming a believer is entirely of God, and man had <u>nothing</u> to do with it. Therefore some people are born to whom God is not going to give the faith to believe, and they will not be of the *elect*. In this view, the *elect* were born destined to be believers and the rest were born destined to never believe in Jesus (and ultimately go to hell).

The other group of Bible scholars says that God wants everyone to be saved and gives everyone the opportunity to choose to believe, yet He knows ahead of time who will make the choice to believe and who will not. This view gives man the choice to have faith or not. In this view, no one is born destined to be faithless. Both sides of the argument have ample Bible verses to "prove" their view. As a Christianese word, all that can be presented here is an over-simplified presentation of a very complicated question of how God works among the souls of men. The definition of *predestination contains some of the elements of the same problem. Max Lucado, Pastor and author, tells a wonderful story about being a casual laborer waiting for someone to hire him, how good it was finally to be "chose."

Christians know that they were chosen (*elect*), and that they owe everything to God's amazing love coming to choose them, regardless of how this word *elect* is defined.

End Times: the time in history that leads up to the end of the world, also known as "the last days." Jesus taught that there is coming an end of this age (Matthew 24:35-25:46). And it will be at that time that He returns, for His *second coming. (Jesus is coming back.) There has always been much curiosity about it. Even His disciples asked Him, "when will these things happen?" (Matthew 24:3). There has been much controversy and confusion about what will happen in the *end times*, the time leading up to the end of the age or the return of Christ. In Acts 2:16-17, Peter declares that the last days, or *end times*, began at the time he was preaching, just after Jesus.

There is no universal agreement among Christians on the *end times*. There have been some popularized interpretations of the way things will unfold in the *end times*, offered by high-profile Christian leaders, however, it is all very open to interpretation.

A few things are known for sure, according to Bible prophecies. (1) Jesus will come back, and He will come at a time no one can predict (Matthew 24:36 and Mark 13:33-37).

(2) He will come as King and as Lord assuming rulership over all (Daniel 2:44-45, Revelation 19:16, Philippians 2:9-11).

(3) There is to be a mass ascension of all believers who are alive at the time, up to meet Jesus in the air (1 Thessalonians 4:13-18). The timing of this event is a matter of controversy. It is popularly called "the *Rapture."

(4) There is to be a "*great tribulation," a time of extreme trouble for all the earth (famine, war, plague, tyrannical government, torment, persecution of Christians, fire, earthquakes, blood and smoke, and the wrath of God). Some think that the tribulation has been going on ever since the beginning of the church until the present.

American Christians tend to believe that it will be a future seven year period and that it has not started yet. What is universally accepted as clear in the Bible is that the righteous will suffer persecution (John 15:20, 2 Timothy 3:12).

(5) The Millenium is a 1000 year period in which Jesus and His faithful will reign on earth and Satan and his forces will be bound (Revelation 20:1-7). Christians disagree on when this will happen, whether it has already happened, whether it is a literal 1000 years or just a long time. All of these possibilities are points of debate.

Most Christians seem to believe that Jesus could return at any time, but they live, pay rent, go to college, and plan ahead as if it is going to be a long time. Peter the apostle of Jesus puts forward the real question about *the end*, the "*day of the Lord." 2 Peter 3:9-15 says, "The Lord is not slow about His promise...but is patient...not wishing for any to perish but for all to come to repentance. The day of the Lord...will come...with a roar...the elements will be destroyed with intense heat......what sort of people ought you to be in holy conduct and godliness, looking for and hastening the coming of the day of God?" Christians ask themselves, "What can I do in the time remaining to ensure that I am in harmony with the heart of God for all people? How can I engage with those whom He loves who have yet to acknowledge Him? I know it is His desire that none will perish."

Enemy: the *devil. Christians commonly know the devil as "The *enemy* of our soul." He is referred to as "the *enemy*" in Luke 10:19. Revelation chapter 12 gives a clear overview of how the devil, portrayed as a great red dragon, is the *enemy* of the church, the faithful believers, and is in opposition to all that is of God. It is clearly a war, there is an opposing *enemy*. Satan, the devil, the *enemy* is to be finally defeated, not by violence (his tactics are violent and murderous) but by believers' faith in Jesus, even in the face of death (Revelation 12:11).

Eternal: without beginning or end. It is important to understand that eternal does not just mean "forever" when Christians are talking about God. Forever means it is never going to end. *Eternal*, when talking about God, means it has no beginning <u>and</u> it has no end. Only God fits that qualification. The Bible also talks about *eternal* life (see the next definition) which is what God promises to believers, but God really is the only one who is *eternal*. He always has been, is not created and cannot be destroyed. God is *eternal*. Christians, who clearly have a beginning, get to enter into *eternal* life, which seems to mean that entering into God's reality includes all of God's astounding *eternity*, not just beginning when the Christian counted the beginning.

Eternal life: life without end. To Christians, this is really important to understand. This term means several things to Christians. It means, "life forever," it also means, "Heaven," and, perhaps the least understood meaning; it also means, "life <u>now</u> with a whole new outlook." Look at these one at a time.

Life forever: dying is one of mankind's big problems; everybody is going to die, but perfectly sane men have spent their lives searching for the "Fountain of Youth," so they would never have to die. Jesus' clearest promise is to make *eternal life* possible. It is written in John 3:16, which is perhaps why that Bible verse is so often quoted: "for God so loved the world, that He gave his only begotten son, that whoever believes in Him shall not perish [die], but have *eternal life*." Obviously Jesus is not promising that people who believe in Him will walk around alive for ever, or we would have some 2000-year-old people here who believed in Jesus back when He first arrived in Galilee. But, in fact, they all died: Peter, James, John, etc. It remains true that all will die.

Eternal life, then, is about spiritual life, not a physical life. Spiritual life is no less important. In fact, it is probably more important because it <u>is</u> forever. Christians believe that man is created to be eternal.

Pastor and author Alan Redpath says, "Two things are eternal; the Word of God and the souls of men. Everything else is temporary." This idea is in agreement with Jesus. He divides mankind into two groups in Matthew 25:31-46. One group, He says is going to eternal punishment, and the other is going to *eternal life*. Both conditions are eternal. *Eternal life*, Jesus states, simply is "with Me in paradise" (Luke 23:43). *Eternal life* is a gift from God by faith in Jesus (Romans 6:23). Even believers still have to die physically, but what they have to look forward to, "on the other side of the veil," (that is, after death) is *eternal life* with Jesus, which leads to the next idea, that *eternal life* means heaven.

Look up *heaven to see all that it means, but basically (and people have been there and come back to this life to tell about it) it is a place that people describe as indescribably beautiful, with light, music, angelic beings, peace, freedom, joy, holiness, no sickness, no sorrow, no darkness, and everything saturated with the awareness of the presence of God and His unending love. Those who go to heaven will stay there forever, eternally; that is *eternal life*. With Jesus, it only gets better after this life.

Eternal life's, third meaning is that even here on earth *eternal life* <u>begins</u> at the moment that a person accepts the offer of *eternal life* from Jesus. It happens when one is forgiven, when one chooses to believe in Jesus (becomes a believer) or, as Christians say it, "gets *saved," which means entering into *eternal life* by faith in Jesus. *Eternal life* is part of the huge package Christians call *salvation.

Eternal life <u>now</u> is the awareness that everything has changed; (1) the believer has a new life in Christ. It is a completely new life, not a make-over.

(2) There is no guilt or condemnation hanging over the believer's past and his deeds.

(3) There is reconciliation between God and the believer, they are no longer adversaries, but now friends.

(4) There is the promise and the experience of supernatural help from God in every area of life.

(5) There is worship, the adoration of God which comes from entering into His presence. (6) There is prayer, communication with God, both to Him and from Him.

(7) There is the Word of God, the Bible to encourage, direct, strengthen, teach and empower the believer. The most important feature of *eternal life* is that it starts <u>now</u>. And believers, full of *eternal life*, do become a powerful influence for good in the world around them now. Eternal life is evident on them, others see it, ask about it, and are influenced by it.

Eternal security: the belief that a believer will remain heaven-bound no matter what future sins may be committed, no matter what lies of the devil may be spoken against him. *Eternal security* is a term that means that once a person is *saved (has given his or her life to God) and has *eternal life (is going to heaven) it can never be taken away, and he or she can never lose it. Many Christians say, "Once saved, always saved."

Some Christians believe in *eternal security*, and some don't. It has been a point of argument for centuries among Christians. Here are some things that are clear in the Bible: A Christian cannot lose her salvation by accident, like tripping over a curb, because she committed a certain sin, and suddenly she is not saved any more without even knowing it. That doesn't happen. If one can lose one's salvation, if it is possible, it is the result of a conscious, determined, consistent effort to reject all of God (Hebrews 10:26-29). Biblical truth also makes clear that the devil cannot rob the Christian of her eternal life.

John 10:28 says, (Jesus speaking) "I give eternal life to them, and they will never perish; and no one will snatch them out of My hand." The devil can't just sneak into a Christian's life and lie to her, trick her, and steal her salvation. He is tricky, but he cannot un-save the believer.

Now consider the common non-Christian idea of, "selling your soul to the devil." This usually refers to what a person does who does not believe in Jesus, but wants something very badly (wealth, fame, success, etc.) and she makes a deal with the devil to get it. The trouble is, the devil is a deceiver, and usually doesn't give what he promises. And even if one has made that kind of a deal, but then *repents, changes her mind and wants to follow Jesus, the deal is off, null and void. The devil has no claim on a person who has turned instead to Jesus. Jesus' authority overrides any claim Satan has on that person.

Also; some people get worried about the "*unforgivable sin" which is clearly the act of *blaspheming the Holy Spirit, or saying bad things about the Holy Spirit (Matthew 12:31-32). People who are worried about that, fear that they do not have *eternal security,* that they may have lost salvation unawares, by mistake. But no, this would have to be a conscious and calculated decision, not a slip of the tongue that the believer did by mistake. If someone is worried about having committed the unforgivable sin, that is a sure indication that she <u>hasn't</u> done it; she still desires God's favor; she has not turned against God.

Notice this also: that committing sin (even a huge amount of sin) does not equal losing salvation (story of the prodigal son, Luke 15:11-32). Some would say, "Well, she sins a lot, and she used to be a good girl, so she must have lost her salvation," and a person like that can sure look like a non-believer. But, the truth is, that person did not gain salvation by stopping sinning; she gained salvation by God's generosity because she believes in Jesus (Ephesians 2:8). She became a child of God.

So she can't lose her salvation by doing sins any more than children are rejected by their parents for being naughty. The door by which believers enter salvation is grace (God's generosity), so the door they get out by, if there is one, is rejection of that grace (Hebrews 10:29).

Eucharist: a ritual meal taken in remembrance of Jesus' saving work (same meaning as *communion). "*Eucharist*" is the word used for "communion" in Catholic and Episcopal churches. (It is originally from Greek and Latin meaning thankfulness and gratitude.) In English, it can mean the ritual, or it can mean the actual consecrated bread that is eaten in the communion ritual. The ritual is the remembering of Jesus' death on the *cross. In remembrance, Christians eat the bread and drink the wine or juice, usually in church, together. This is one of the few rituals that Jesus instructed for believers. For Christians it has the powerful effect of leading them into deeper relationship with Him, and even imparting to them renewed faith and strength for life.

It began as a tradition the last time that Jesus ate a meal with His followers (known by Christians as the last supper). Jesus took some of the bread that was for dinner and said, "This is My body," and He took some of the wine and said, "This is My blood of the covenant which is poured out for many for forgiveness of sins." And He instructed His followers to eat and drink as a way of remembering Him, remembering His death on the cross, remembering and being thankful that He gives forgiveness and new life.

Evangelical: churches or Christians who believe that people establish their relationship with God only through believing in Jesus. (Non-evangelical churches may believe that one gets restored relationship with God through church membership or church rituals.) Christians talk about *evangelical* churches, usually meaning any type of Christian Church whose people want to tell everyone about Jesus (they want to *evangelize; they want to "preach the *gospel").

Evangelical usually does not include Catholics or Episcopalians, even though those groups may be just as passionate about the gospel and evangelizing in their own way. *Evangelicals* also do not include *cults (groups which pose as Christian, but have a very different message than *evangelical* Christians).

What the cults teach is different from the gospel spoken of by *evangelical* churches. *Evangelicals* have clear definitions of God and His work and about Jesus and who He is. This is all in agreement with time-tested, traditional and Biblical Christian thinking. Cults are not biblically accurate (although they may use the Bible or their own version of it). They differ significantly from traditional Christianity, and are therefore not *evangelical*.

The term *evangelical* is also used to refer to *evangelical* Christians meaning sort of like "standard" Christians. Most of the mainline church groups (*denominations), Methodists, Presbyterians, Baptists, etc. would be referred to as *evangelical* churches and their people would be considered to be *evangelical* Christians.

Evangelist / evangelize / evangelism: those who tell the good news or teach others the way to tell the good news (the Gospel). An *evangelist* tells people the good news that God loves them and forgives them through believing in Jesus. And *evangelist's* message can take many different forms, but always has an effect on people: it makes them want to come to God, and it portrays God in a way that is attractive and desirable, often even to people who have resisted the message of the Bible or the church for a long time. It makes people feel an urgency to know God and find His forgiveness, and His love. The *evangelist's* message helps people trust God and feel free to approach that awesome throne, even with their load of guilt and shame, knowing and believing they can be set free and come to the knowledge of the truth.

Evangelists also love to teach other Christians how to *evangelize*, how to lead people to trust in Jesus.

Some *evangelists* are like Billy Graham, speaking to big crowds, but most *evangelists* just speak to one person at a time, to a neighbor, a co-worker, a hitch hiker. Most people who become Christians do so because some one person *evangelized* them, talked to them about Jesus.

People may say, "Don't talk to me about religion," but the true *evangelist* can find a way to talk about Jesus without causing hard feelings. Later, when people have become Christians, they are thankful and remember forever the people who told them about Jesus in a manner that they could listen and understand. They will thank the *evangelist*, if they do come to believe in Jesus, for confronting their unbelief, for being bold enough to cross that boundary of, "Don't talk to me about religion," or for being willing to risk losing the friendship, or to look like a fool. It is a gift from God to be able to *evangelize*. (See *Spiritual Gifts.) Ephesians 4:11 is about the gift or office of the *evangelist;* Acts 8:26-40 is a story about Philip the *evangelist* in action; in 2 Timothy 4:5, Paul writes to a young Christian named Timothy and encourages him to be the *evangelist* that God has gifted him to be.

Evil one: Satan, the devil, Lucifer, the enemy. See *devil for complete explanation. He is referred to as the *evil one* because he is exactly that. Everything he does is ultimately evil towards mankind, and towards God, and he has a consistently evil agenda. He may come across as charming and helpful when people first encounter him, but it is a trap. He generally uses temptation greed, ambition, pride, and deceit to get people on the wrong track in life.

He especially accuses Christians all the time, whether they've done anything wrong or not, so much so that he is called "the accuser of our brethren" (Revelation 12:10). He lies all the time trying to promote fear or to mislead people, especially believers. Why believers? Because the *evil one* sees Christians as his primary threat. The Bible says that the *evil one* will eventually be defeated by the Christians' faith in Jesus.

Revelation 12:10-11 says that the Christians will finally overcome the devil "by the blood of the Lamb, and because of the word of their testimony," even when facing death. The *evil one* works constantly to turn Christians against God, or to destroy their faith, in order to attempt to prevent that prediction in Revelation from happening.

However, Jesus gives Christians authority over all the power of the *evil one* (Luke 10:19 says, Jesus speaking, "Behold I have given you authority...over all the power of the enemy, [Satan, the devil, the *evil one*] and nothing shall injure you,") which means they don't have to submit to any of the *evil one's* tricks. Believers in Jesus don't have to give into temptation, believe his lies, be subject to fear, come under his condemnation, or buy into his program of complaining, criticizing and being negative. He is an already-defeated enemy, according to the Bible. (Colossians 2:15 says that Jesus "disarmed the rulers and authorities [the devil and his demons]. He made a public display of them [in the spiritual realm] having triumphed over them through [the cross]."

Evil spirit: a being without a physical body which works to injure, sicken, terrorize, or defeat people, especially Christians. (See *Demon.) These spiritual beings are allies of the devil, mostly invisible except when it is helpful to their work to be seen either as a deceiving angel of light (2 Corinthians 11:14-15) or as a threatening presence to frighten people. One of Jesus' more common miracles was to "*cast out a demon" (Matthew 18:18). Jesus demonstrated His spiritual authority over all things in this way, and He taught His followers to do the same thing (Matthew 10:10).

Exodus: the departure of God's chosen people from Egypt, or the Bible book about that event. *Exodus* was an event in the Bible that happened about 3500 years ago, and the second book of the Bible has the title, *Exodus* because it is the historical account of it. What happened was that the Jews were held in slavery in Egypt for hundreds of years.

When God brought them out of Egypt and set them free from slavery through Moses' leadership, it was called "the *exodus*" (think, "exit"). Hundreds of thousands of people in a huge crowd had to hike from Egypt to the land that God had promised them (the *promised land, which is now the nation of Israel, and is still mostly Jews).

So when Christians talk about the *exodus* it is that story, or the book about it, to which they are referring. And it is an important story, not only because an entire race of people (perhaps close to a million) made this journey with God's help, but also because freedom from slavery is an idea that is parallel to freedom from doing wrong (sin). In Christian thinking, sin enslaves people. Think especially of addictions of all kinds, and think of selfishness, greed, and abuse of power. People become enslaved to these behaviors because, in all these areas, there is a pay-off for behaving that way, so it is hard to stop, hard to break free, and getting free takes God's help. The story of *Exodus* tells Christian believers that no matter what the slavery is, God can and will set them free. And the story of *Exodus* is the story of getting to a better place, "a land flowing with milk and honey" (Exodus 3:8). Christians see the *exodus* as a parallel to their own journey from slavery of the wrong things to a new life of doing well, and their personal *exodus* will lead ultimately to heaven and perfection in the presence of Jesus.

Exorcism: the work of an exorcist, that is, negotiating to get demon influence out of a person. Sometimes Christians use this word to mean "*casting out a demon," or "*deliverance," but theologian Mike Webster teaches that it is actually the wrong word to use for those activities, and has quite different in meaning. Casting out a demon or deliverance are Christian terms that mean what happens when believers speak in the authority of Jesus to <u>command</u> an evil spirit to leave a person.

Exorcism is a term from other belief systems (religions), meaning the magical or superstitious rites and ceremonies that are used to try to remove evil spirits from a person's life. Evil spirits, or *demons, are spiritual beings, invisible usually, that cause problems in some people's lives, usually using fear as their primary weapon. Many of the religions of some cultures involve putting curses on people, which is asking an evil spirit to attack someone.

People who are the victims of curses of course want to get rid of the evil spirits and they will use some form of *exorcism* if they are not Christians. Exorcism will use some particular formula to coax the evil spirits to leave.

Evil spirits will sometimes move or obey in response to those formulas, which is why black magic and witchcraft is so full of strange ceremonies that have to be done at a certain time (midnight, under the full moon, etc.) or a special place (a certain tree, or in a cave) with certain ingredients and procedures. There is power in those things in non-Christian beliefs. Curses, spells and witchcraft are real phenomena. However, Christians believe that the power of Jesus is infinitely greater, and it is Jesus' authority that Christians use to get rid of evil influences. Jesus is the higher authority, and all spirits must obey Him eventually.

There is a story in Acts 19:13-19, in which a group of *exorcists* had begun to use the name of Jesus as their new formula to get rid of demons. The *exorcists* themselves did not personally believe in Jesus. Apparently it worked for a while, until they came across some demons who knew that the *exorcists* did not really know Jesus, and therefore they did not really have authority over the demons. The demon- possessed man, under demonic power, physically beat up all seven of the *exorcists* and ran them out of the house. For Christians, it is all about relationship; one must really know Jesus to use His name in authority, and *exorcism* is just playing the evil game of who has more power. Jesus, the ultimate authority, has power over all the false powers of the world.

Faith: a firmly held stance or position, coming from the heart (as distinct from in the brain); belief and trust in God. The things that one believes do not have to be based on facts, and certainly do not have to be based on things that one understands. (One gets on an airplane without any understanding of aerodynamics. That is an act of *faith*.) *Faith* is, in part, an abandonment of logical understanding and a devotion to spiritual understanding.

The human spirit is able to understand things that the brain does not understand. God is not someone that the brain can fully understand. At some point one's position regarding God must be based on *faith*. That firmly held position in the heart, in the spirit, is *faith*. There is a passage in 2 Corinthians 4:18 that says, "look not at the things which are seen, but at the things which are not seen; for the things which are seen are temporal [temporary], but the things which are not seen are eternal." Pastor Bill Johnson of Redding CA says, "Faith sees and responds to unseen realities."

For Christians, the most important part of this is that everything one receives from God is by *faith*. God promises many things, but without *faith* those things will be missed. Believers do not get God's good grace by earning or deserving it, but they get God's goodness only by *faith*.

The only clear definition of *faith* in the Bible is in Hebrews 11:1; "*Faith* is the assurance [substance] of things hoped for, the conviction [evidence] of things not seen." That could be paraphrased as, "If you can believe and trust it, that is all the evidence you need that it is really there." The New Living Translation says, "Faith is the confidence that what we hope for will actually happen; it gives us assurance about things we cannot see." Renowned *faith* teacher Kenneth Hagin says, "*faith* is born of the spirit." It is not a mental exercise. It is a gift that comes from God and resides in the spirit of a person.

The Holy Spirit builds *faith* in a person, using the Bible, worship, and preaching (the proclamation of God's truths).

God also uses *prophecy (words spoken which declare God's truth over someone's life), and *evangelism (clear teaching about the necessity of a relationship with God), to plant seeds of *faith*.

Christians have to unite *faith* with what they have heard about God, even though they can't see anything concrete. So somehow they must be persuaded to believe and trust, and that is the Holy Spirit's work.

Christians must come to the place of longing for and trusting in that which they cannot prove. Part of *faith* is making a choice to believe, to say, "I accept that it is true and I put my trust in it." Christians believe that God alone can bring a person to that point, to *faith*.

Jesus' having come to earth is a great help in finding *faith* because He was seen, touched, and heard. He is an undeniable historical figure. It was a long time ago, but the historical record in the Bible is the most reliable and accurate ancient document in existence. (The book, "Evidence that Demands a Verdict," by Josh McDowell is a good help in understanding this.)

So Christians tend to say, "All you have to do is believe in Jesus." *Faith* in Him is all one needs in order to move into all that God promises. *Faith* needs to be watered and tended so that it will grow into an unshakable *faith*. Some of the many benefits that come by *faith* are also defined in this book: *salvation, *sanctification, being filled with the *Holy Spirit, being *born again (new life), *forgiveness, *atonement, *reconciliation, *victory, *light, *Kingdom of God, *adoption, *wisdom, *resurrection, *eternal life. All of these things are promised by God to those who have *faith* to receive them.

Psalm 91:14 says, "Because he has loved Me, therefore I will deliver him; I will set him securely on High, because he has known My name." In the NLT Study Bible, notes on Hebrews 11 say that "*Faith* is unhesitating action taken on the basis of what God has made known."

Fallen / the fall: man's *fall* from a place of perfect relationship with God, to a place where the relationship is broken but in the process of being restored. See also the *Garden. Christians say that man has "*fallen*" from grace (or *fallen* from favor with God). In the *fall*, God's love did not change, but man's obedience and submission to Him *fell* drastically. This *fall* happened to Adam and Eve, the first people that God created, according to the creation story of the Bible. (The full story is in Genesis chapters 2 and 3.)

Before the *fall* there was perfect love between God and Adam and Eve. All was well with the world: no death, no danger, no fear, no crying. After the *fall*, which happened because Adam and Eve chose to listen to the devil and disobey God, communication with God broke down and the world was changed. Now death, fear, and sorrow came into the world, and it has been that way ever since. (See *curse). You will hear Christians say, "we live in a *fallen* world," referring to how things are bad now in comparison to how Adam and Eve existed at first in the *Garden of Eden.

Ever since the *fall*, people are no longer innocent, but born sinful (prone to do wrong things). Psalm 51:5 says, "I was brought forth in iniquity, and in sin my mother conceived me." All people will sin. Every child lies, steals, hurts other children, and that sort of thing, just naturally. That is the product of the *fall*. It is the *sin nature, as Christians say, the nature of man is to be selfish, greedy, and willing to hurt others in order to get more for the self. Romans 7:14 says, "We know that the law is spiritual, but I am of flesh, sold into bondage to sin."

The good news or the *Gospel, preached by Christians, is that people don't have to stay in bondage to sin. People can be restored to good communication with God and restored back to His *grace, that is, the opportunity for them to become like Jesus. People live in a *fallen* world, but they don't have to live out *fallen* lives.

Christians get to live above the *fall*, in newness of life, with good communication with God, and with promises of protection from the effects of the *fall*, including *death and sickness. Instead of death, Christians get *eternal life, and instead of sickness Christians may receive healing. Instead of broken relationship with God, the love of God can be restored.

Fate: an unchangeable future, a chain of events that cannot be altered. *Fate* is not a Christian idea, because *fate* means something is going to happen to a person, and there is nothing one can do to stop it; it is *fate*.

Christians don't believe in *fate*. They believe that people make choices that change things. One of the choices is whether to have faith in God or not. A definition of *fate* is only included here to clarify how different it is from the Christian ideas of *destiny, *free will, and the *will of God.

Basically Christians trust God rather than believe that everything in life is determined beforehand by *fate*. There are, of course unstoppable events; think of an earthquake. However, Christians face such dangers <u>not</u> with the idea of *fate*, but with faith in the influence of God in any circumstance. However God's influence on a believer is not usually as if He takes the steering wheel. A Christian can choose her path, good or bad, obedient or disobedient, wise or against all wisdom. So there is no *fate* in Christian thinking about life. There is *destiny, which is the idea that God has a plan for a person's life, but one can always decide whether or not to choose that plan. Similarly, there is *calling, which is the idea that God has given certain talents to a person to use in service of God and in relationship to God, but again, one may always choose to use those talents for other purposes, <u>or</u> may choose to pour all of her life into fulfilling that calling.

In Christian thinking, it is not one's *fate* to be rich, poor, or survive or die in an earthquake. God is involved, and so are the will and the mind of the believer. People who believe in *fate* believe that God (or *fate*) must be the cause of everything that happens.

Christians understand that not everything that happens is God's doing. There are usually human choices involved, and God has given the needed wisdom to make good choices. God will occasionally tell believers something that is going to happen (even earthquakes) but the believer's response to that prediction is very important to the outcome. God gives instructions, and people get to choose whether or not to follow those instructions. Pastor Shawn Bolz tells the story of an earthquake God warned him about in his book *Translating God*, and how people made good choices on the basis of God's warning.

Father: the central idea of God, as a caring provider, protector and source of wisdom. Often Christians pray, beginning with *"Father,"* meaning God, as in the prayer that is commonly called "The Lord's Prayer." It starts with, "Our *Father* who is in heaven," (Matthew 6:9). Christians pray to the *Father* often because Jesus teaches in the Bible that God is the Heavenly *Father*. In Matthew 23:9, Jesus says, "Do not call anyone on earth your *father*; for One is your *Father*, He who is in heaven." Furthermore, many Christians have really come to understand Him as *Father*. He has that role in their lives as One who loves them and is provider, protector, and wisdom-giver. When a person becomes a Christian, he is *adopted into God's family, and God is the *Father*. (Romans 8:15-16).

So, if God is the *Father*, then who are His children? Christian thinking says not all people are children of God, contrary to popular thinking. All are created and loved by Him, but one becomes a child of God by receiving Jesus. (Receiving Jesus means believing that He is all that He claims to be in the Bible. See *saved.) John 1:12-13 says, "But as many as received Him, to them He gave the right to become children of God, even to those who believe in His name, who were born, not of blood nor of the will of the flesh nor of the will of man, but of God."

Human fathers are, at least in fairy tales, supposed to be loving, wise, strong, wealthy, protectors, helpful, always favoring their children, and there for the family. In reality, God is the only one able to perfectly fill all these roles. Fathers in this earthly realm fall short. They do not necessarily do all things well. If men are hoping to be really good Dads, God is the ideal pattern. Everyone has had a father, and many earthly fathers have done poorly, but the wounds that may have come as a result of poor parenting may be healed by the Heavenly *Father*. Psalm 27:10 says, "For my father and my mother have forsaken me, but the Lord will take me up." And He will do so perfectly.

Fear: being afraid; the response to perceived danger. (This is a separate idea from the *fear of the Lord, see separate definition below) There is a very important perspective on *fear,* in Christian thinking. In 2 Timothy 1:7, it says, "God has not given us a spirit of timidity [*fear,* cowardice] but of power (courage), and love, and discipline (sound mind.)" *Fear* can come into people's lives and upset everything. As the verse makes clear, *fear,* or being afraid, is not from God.

What is from God is courage, clear headed, love-driven decision making and good direction. Christians don't have to live their lives in *fear* of anything, even death. *Fear* always works against the boldness (courage) that God would have for believers. Love and good judgment is what God has for His children. When *fear* comes in, Christians are to resist allowing it to have any rulership over their lives. They can go ahead with whatever God has directed them to do. Christians are not to make decisions on the basis of *fear*.

This is a life transforming idea for many. Go ahead in spite of *fear*. *Fear* is not from God. What God has told the believer to do, must not be stopped by *fear*. When Christians are afraid, they read Psalm 91 for encouragement. Here is an excerpt: "You will not be afraid of the terror by night…you have made the Lord, my refuge, even the Most High, your dwelling place. No evil will befall you."

Hebrews 2:15 says that Jesus has set free "those who through *fear* of death were subject to slavery all their lives."

God's cure for *fear* is the love of God, according to 1 John 4:18, "There is no *fear* in love; but perfect love casts out *fear*, because *fear* involves punishment, and the one who *fears* is not perfected in love." This is part of a long passage (4:7-5:3) that explains the place of love in the life of the believer. Under the big umbrella of God's perfect love, there is no *fear* of judgment or punishment.

This definition is not about the *fear* that one experiences when in real danger. *Fear* can help a person run from real danger: that is the healthy side of *fear*. Rather, it is about how Christians are freed from the *fear* that can paralyze a person's life and keep him or her from doing what it is that God has made clear he or she is to do. There is a kind of *fear* that says, "What if...?" That kind of *fear* is what can keep people from doing what they want to do, and/or what God wants them to do. It is this *fear* that can be overcome by relying upon the full love and partnership of God.

Fear of the Lord: one's perspective on God that includes awe, respect, love, and terror. Fear of the Lord is a central position of total submission to God and trust in Him. For a Christian, the *fear of the Lord* is a basic foundation stone of relationship with Him. A believer's relationship with God is not founded upon a best-friends-forever idea, or a casual, "God is there when I need help with my life." Christian relationship with God starts with the recognition of who He is: awesomely, eternally powerful, knowing the thoughts and intentions of one's heart, and bringing each person to account for his deeds. Though He always in mercy, He is also always capable of the strictest kind of judgment.

There is much instruction in the Bible about the meaning of this concept. Proverbs 9:10 says, "The *Fear of the Lord* is the beginning of wisdom." Proverbs 8:13 says, "The *fear of the Lord* is to hate evil." Proverbs 14:27 says, "The *fear of the Lord* is a fountain of life."

Matthew 10:28 says, "Do not fear those who kill the body, but are unable to kill the soul; but rather *fear Him*, who is able to destroy both soul and body in hell."

Believers are not supposed to be afraid of God, nor are they supposed to be living in terror because of God. But Christians are to have a reverence or a respect for Him that goes beyond honor and into fear. *Fear of the Lord* is not dread, or terror. Unbelievers sometimes experience dread or terror of God (2 Chronicles 17:10).

Fear of the Lord is a reverence always accompanied by the awareness that although eternal life is available in Christ, God also can put a soul in hell for eternal destruction, eternal fire, eternal punishment (Matthew 25:46, 2 Thessalonians 1:9). This is the terror part of the *fear of the Lord*.

Think of the hush that comes over a room full of people when the CEO walks in. He can fire anyone in the room, or he can give promotions and raises, so he is *feared* and honored. That bears some similarity to the *fear of the Lord* if you multiply that respectful hush many times. In fact, it is quite normal in Biblical accounts, when God appears in visible form, for all who are present to fall on their faces in a holy *fear of God*. There is no cockiness, like "Hi God, good to see You!" Isaiah 6:1-5 tells about Isaiah's first encounter with God; Daniel 10:5-9 is the account of Daniel and his friends, and upon experiencing God, they either run away or are immobilized; Ezekiel Chapter 1 is a very detailed description of an appearance of God, and by the end of the experience, Ezekiel is lying face-down, Revelation 1:12-17 is John's encounter with God, and John is soon lying face down, in the *fear of the Lord*.

Fellowship: time together sharing everything, whether with God or one another. *Fellowship* to Christians means being together with God or with other Christians. Like any friendship, it is encouraging. Unlike normal friendship, which is a natural human activity, *fellowship* has a supernatural element because it includes the presence of God.

Fellowship brings encouragement on a deeply spiritual level. There is a special Greek word in the original writing of the Bible, *koinonia*, which includes a meaning of partnership, socializing, communication, companionship, and participation. All of that is going on in *fellowship* with the Holy Spirit of God present in the experience. *Jesus* says, "where two or three have gathered together in My name, I am there in their midst." So Jesus is there spending real time with any get-together of believers.

Fellowship is one of the most important elements of the lifestyle of a Christian. Beyond Bible reading, prayer, and serving (the primary ways Christians maintain a walk with God) being in *fellowship* regularly encourages one's faith. It is the rare person who can survive as a believer in this world without *fellowship*, especially if he is not praying, reading, or serving.

Christians find that when they are down, feeling low, maybe they don't feel like seeking *fellowship*, but that is when it is most needful and helpful. Christian friends, one- on-one, or in groups, offer the best possibility for obtaining rekindled faith and hope.

Firstborn: the eldest child, a position of responsibility and authority. Jesus is referred to as "the *firstborn*" several times in the Bible. Colossians 1:15 says, "He is the image of the invisible God, the *firstborn* of all creation." *Firstborn* is a title, a position of authority, and for Jesus it means the *firstborn* of God, a place of equality with the Father (God.) In Hebrews 1:6, the *firstborn* (Jesus) is described as One Whom the angels will worship (the angels only worship God, no other, therefore Jesus is God). *Firstborn,* in the Bible, referring to Jesus, in no way diminishes Jesus to be a mere man. He <u>was</u> born (that's what is celebrated at Christmas, baby Jesus was born). And He was indeed the first child born of Mary (later there were other children). All that is true, but being Mary's first child is not what *firstborn* in the Bible means when referring to Jesus as the *firstborn*.

Greek was the language in which the New Testament (the part of the Bible written after Jesus) was originally written. There still exist actual copies of most of the New Testament, handwritten in Greek, copies made long before the printing press was invented. Theologian Mike Webster explains that in those writings, there are two Greek words that could be translated into English as *"firstborn."*

One of the Greek words, "protoktistos" really means "first created," just the first child in the family. But that word is not the one used in the Bible when talking about Jesus as the *firstborn*. The other word, "prototokos" is the word that means a position of authority. That second word is the only one ever used to refer to Jesus as the *firstborn*.

This is an important point because some *cults (groups posing as Christians, but not believing the same things about Jesus) say that because Jesus was *firstborn*, that means He isn't God because He had a beginning and was just the first child born in a family. It is an important belief in Christianity that Jesus is God. God has no beginning and is not created; He is eternal. Jesus is eternal. He was not created; He has always eternally been the "prototokos," the *firstborn* as a position of authority equal with the Father. He has "first place in everything" (Colossians 1:18). He was always "with God, and was God." (John 1:1-14), and after Jesus went to the *cross and died and was buried and was resurrected (raised from the dead), Ephesians 1:20-23 says that Jesus resumed that place of authority and was, "seated... at His [God's] right hand in the heavenly places, far above all rule and authority and power and dominion, and every name that is named, not only in this age but also in the one to come. And He [God] put all things in subjection under His [Jesus'] feet, and gave Him as head over all things to the *church, which is His *body, the fullness of Him, who fills all in all." That is the place of the *firstborn*, Jesus, eternally existing, and also born as a man to live on earth.

First fruits: the ceremonial first-harvested portion of the crop. In the country of Israel, back in the days even before Jesus, when the crops were ready to be harvested, the very first grain cut was ceremoniously offered to God, in thanks for a good harvest, and that first, early, ceremonial harvest was called *first fruits*. Christians use *first fruits* to mean the first of something of which a lot more is expected to come.

Christians use these words to refer to Jesus, because the Bible refers to Him as the *first fruits* of those to rise from the dead (1 Corinthians 15:20-23). Jesus was the first, and there are millions of others, believers, who will also be raised from the dead because of Him.

Interestingly, the very same day that Jesus was actually raised from the dead was the day of celebration of *First Fruits* (a national holiday) in Jerusalem. Fifty days later (another national holiday called Pentecost) was the day when thanksgiving for the rest of the harvest was given ceremonially in Jerusalem. And on that day, Pentecost, was the day the church began, because God's Holy Spirit showed up in a powerful way to a gathering of the disciples, and they began to proclaim the good news and convince people to believe that Jesus is the *Messiah, the Expected One. (You can read the story in Acts chapter 2.) Three thousand people became Christians on that day; they believed in Jesus, so it was the beginning of the church. It was the beginning of a worldwide movement of God, now called Christianity, the first gatherings of people who believe in Jesus to celebrate Jesus and celebrate the harvest of millions brought into the knowledge of God. So, to follow the analogy, Jesus is the *first fruits* and the church is the harvest. In 1 Corinthians, Paul uses that idea, writing, "the household of Stephanas, that they were the *first fruits* of Achaia," meaning that this household was the first of probably thousands who eventually became Christians in that region.

One further meaning of *first fruits* is the Holy Spirit. Romans 8:23 says, "...we ourselves, having the *first fruits* of the Spirit...wait eagerly for our adoption as sons, the redemption of our body." Christians receive the indwelling of God in themselves, the Holy Spirit. He is the *first fruits*, the earliest sample of the incredible transformation of character that begins when one believes in Jesus and eventually ends with translation into heaven, either when the believer dies, or when Jesus comes back, whichever happens first.

When a Christian says something about *first fruits*, it means that this was the first of something really big that will come after that *first fruit*. Maybe it is the first people in a new church. Maybe it is a small business venture that this Christian believes God is going to prosper, and he calls the earliest signs of profit, the *first fruits*. Maybe it is the expectation of ever-greater manifestations of the power of God. For Christians it is a hopeful term, an expectancy that God has a lot more to come after the *first fruits*.

Fish: in Greek, an acronym for Christianity. The *fish* became a symbol of Christianity. Here's why: the word for "*fish*" in Greek, the common language of Jesus' time, comes out roughly "*IXOYE*" and it is pronounced "*ichthus.*" These five letters in the Greek language for "*fish*" were an acronym; that is, each letter is the first letter of a word, and there are five separate words. The five words in English are *Jesus, *Christ, *God's, *Son, *Savior. If anyone agrees with the proper Christian definition of each of these words, that means he is a Christian. So the *fish* symbol came to be a sign of Christianity. In the early days of the church it was used during times of persecution as a code word to communicate between Christians when it might have been dangerous to speak publicly about Jesus. Today, the *Ichthus fish* is seen on bumper stickers, posters and advertisements to say, "I am a Christian."

Flesh: the lower, sinful (wrong-doing) human nature. (Also see *carnal). *Flesh,* to a Christian, means either the influence of one's body (instead of the influence of the Spirit), or it means one's natural self-reliance (instead of relying upon God). A person's *flesh,* in the Biblical sense, is that part of one's life where the appetites are centered. The appetites for food, comforts, pleasure, money, sex, power, fame, achievements, etc. are desires that are not spiritual, but *fleshly* or *carnal.

The *fleshly* person will "live for his belly" as Tolstoy puts it. For non-Christians, that *flesh* will be the thing that makes the decisions, hour by hour, day by day.

For the non-believer, even long-range goals of one's life are decided by the *flesh.* In a Christian's life, faith in Jesus no longer allows the *flesh* to take the lead. The *flesh* will always lead in the opposite direction from a spiritual life in Christ. Romans 8:5-7 says, "For those who are according to the *flesh* set their minds on the things of the *flesh,* but those who are according to the Spirit, the things of the Spirit...the mind set on the *flesh* is hostile towards God." A Christian has set his mind on the things of the Spirit, and the things of the *flesh* are no longer the focus of attention.

Christians also call the *flesh* the "*old man" (old, only because it existed before the new man), or they call it the "*natural man" (natural, normal, before the supernatural influence of Jesus). Christians believe that *flesh,* the old man, dies (in a spiritual sense) when one believes in Jesus. Romans 6:5-7 says, "our old self was crucified with [Jesus] in order that our body of sin might be done away with."

When someone begins to have faith in Jesus he receives new life. The old life passes away. "Living for the belly" stops. Self-reliance is no longer the norm. 2 Corinthians 5:17 says, "Therefore if anyone is in Christ, he is a new creature; the old things passed away; behold, new things have come." Things that used to be attractive and even irresistible when living the *fleshly* life will lose their glitter after the *flesh* has died and the old man is replaced by the new man.

Christians sometimes wonder whether the old man is really dead because old temptations that had gone away sometimes begin to tempt again. The death of the *flesh* is a spiritual stance of faith; it is not based on anything visible. Romans 6:11 says, "consider yourselves to be dead to sin, but alive to God." Christians put the emphasis on being alive to God rather than on struggling with temptations.

Romans 13:14 says, "put on the Lord Jesus Christ, and make no provision for the *flesh* in regard to its lusts." Paying attention to the Spirit at all times and being "alive to God" builds faith and reminds the believer the *flesh* is dead.

Forgive / forgiveness: to release someone from guilt, to decide against taking revenge, to decide not to think or talk about wrong suffered at the hands of another. Christians are instructed by Jesus to *forgive* those who have done wrong to them. True Christians are known around the world for radical *forgiveness*. Christians have granted *forgiveness* to the murderers of their children. Christians will choose to die at the hands of terrorists rather than take revenge.

In the prayer that Jesus taught in the Bible (Matthew 6:9-15, known as the *Lord's prayer) He instructs believers to pray to God; "*forgive* us our debts [our wrongs against God] as we also have *forgiven* our debtors [those who have done wrong to us.]" Jesus goes on to teach that if believers *forgive* others they will be *forgiven* by God, but if they do not *forgive* others, God will not *forgive* them. Forgiveness is so central to the heart of God that it is not going to work for anyone to try to be a friend of God but not a forgiver of others. It is the reason that *unforgiveness,* or refusing to *forgive,* is such a bad thing in the Christian's life. (*Unforgiveness* can be used as a foothold for the devil to come in and make trouble in a Christian's life. See *deliverance.)

Forgiving is a choice a person makes, not on the basis of how she feels about the person she is *forgiving*. If she waits until she <u>feels</u> like *forgiving,* it may never happen.

In American culture, it is often thought that *forgiving* someone can't happen until the *forgiving* one really means it, really <u>feels</u> *forgiving*. But *forgiving* is not an emotion, it is a decision, a point of obedience for the Christian. The Christian *forgives* because Jesus says she must. Jesus doesn't say that the one who is being *forgiven* has to come and apologize first. Jesus does not say that someone has to deserve *forgiveness*, in order for *forgiveness* to be granted. Christians can just make the choice to let it go. Let go of all the hurt, grudges, and anger, and Christians say the words before God: "I *forgive*," and then behave in a manner that does not bring up the offense again. It is *forgiven*. The act of *forgiveness* is met with God's help in the innermost being to soothe the pain and release the grudge-holding, and the need for revenge. Getting over those emotions is God's work once the decision has been made to *forgive*. It is possible for the Christian to be freed from the torment of unforgiveness. Someone has said that not *forgiving* another person is like taking poison and expecting that other person to die. Unforgiveness only hurts the one who refuses to *forgive*.

The same process is used in *forgiving* oneself, often the hardest person to *forgive*. It's very important for the Christian to *forgive* herself. Holding a grudge against herself will not help her to do better in the future, but *forgiving* herself will. And since the believer has received God's *forgiveness*, there is no reason to delay *forgiving* herself. Unforgiveness of self denies the power of God's *forgiveness*.

Christians choose to be *forgiven* by God. Sometimes a person's guilt is so strong it is possible to think that even God could not *forgive*. But if one can pray, "I am <u>willing</u> to be *forgiven*, or to *forgive*," that will be more in agreement with the Spirit of God, who is totally *forgiving* on the basis of the *cross. Christians are *forgiven* by faith in Jesus; that is the great promise of God through Jesus, "I will *forgive* you." And God promises never to bring up again those old wrongs, once forgiven.

God writes in Isaiah 43:25, "I am the one who wipes out your transgressions for My own sake, and I will not remember your sins." And Psalm 103:12 says, "As far as the east is from the west, so far has He [God] removed our transgressions from us."

Forgiving and being *forgiven* is essential to the lifestyle and mindset of the Christian. It is what Jesus came to do: to *forgive* so that believers might go free. And Christians are to be "*forgiving* each other, just as God in Christ also has *forgiven* you" (Ephesians 4:32). *Forgiveness* is a world-changer.

Fornication: sexual intercourse between people who are not married. Much instruction in the Bible says not only that this is wrong (a sin) but also that it is damaging to the persons involved. 1 Corinthians 6:15-20 explains that the sex act makes two people into one, the same as in marriage, "they shall become one flesh" (Genesis 2:24). In the heart of a Christian, the intimacy and closeness of the act of love-making validates that it is singular, meant for marriage. But when it is *fornication*, there is no marriage, just the one-flesh experience completely separate from any commitment or pledge of an exclusive and permanent relationship. There are lasting and painful consequences to this kind of behavior. In the Christian view, *fornication* cheapens rather than deepens the relationship. *Fornication,* not having the commitment of marriage, is only a temporary thrill. That leaves people confused, because a person's entire being is pre-programmed by God to know that sexual union is something special that is only to follow after the deepest development of a love relationship and the public declaration of the permanence of that relationship (marriage). Sexual union in marriage deepens the relationship because it is in the context of commitment, safety, trust and permanence.

Fornication becomes a huge temptation to most young people at some time because the body becomes sexually driven before the maturity is present to make a decision about marriage.

God says to "flee from youthful lusts," (2 Timothy 2:22). How to really get the mindset to do that is very clear in the book: *"Purity, the New Moral Revolution"* by Kris Vallotton. There is a lot more to it for the Christian than just resisting the act of intercourse until marriage.

There is very healthy power in the married sexual relationship for positive, creative, mutually beneficial advances in love, and it is an essential part of a good marriage. There is an equally great power to destroy self-respect, create guilt and shame, and generally just mess up lives when it is done out of God's order and design. A biblical view of *fornication* is quite opposite of the popular ideas of our culture. It is not an option in God's mind, not a way to see if two people are suited to be married, not a game or a means of recreation; it is not to be laughed at, pursued or encouraged outside of marriage. It is destructive.

God also outlines what happens as a result of *fornication*. Proverbs 6:24-35 and Proverbs 7: 5-27, say things like "an arrow pierces through his liver... it will cost him his life." See also 1 Corinthians 6:13-18, and 1 Thessalonians 4: 3-8. Also see *adultery.

Free: four areas of freedom to the Christian: (1) freedom from cultural pressure to conform, (2) freedom from the lower nature (the *flesh), (3) freedom from fear of the condemnation or judgment of God, (4) freedom from the accusations of the devil.

(1) All people live under tremendous pressure from the culture around them to conform. Usually they do not recognize the pressure; they just go along with it. The Bible says, "do not be conformed to this world, but be transformed by the renewing of your mind, so that you may prove what the will of God is" (Romans 12:2). Believers are promised by Jesus that they will be *free*. Jesus says to those who believe in Him; "you will know the truth and the truth will make you *free*" (John 8:32).

People who come to believe in Jesus go through a process of gradually shaking *free* from that pressure of the culture around them, which becomes unwanted once they have become aware of it.

(2) The lower nature is in command until Jesus comes in. Jesus says, "everyone who commits sin [wrong] is the slave of sin" (John 8:34). Slavery is clearly the opposite of *freedom,* so *freedom* from slavery to sin is another kind of *freedom* that Christians experience. Before Jesus sets people *free,* they are slaves of sin according to Romans 7:14. Human beings <u>will</u> sin. People cannot <u>not</u> sin. Every child lies, hits other children, or steals things, etc., things all recognized as wrong, as sin. They can't help themselves, and it goes into adulthood many times. Without the intervention of Jesus they keep on sinning and keep on justifying why it's okay that they do that. So Christians are to be *free* from that slavery to sin, that cycle of doing wrong that they know is wrong, and *free* from the habit of trying to justify it to escape the guilt.

(3) Yet another way that Christians are *free,* according to Romans 8:1-2, is that "there is now no condemnation for those who are in Christ Jesus." The passage goes on to say that "the law of the Spirit of life in Christ Jesus has set you *free* from the law of sin and of death." The *law says, "If you sin you die." (Paraphrased from Hebrews 10:28 and Deuteronomy 17:2-6, that is the law of sin and of death). This is the judgment of God. But the passage in Romans says that the new law of the Spirit of life replaces the law of sin and of death (it was new when Jesus died and rose again). Because of Jesus on the *cross, the wrongs are forgiven instead of requiring death. And instead of death, the believer (anyone who receives that offer as true) gets life, gets free. Romans 8:6 says, "the mind set on the Spirit is life and peace." *Freedom* is a whole new world. Instead of cringing every time they do something wrong, expecting severe punishment, Christians can receive the forgiveness of God and move on with the help of the Spirit of God (see *Holy Spirit) more in harmony with God.

Some Christians don't understand this, and they become legalists. There is a full definition of *legalism, but basically it means they are not receiving *freedom* from the law of sin and of death. It seems impossible to them, that God could be that generous, but He is. Legalists believe that the only way to please God is by obeying the *law. But the law of the Spirit of life, says that the requirement for pleasing God is faith (Hebrews 11:6).

(4) Another great area in which Christians are *free* is *freedom* from having the devil's influence in their lives. The devil jerks people around like a dog on a chain; one minute tempting them, (lying to them about what they are missing if they choose God's way) and then accusing them of wrong things they have done if they give in to that temptation. The devil also lies to people about who they are, making them feel like dirt and then condemning them. The devil can make people feel guilty (many people walk around with a load of guilt over things that they aren't really guilty of doing). The devil can also make people feel proud (we all know people who are proud and arrogant but they aren't even nice people). Christians learn how to live in this *freedom* rather than continue to believe the devil's lies. Everything that sounds like accusation or condemnation, or is discouraging, depressing and dismaying is probably the devil lying. Those things need to be silenced by listening to the truth ("the truth shall make you *free*"). Also, "Resist the devil and he will flee from you" (James 4:7).

Free will: the ability to choose what one will say, think, or do. "God has given mankind *free will*," is something Christians say. What they mean is that no matter how God wants people to live, they can always make up their own minds, perhaps even in a way that is very much against what God desires. Example: God says, "don't tell lies," and even with that commandment ringing in people's ears, they might decide to lie anyway (and have some kind of excuse for why it was alright in this situation).

That's *free will*. Even though God wants people to never steal, they always have the choice whether or not to decide to steal.

It has become a debate among Christians whether *free will* really exists or not. One reason for the debate is that mankind, before believing in Jesus, is "sold into bondage to sin" (Romans 7:14). Bondage equals slavery, therefore the slave does not have *free will*. So how does one in such a condition choose to believe in Jesus? Some say that it is only by God's choice that one is able to come to faith in Jesus (this is the argument of *predestination). Others say that even fallen man is able to be drawn to faith in Jesus and it is a *free will* choice. This debate is complicated, centuries old, and will not be settled in these pages.

The argument on the side of the existence of *free will* says, particularly for the Christian, that it means believers aren't robots. If believers did not still have *free will*, they would not be able to choose to do right or wrong, but apparently they still can and do. If there is no *free will*, they would automatically do everything exactly as God wants, but they wouldn't quite be human, and they couldn't love. Love is not love if one cannot choose to not love. With *free will*, a person may choose the ways of God, and a person may choose to respond to the love of God with love in return.

So *free will* is at the same time a blessing and a problem. It is a problem because people have the option to do wrong things (sin). It is a blessing because when people choose to do the right thing, against all temptations, it expresses a very high level of love, respect, and trust in God. In this view, the richness of the life of the Christian is based upon that love and respect and trust, and upon that obedience and submission. Many are the benefits of obedience and submission for the Christian in relationship to God, but it is only possible through making *free will* choices.

Fruit: good things that come from good trees, as symbolic of the good things that come from the lives of good Christians. Trees bear *fruit*, some is good *fruit*, some is bad (peaches-good, crabapples-bad). Christians talk about the *fruit* of their lives. A good Christian life bears good *fruit*, like a good tree bears good *fruit*. That means there is something good that comes out of that life. *Fruit* to a Christian life means things like: loving the unlovely, being kind, being patient, feeding the hungry, giving clothing, giving counsel, helping people out of a bad situation, being a Pastor, teaching the Bible, helping people come to believe in Jesus, building a fellowship or a church. Titus 3:14 says, "Our people must also learn to engage in good deeds to meet pressing needs, so that they will not be un*fruitful*." *Fruit* is visible; hopefully there is plenty of it; it is good and sweet; there are no worms in it, and it is enjoyed by all.

Christians also talk about the "*fruit* of the Spirit." The *Holy Spirit lives in a Christian which results in a changed life, especially in the direction of doing good. The living Holy Spirit (God Himself) inside of a *believer brings forth these *fruits*: love, joy, peace, patience, kindness, goodness, faithfulness, gentleness, and self-control. This list is in Galatians 5:22-23. These *fruits* are what sweeten a Christian's life. The first *fruit* is love. Helping someone in any way without love is worthless, according to first Corinthians 13:1-3. So *fruit* comes from the Christian life by first letting the Holy Spirit bring out the *fruit* of the Spirit, then the other good things, other *fruits*, will begin to happen also.

Fundamentalist: a Christian who is devoted to the fundamental ideas of Christianity. Certain Christians are labeled by others, or by themselves, as *fundamentalists*. There is disagreement in American society about whether it is a good thing or a bad thing to be a *fundamentalist* Christian, because it has come to mean something different than it meant originally.

Fundamentalists started out as a movement to clarify and promote the unquestionable *fundamentals,* or basics of Christianity. It began, because there were increasing numbers of people who were questioning those basic, foundational Christian beliefs.

In the original thinking of *fundamentalists*, the fundamentals are: (1) The inerrancy of the Bible: this is the belief that the entire Bible in its original manuscripts (the actual pages written by the various authors) is entirely accurate, without any errors. We do not have any of those original manuscripts, so the idea cannot be really verified, but the point is that God had a clear, accurate message to give to mankind, and that message still exists in our Bibles today. (2) "Sola scriptura" is the second point of *fundamentalists.* It is Latin, meaning that only the Bible is needed to tell a person everything he needs to know for life and for *salvation. No other writings, no special people, no special add-ons of any kind are necessary in order to be able to become a Christian and live as a Christian. (3) The virgin birth of Jesus. This is the belief that Jesus' mother, Mary was made to conceive a baby by the power of the Holy Spirit, by God, miraculously, and Jesus is therefore the son of God. So, to put it bluntly, Jesus is not a bastard child, conceived out of wedlock. He is not Joseph and Mary's son, and God didn't have sex with Mary; it was a miraculous conception. She was entirely a virgin until Jesus was born. (4) Substitutionary atonement is the basic idea of what happened on the *cross when Jesus died. He was a substitute for all mankind. He died for the sins of all people so that people don't have to die for their sins. By faith in Jesus' substitution, people can have life in heaven forever. And it means that Jesus got believers back in favor with God. Also because of that substitution, Christians are *adopted into God's family, and they are *reconciled (made friends again) to God. Jesus is the only way for that to happen. Nothing one could do could bring one into that depth of relationship with God.

These are all solid core beliefs of Christianity worldwide. They are accepted, agreed upon, and based upon the Bible. So these are not the problem. The problem seems to be that some *fundamentalists* have been bullish about their beliefs and have become especially offensive to some unbelievers. When that happened, popular opinion turned against the *fundamentalists*. They get labeled as "narrow minded." However the intention of the original movement was simply to preserve the integrity of Christian beliefs. The fundamentals of Christianity present a superior reality to the world, and of course it is going to be subject to criticism by others whose existing realities are challenged.

Garden: the place that God created for the first man and woman, the "Garden of Eden," where they were to multiply and fill the earth. They were to cultivate and keep it in perfect partnership with God (Genesis, chapter 2). It was God's intention from the beginning that the twisted ways of the devil, who was apparently already there, would be overcome by mankind through perfect cooperation with God and through mankind carrying the delegated authority of God. However, mankind fell into the devil's ways and lost the ability to carry out the assignment in cooperation with God in God's authority. Ever since that time, restoration of the original relationship between man and God, and restoration of the original God-given authority has been in process. Since the time of Jesus, He has given to believers that place of partnership and the authority to overcome the devil.

So when Christians refer to "*the Garden*" they always mean that place where the love and trust between God and man was perfect. There is a longing for restoration of that perfection, and that is God's goal too. In the life of faith-filled Christians, there are times when God's presence is overwhelming in His goodness, and perfect open communication with God is realized. There are times when God's love so saturates the room that it is like it must have been in the *garden*.

It is clear that heaven will be the full restoration of that perfection, but it is also intended to be in the present, in this life. Jesus instructs His disciples to pray, "Your will be done on earth as it is in heaven" (Matthew 6:10). Pastor Bill Johnson wrote the book, *When Heaven Invades Earth* on that idea.

Gentile: anyone who is not of the Jewish faith. God always intended that all people come to know Him, Jews and *Gentiles* alike. Jewish people were to be His spokesmen in proclaiming God's goodness and power to all mankind (Gen 12:3, Romans 15:7-12). God chose Abraham to be the father of a great race of people who became known as the Jews, or Hebrews. Their assigned task was to be a blessing to all peoples of the earth. They were a particularly blessed people in that God showed His power on their behalf, demonstrating through them that He is good.

By the time of Christ, the Jews had established decrees that separated them from the *Gentiles,* having no association with them at all if possible. *Gentiles* were viewed as unclean, stained by ungodliness. This discrimination against *Gentiles* was not God's original intention. When Jesus came on the scene, He broke those traditions of segregation. It was difficult for His disciples to overcome their prejudice against *Gentiles* at first. See *great commission and read the story of Jesus with the woman at the well (John 4:3-42). The *Gentile* woman in that story is just one example of how Jesus was quite open to dealing with *Gentiles* and giving them the same message He gave to the Jews. He went into *Gentile* territories often and taught the people and healed them, showing that He had no prejudice against them (Matthew 4:24-25, Luke 6:17-18).

Jesus' goal is for all people everywhere, of all languages, tribes, races, and nations to come to know Him by faith. He sent His disciples out into all the world to make disciples among the Jews and the *Gentiles,* baptizing them into the faith. That has been going on for 2000 years and eventually every person will have opportunity to come to believe in Jesus.

That will happen according to Revelation 7:9-12, Ephesians 3:6-10, Galatians 3:26-29. See also *heathen.

Gift (spiritual gift): an empowerment from God; an ability given by God to His servants to carry out His work. When Christians say, "He/she has a *gift*," or, "It's one of my *gifts*," they are talking about *spiritual gifts*. A *spiritual gift* is a gift from God. It is an empowerment by God to do something that one cannot do in one's natural strength. Pastor Alistair Beg states that, "God gives extraordinary *gifts* to ordinary people for out-of-the-ordinary purposes." *Gifts* are not talents. Talents are given by God too, but they are natural (naturally in the body, like the talent of an athlete or a musician) not dependent on a relationship with God. (Although a relationship with God can also dramatically amplify a natural talent.) *Spiritual gifts*, come to those who have a love-relationship with God, and these *gifts* are used by God, through each person, to teach, heal, have insight, lead, etc. In the gathering of Christians together, each person comes with his or her *gifts*, and it becomes a place where God goes to work to help people in many various ways. In all these things God is made great and people get to partner with Him. No *gift* is more special than another. John Wimber, a famous Pastor, used to say, "The best *gift* is the one that is needed at that moment." No person is considered better or lesser than another on the basis of his or her *gifts*. Paul does write that he wishes everyone spoke in tongues (one of the *gifts*) and even more that all would prophesy (1 Corinthians 14:5). There is also an exhortation in 1 Corinthians 14:1-12 to seek for *gifts* that *edify (teach, build up), that these are the most to be desired, perhaps the most helpful because it is so important to build one another up.

If God can work a miracle of healing through someone's prayer, that is a *gift* of healing. If someone has mercy at a level that is beyond the natural, far above and beyond what normal people would do, that's a *gift* of mercy. If someone explains Jesus in a way that inspires people to want to give their lives to Jesus, that's a *gift* of evangelism.

There are four places in the Bible that refer to *spiritual gifts*. Each place includes a partial list of some of the *gifts*, not as a list really, but to teach about them. Ephesians 4:11 talks about *apostles, *prophets, *evangelists, *pastors, and teachers (These are sometimes referred to as "the five-fold ministry.") Romans 12:6-8 lists prophecy, service, teaching, exhorting, giving, leadership, and mercy. 1 Corinthians 12:8-10 lists word of wisdom, word of knowledge, faith, healing, miracles, prophecy, discernment of spirits, tongues, and interpretation of tongues. 1 Peter 4:10-11 is a general teaching about speaking and serving. These are not meant to be complete lists, and there is some overlap and repetition between the lists. Also, it seems that there are other *spiritual gifts* that are pretty obvious, but not listed anywhere, such as preaching, hospitality, and worship-leading.

Spiritual gifts are to be sought after by Christians. They are one of the primary means by which it is demonstrated that God is at work, rather than merely the influence of persuasive people. Jesus Himself used the miracles that He accomplished to demonstrate His identity as sent from God. Jesus said, in John 10:37,38, "If I do not do the works of My Father, do not believe Me; but if I do them, though you do not believe Me, believe the works, so that you may know and understand that the Father is in Me, and I in the Father." There is much written about the *gifts of the Spirit*. Be aware that not all authors agree on details like how many gifts there actually are, and how to receive them. It might be best to read more than one author for an in-depth understanding of the *gifts*.

<u>Glory</u>: the recognizable influence of God. There are two ways this word is used: First, when something wonderful happens, Christians give *glory* to God. That is, they give credit to God, they honor and approve Him, and they do so by saying, "*Glory* to God!" Christians recognize and celebrate the *glory* of God, the power and influence of God. Christians don't seek their own *glory* (honor and approval) but are eager to proclaim God's *glory*.

In this meaning of the word, God's power and influence is being recognized, appreciated, and applauded. The second meaning is God's splendor, wonder, majesty, holiness, and superiority sometimes actually seen, heard, or felt, in one's natural state, just as one would observe anything else in the world, like a waterfall or a concert. It is clear in the Bible that God is *glorious.* He is splendid and completely different from anything else that one can experience.

Christians will talk about the *Shekinah *glory*. That is the visible divine presence, usually like a smoke, fog or light, or both, which are a tangible evidence of His presence. The Hebrew word translated "*glory*" speaks of something with weight and substance, something that is real. God's *glory* is definitely able to be perceived. 1 Kings 8:10-12 tells of how that *glory* cloud filled the temple when Solomon dedicated it. Moses saw this *glory* on the mountain early in the book of Exodus (19:16-20). In fact, the *glory* of God that was experienced in that account included trumpet blasts, lightning, thunder, fire and smoke seen by all the people of Israel. The pillar of cloud that led the people in the desert (Exodus 13:21-22) and hovered over the tabernacle, (Exodus 40:34-38) which was the place of God's presence, was the *glory* of God and everyone saw it. As Pastor Bill Johnson says: "some people just saw smoke and some people saw God." How a person perceives *glory* has to do with one's present position spiritually. A closed mind will not recognize anything but smoke, or a curious unexplainable something. However, if a believer accepts the idea of God showing up, he will indeed see God in some kind of way, God's *glory*.

Ezekiel Chapter 1 is an interesting and detailed description of when the prophet saw God and His *glory*. In Chapter 10 of Ezekiel, he sees God's *glory* again, this time, the *glory* is departing from the temple because He was not being recognized or worshiped. In Luke 2:9 the shepherds saw the *glory* of God shining around them and an Angel announced Jesus' birth to them.

The *glory* of God can also be just an overwhelming awareness that God is present, with nothing seen or heard, but an unmistakable recognition of the Presence. His power and holiness and splendor sometimes become so intense that one can't move, can't speak, can't stand, so people do what people always do when God appears; they lie face down on the floor, and soak in His goodness, or tremble in fear.

God's *glory* is most often recognized when believers are singing, praising, worshiping, and adoring God. God's *glory* is often most intense in a group of people, a gathering of believers agreeing together on God's majesty, focusing on Him, acknowledging Him. God's *glory* is the influence of God. God's *glory*, which fills the earth (Isaiah 6:3, Habakkuk 2:14) is His influence, His wonderful, transformational presence. When a Christian *glorifies* God, he acknowledges God's stunning power, declares it, and celebrates it. When God comes to touch people's lives, to speak to them, or to change the way they see things, it is *glorious*, it is wonder-full. Experiencing God's *glory* will mean changes for people because of God's influence.

Following is a short list of places in the Bible to read about *glory*. Exodus 33:18-23, Exodus 40:34-28, 2 Chronicles 7:1-3, Isaiah 6:1-4, Ezekiel 1:1-28, Ezekiel 8:4, Ezekiel 10:4-5, Ezekiel 43:1-5, Matthew 17:1-8, John 1:14, Acts 22:6, Revelation 1:10 (includes glory in a sound, a voice or a trumpet or thunder). Revelation 15:8.

God: the spiritual being who is omnipotent (all powerful), omniscient (knows everything), omnipresent (everywhere all the time), and eternal, that is, He has no beginning and no end. When a Christian says, "*God*," He is not a vague and poorly defined being. To Christians, *God* is not a mysterious power out in the universe somewhere. A lot of people say, "I believe in *God*," but it is quite important to know what they mean saying "*God*." To a Christian, *God* is personal; He is a person, not in bodily form except in the person of Jesus when He walked this earth.

God is personal; He lives in relationship with people, loving, forgiving, merciful, powerful, wise, and fatherly. He is near; He is the provider and the healer; He gives peace; He delivers from danger; He is a refuge in time of trouble, and a comfort in sadness. He gives purpose in life. He blesses His people, and expects His people to be a blessing to others, even to those who reject Him. *God* is good, all the time.

At the same time, *God* is transcendent, meaning He is above everything, and certainly mysterious, certainly undefinable in many ways. Christians say He cannot be put into a box. A thorough study of the Bible will give much definition of *God* <u>and</u> will raise many questions about the *Godhead. Christianity is not a *religion constructed around man's guesses about *God*; it is a relationship with *God*, and authored by God. It was His idea from the beginning, and He has revealed Himself gradually over thousands of years, yet there is infinitely more to know about Him.

Now *God* to a Christian can mean *God* the father, or Jesus (*God* the son), or *God* the Holy Spirit, or the *Godhead, which includes all of the Father, Son and Spirit. This is not three gods (see *Trinity). When Christians just use the term "*God*" it doesn't necessarily mean specifically Father, or Son, or Holy Spirit. Nor does it really matter most of the time, because they are One. For more on *God* see *Father, *Jesus, and *Holy Spirit.

Christians also use the term "god" with a small 'g' meaning something that others consider to be a god or treat like a god. This can be anything that gets all of a person's time, money, or devotion (a car, a job, a lover, etc.). Often it can be something like an *idol, a statue or a shrine, as typically used in the world's religions, but these things really have no comparison to *God* in power, influence or relationship. There is often spiritual power there (in an idol), but if it is a statue, or a shrine, it is limited to that place; it is not really *God,* who is without limits (See *idol). 1 Corinthians 10:19-21 says that the power of idols is *demonic, that is from *Satan.

Revelation 9:20-21 says that people who worship idols are worshipping demons. Psalm 115: 4-8 is a description of what an idol really is.

Godhead: all of God, the divine ruler. Occasionally you will hear Christians use this term, and to the Christian basically it means all of God, that is, God the Father, God the Son (Jesus) and God the Holy Spirit. God, who is only One, includes those three names (see*Trinity.) Christians talk about them like they are three individuals, but they also understand that there is only one God, a *Godhead*. Absolutely central to Christianity is the belief that there is only one God, in contrast to many other religions which believe in multiple gods.

Godhead means God in His largest definition, nothing left out in His place of power and authority. It is used to emphasize the totality of divinity. Colossians 2:9 in the King James Version of the Bible speaks of Jesus as the "fullness of the *Godhead* bodily." (The same verse in the New American Standard Bible says, "In Him all the fullness of *deity dwells in bodily form."). This means that Jesus expresses all of God on a human level, in a way we can see, since He took on human form. God the Holy Spirit also expresses all of God but on a spiritual level. Christians experience the presence of God by the power of the Holy Spirit. They find deep understanding, spiritual power, the experience of being adopted, and all manner of other benefits by the presence of the Holy Spirit living inside them. Similarly, God the Father expresses all of God in a fatherly way. (Wherever an earthly father might not be perfect, God is able to be perfect as a Father.) He is the model of fatherly love, forgiveness, and righteousness. Even if a Christian's earthly father was untrustworthy, that Christian can learn how to trust God the Father to be totally good. Pastor Bill Johnson says that one of the messages of Jesus is, "If you like Me, you're going to really love My Father, because He's just like Me," and all One with the *Godhead*.

Gospel: good news, news of what God has accomplished through Jesus for all who will believe. *Gospel* is an old English word, which would be "good news" if it were translated into modern English, but even in many modern English Bibles it is not translated into "good news," but remains "*gospel.*" There is a reason for that. The good news of the *gospel* is so distinct from just any other good news that it is helpful that it has its own distinct name, "the *gospel.*" Most often, the *gospel* refers to the central message of God through Jesus: that God loves, and that He is coming to the afflicted with relief, to the brokenhearted with healing, to the captive with liberty, and to proclaim the favor of God. This is from Isaiah 61:1-2. Jesus read this passage from Isaiah when He began His ministry, thus predicting that He was bringing good news, the *gospel* (Luke 4:16-21).

The *gospel* is also the Christian's message about Jesus: (a) that He is God (He came to carry out all of the Isaiah promise above), (b) that He died to forgive the sin of mankind, (c) that He rose again, and was seen alive by many (1 Corinthians 15:1-8) which demonstrated a victory over death. People who believe the *gospel* "shall not perish, but have *eternal life," according to John 3:16. Eternal life means life after death, that is, the life in heaven that one goes to as a believer in the *gospel* (see *eternal life). Christians believe the *gospel* and believe that, by the *gospel*, they have been forgiven of all wrongs done and can get reconnected with God again, and can receive freedom from fear of death, all by believing the *gospel*.

The *gospel* also says that those who believe this good news can have new life (see *born-again). The *gospel* says that believers can really stop doing things that they wish they could stop doing, and that they can "turn their eyes from darkness to light and from the dominion of Satan to God" (Acts 26:18). This transformed life is available because God gives it as a gift if one just believes in Jesus. And that is the *gospel*.

When Christians talk about spreading the *gospel*, that's what they mean: telling this good news of forgiveness, God's favor, and the promise of heaven to all who will believe.

The *Gospel* can also refer to any one of four books of the Bible: Matthew, Mark, Luke, and John. These four books are commonly referred to as the *Gospels* because they are the narrative of what Jesus did.

Grace: the unexplainable generosity of God above and beyond all human expectation, that is, the generosity of God not as a reward, and given even though punishment might be expected by the one receiving *grace*. It is *grace* that sets Christianity apart from any other world religion. Jesus brought *grace* into full view. It was always God's way of dealing with mankind, but most of God's people (the Jews) before Jesus required obedience to the laws of God as the way to get God's favor. Jesus fully made possible the way of *grace* and it became the defining characteristic of Christianity. The centerpiece of *grace* is that it is un-earned. All world religions, Muslim, Buddhist, Hindu, etc., have requirements to perform, and they believe that if one does those things, then one earns the promises (heaven, nirvana, bliss, whatever).

Christianity does not operate that way; it is a relationship of faith. When one enters into relationship with God by faith, by believing in Jesus, God freely gives all the promises of God by *grace* (2 Peter 1:2-4). Well-known Pastor Mike Bickle says that the scandal of *grace* is that it is not fair. Fair, in merely human terms, would be that people who do wrong things get punished. *Grace* takes punishment out of the picture for the guilty ones who choose to believe. By faith they receive forgiveness instead of punishment.

God wants to be in relationship with His people and He does that by giving relief from affliction, granting His healing to the broken, His liberty to captives, and His love to all. He takes the risk that such an offer through the *grace* of Jesus will be refused, or, if it is accepted, that the one receiving the freedom and healing will not stay in relationship.

More than just God's undeserved favor, *Grace* has power to carry the believer, the receiver of *grace*, into a new reality. Pastor Bill Johnson says that *grace* is unmerited favor that brings the enabling presence of Jesus so that believers can taste life in its fullness. According to Guy Chevereau in his book, *Turnings*, *grace* gives believers the ability to be more like Jesus. Well-known Pastor/teacher Graham Cooke says, "*Grace* is the empowering presence of God that enables you to become what God sees when He looks at you." God, by *grace*, sees the believer as already perfect, and empowers that person to become increasingly perfect. Furthermore, in any situation, by *grace*, a believer can respond to people, relate to people, and minister to people like Jesus does. It is *grace* that allows Christians to do that, and it comes across to others as surprising, unnatural, undeserved, even miraculous, more than a little like Jesus. *Grace* is the power to live above the natural, above pain, above tragedy above temptation, above failure, and *grace* is the ability to be there for others going through it too.

Grace is a gift from God. People are "*saved by *grace* through *faith," (Ephesians 2:8). God chooses to forgive those who have done wrong and give them new life. That's *grace*. God also chooses that the only requirement to get all of that from Him is faith; one must believe, and He even grants the struggling unbeliever the faith to believe. *Grace* eliminates all these words: good-enough, nice-enough, smart-enough, spiritual-enough, qualified, accomplished, deserved, earned, entitled. One does not have to be any of those things in order to receive all of God's love, all of God's favor by *grace*, just believe.

"Amazing *Grace*, how sweet the sound that saved a wretch like me, I once was lost but now I'm found, was blind but now I see." These are the words of John Newton's famous Christian worship song, "Amazing *Grace*," sometimes called America's most beloved song.

Grace (prayer before a meal). When sitting down to a meal with Christians, someone says, "Who will say *grace?*" A prayer is spoken, everyone says "*amen," and then everyone can eat. This strong Christian tradition of praying at meals comes primarily from a couple of Bible verses. In Exodus 23:25, God states that if people will serve God, He promises to bless their food and water and to remove sickness from among them. In 1 Timothy 4:3-5, God declares that all food is good to eat if it is *sanctified (made holy), by thanksgiving prayer. Given these verses, saying *grace* is not an empty ritual. Christians believe it keeps them safe from sickness and physically blessed by their food if that prayer is offered in faith. Christians really depend on God to protect them by believing in this promise. Missionaries have done it for hundreds of years, eating all manner of unusual things and foods not prepared in a sanitized "class A" kitchen, usually without any harm as they depend on God to keep sickness away by saying *grace*.

Great Commission: an important assignment that Jesus gave Christians to do: tell the whole world about Him. He gave Christians authority to do this assignment and very clear instructions. The *great commission* is most clearly seen in Matthew 28:18-20, the last verses of Matthew; Jesus said, "All authority has been given to Me in heaven and on earth. Go therefore and make disciples of all the nations, baptizing them in the name of the Father and the Son and the Holy Spirit, teaching them to observe all that I commanded you; and lo, I am with you always, even to the end of the age." So Jesus *commissions* His people to go with His message.

This is why Christians can be found in every corner of the world, people who have gone just to tell the people there about Jesus. These Christians who go are called *missionaries. They may be nurses, teachers, engineers, farmers, or pastors, but their main purpose in being where they are is to carry out the *great commission*.

There are many dark corners still in the world where there are people of other languages, or people of other cultures who know nothing of Jesus. Even in the U.S.A. there are people do not know anything about who Jesus is. According to the *great commission,* someone needs to go to them so they can hear the *gospel, the good news of forgiveness, love, and new life by faith in Jesus. Jesus commands Christians to go. Not everyone can or will go, but they are to help financially support and pray for those who do go.

The *great commission* is not a new idea from Jesus. It was God's intention all along for all peoples of the earth to come to know Him. It began in Genesis 12:1-3 as God gave the assignment first to Abraham and his descendents. Isaiah 66:18-23 also talks about it, saying, "The time is coming to gather all nations and tongues. And they shall come and see My glory." Jesus teaches about the *great commission* in each of the four *Gospels (Matthew, Mark, Luke, and John). The early Christian church began to go. Peter went (Acts chapter 10 and 11.) Barnabas and Saul (Paul) went (Acts 13 and 14). Later Paul went out twice more on missionary journeys to what is now Europe and present-day Turkey. There is an amazing book, *From Jerusalem to Irian Jaya,* by Ruth Tucker, which tells the history of Christianity through the stories of the hundreds of missionaries who obeyed the command to go and obey Jesus' *great commission.*

Great Tribulation: a time of severe trouble, worldwide, that Christians believe will happen before Jesus' *second coming, that is, before He comes back to establish His kingdom. Christians call this time of trouble the *great tribulation.*

In John's Revelation, the last book of the Bible, John writes that he sees in the future, a group of people in white robes who have, "come out of the *great tribulation*" (Revelation 7: 13, 14).

The language in this passage indicates that these people went through the *great tribulation* experiencing persecution, thirst, starvation, and severe heat. In fact, it is likely many were seen there in John's vision because they will have been killed for their faith, or were *martyrs (Revelation 6: 9-11).
   Most Christians see the *great tribulation* as a time of persecution for Christians: being discriminated against, being prohibited from access to food, water and shelter, and even being killed just because they believe in and worship Jesus. Christians all over the world in various places and various times through history have certainly experienced and are still experiencing today, this kind of persecution. Pastor Jack Hayford points out that, in most of the world, Christians believe that the *great tribulation* has been happening ever since the first century. However, popular American teachings attempt to prove that the *great tribulation* is going to be only for seven years, and it hasn't started yet. Another group of scholars believe that what is called the *great tribulation* already happened in 70 AD when Jerusalem was destroyed by the Roman army and a million people were killed. These widely differing opinions are just that, opinions and interpretations of the Bible. This is one area in which the Bible is not clear. There are lots of hints, but no one interpretation seems to include all the possibilities. The essential truth is that God is with the believer in all *tribulation*, all suffering. God counts every tear (Psalm 56:8), and God ultimately brings the suffering ones to comfort and safety (Revelation 7:14-17, Psalm 12:5). And there will eventually be an end to the *tribulation*, and the establishment of God's Kingdom, the new Heaven and the New Jerusalem (Revelation 21:1-4).

Hades: another word Christians use for *hell. It was originally a Greek word, at the time of Christ, meaning the grave, where the dead are; a dark, joyless place, ruled over by the enemy of all life, the devil. It was the Greek's view of where everyone went when they died. It sounds pretty similar to today's common notion of what *hell is.

Hebrews, or Jews had the term Sheol, for the grave, but it was different from the Greek idea. In the way Jesus presented it, the good people went to "Abraham's Bosom" in Sheol, and the bad people went to Gehenna (also called Hades), the name given for a place of torment in Sheol (Luke 16:19-31). (Gehenna was fittingly also the name of the local garbage dump near Jerusalem where there were fires, burning trash, and continual pall of smoke.) All those who died, were in Sheol, either suffering or being comforted, according to the Hebrews, until the final *judgment day.

Christianity sees hell or *Hades* (same thing) as the place where those not blessed by God go when they die, and heaven as the place where those go who died believing in Jesus. Believers, then, go directly to His presence, no longer having to wait in "Abraham's Bosom," as the Hebrews believed.

The reason for the use of the Greek word *Hades* in modern Bibles is complicated, but it is enough to explain it was used by the original writers, writing in Greek. Sometimes it was translated into hell (in the King James version of the Bible) and sometimes just left as Hades in the modern translations.

Hallelujah: Hebrew word meaning, "praise the Lord." It has been said that there are three words understood around the world in many languages. Those three words are, "amen, *hallelujah*, and Coca-Cola!" *Hallelujah* is such a common Christian word that it is as familiar as Coca-Cola.

Christians use the word *hallelujah* to mean, "hurrah!" or "oh good!" Its literal translation is "praise the Lord." In most Bible translations you won't find *"hallelujah"* in the Old Testament (the part of the Bible written before Jesus). But wherever it says "Praise the Lord" that was *"hallelujah"* in the original Hebrew language.

Christians say "praise the Lord" or *hallelujah* in order to say "God is so good that I want everyone to know that He is good, and that He is worthy of the praise that we give Him."

Hallelujah is *praise, a response to the nature of God. It is spoken to God as much as it is to man. It has come into common usage among Christians around the world, and it is a way to say "Yay!" from a Christian perspective.

Healing: miraculous recovery from physical, mental, or emotional distress; God-given intervention for health and well-being. In Christian belief and experience, God *heals* people today and every day all around the world through the prayers of faith in Jesus. God does not *heal* every time someone prays, no matter who prays, but he does often *heal* unmistakably and miraculously. There is no formula for *healing*, no set of certain words that must be said, no certain thing to recite, no certain place to go or certain hand motions to make, or a minimum length of time required in prayer. The only requirement is to believe that Jesus is the Son of God, and that God *heals*; it is part of what God has for mankind. Even so, there is no guarantee.

People who see a lot of success in answer to their prayers for *healing* are people who believe that it is always God's will to heal and that it is never a mistake to ask for *healing*. There are many things that can hinder God's miraculous intervention of *healing*, things such as unforgiveness, unbelief, unconfessed wrongs done, resistance to change, etc. However, when Jesus, as the God-man on earth, prayed for *healing*, it happened every time unless there was unbelief (Matthew 13:58). Blind eyes saw, deaf ears heard, the lame walked, lepers were cleansed, demon-possessed people were delivered, and the dead were raised to life again. Jesus never included the phrase "if it is Your will" when He prayed for *healing*. He just spoke the *healing*, for example, Jesus told a man with a crippled hand to, "Stretch out your hand!" and his hand was restored. He instructed His disciples and Luke 10:9 to go out among people and *heal* the sick. He didn't add "ask if it's God's will for them to be *healed*." It is apparently always God's will to *heal*.

Part of Jesus' work on the *cross was to make *healing* possible when people pray in faith (Mark 16:17-18). Many Bible scholars say "the *healing* is in the atonement," which means that just as people are saved by faith in Jesus, also people may be *healed* by faith in Jesus. Excellent books on *healing* include *When Heaven Invades Earth* by Bill Johnson, and, a daily devotional *Health Food Devotions* by Kenneth Hagin.

This is a raw nerve among some Christians who teach that miracles ceased when the original twelve apostles of Jesus died. Pastors or teachers who hold that belief do not see miraculous healing in their churches. People who have been *healed* or witnessed healing in the name of Jesus might use the anonymous quote, "A man with an experience is never at the mercy of a man with an argument."

Heart: the center of one's emotional, rational, and spiritual being. When speaking of the invisible driving factors of life, people use various terms such as *heart*, *soul, *mind and *spirit. Each of these words is defined separately in Christianese. They are not synonyms.

"*Heart*," as a Christian word, obviously does not usually refer to the blood pump in a person's chest, but rather to the center of one's emotional and spiritual being. A Pastor named Wayne Barber puts it well: "your *heart* refers to the deepest recesses of your life...the control room of all you do." This "control room," the *heart*, is spoken of much in the Bible because, obviously, it is important to know what is in there. This *heart* makes decisions for life. Christians work on putting Jesus in the control room.

Proverbs 4:23 says, "watch over your *heart* with all diligence for from it flow the springs of life." The Bible talks about Jesus dwelling in the *heart* of the believer (Galatians 4:6, Ephesians 3:17). There are several warnings in the Bible about the dangers of a *heart* without God at the center, that is, living with the natural *heart*. Jeremiah 17:9 says that "the *heart* [apart from the influence of God] is more deceitful than all else and is desperately sick; who can understand it?"

Proverbs 28:26 says, "He who trusts in his own *heart* is a fool." Jesus says, in Luke 6:45, "the mouth speaks from that which fills the *heart*" (good or evil). Christians learn gradually to trust Jesus living in their *hearts* more than they trust their natural *hearts*; they learn to go by God's instructions, not by their longings. Christians call this, "having the *heart* of God."

So the advice given by so many TV shows and movies, "just follow your *heart*," is not in agreement with what the Bible would recommend for making good choices. It is possible for a Christian to have a well-watched-over *heart* that will not lead him or her astray. It is the Christian's goal to have a *heart* so submitted to God that he or she is drawn to what God is drawn to. That heart will benefit. Pastor Bill Johnson states, "What we do in stewarding [taking care of] that one place [the *heart*] determines the outcome of our lives."

Heathen: any person who is not a Christian. *Heathen*, depending upon the context, can mean either people who are non-Christians (when spoken by a Christian), or it may mean non-Jews (when spoken by a Jew). People don't use the term much these days, but it was used in the King James Bible, one of the earliest English translations of the Bible, so it became a word used sometimes in Christian conversation, although it is not in most modern translations. Sometimes it is used for humor because it comes across as a put-down, not a polite word to use in speaking about other peoples. It is similar to the way radical Muslims refer to everyone else as "infidels."

Heathen tends to mean also that these people practice other religions; *heathen* religions, or *heathenism*. *Heathenism* usually includes all forms of idolatry; worshiping idols, sacrificing to idols, or worship of any non-Christian god.

Heaven: the place where God is and the eventual destination of Christians after they die. "*Heaven*," in popular usage, has come to mean any place where everything is wonderful: "Our vacation to Hawaii was like *heaven*." But to Christians, *heaven* is the eternal spiritual realm where believers go after this life.

Heaven is the place where Jesus lives and is King now and for eternity. There are a lot of speculations or guesses about how *heaven* will be, and people have a lot of questions that the Bible doesn't answer; "If a baby dies and goes to *heaven*, will it be a baby forever in *heaven*?" Or, "Do people really get to have wings and play harps and sit on the clouds?"

What the Bible does clarify is that *heaven* will be an eternal existence, that is, without end, no death. In *heaven* there will be no more wrongdoing like meanness, lies, selfishness, perversion, or lovelessness. There will be only holiness, perfection, peace, and beauty. There will be no more sickness, no more pain, no more crying, not even any more darkness, because the presence of Jesus will be the actual visible light of *heaven* all the time. Even Christians have difficulty imagining such an existence, so very different from what is experienced here on earth. In heaven there will be no more confusion about matters of faith, because everyone who is there will not only see God face-to-face but will be transformed to be like Jesus. Heaven's population will be perfect toward God, perfect toward one another, loving and forgiving at a level that is unimaginable in this life. Christians believe that it is possible for anyone to get to *heaven* simply by believing in Jesus Christ, *accepting Jesus. It is the gift of God which one receives by faith.

Some who, through various experiences, have been to *heaven* and returned have written books and made movies about the experience. *Scenes Beyond the Grave* is a classic book by Marrietta Davis from 1853 when she fell into a trance for nine days, and when she came out of it she described what she experienced in *heaven*. A more modern one is *90 Minutes in Heaven*, both the book and the movie, by Don Piper. Also as book and movie, *Heaven is for Real*, relates the experience of a little boy. Christians believe that God wants people to have the promise and expectation of *heaven*.

Revelation, Chapters 4 through 12, and 19 through 21 include a lot about *heaven*. Some passages are written as viewing things happening in *heaven*, and some passages are looking from *heaven* to things happening on earth. Matthew 5:10-20 speaks of *heaven* as the destiny of the faithful.

Hebrew: a specific ethnic group of people who originate from the Middle East, or the ancient language of those people. *Hebrews* are people who are descendants of Abraham (the first man chosen to deliver God's blessing to mankind (Genesis 12:1-3). They are also called *Jews, *Israelites, or children of Israel. Without going into a lot of history (which is in Genesis in the Bible), God chose to bless Abraham and promised Abraham that He would bless him and his descendants, and make them a blessing to all of the peoples of the earth. *Hebrews* are God's "chosen people" (not to be confused with "favorite people"). God does not have a favorite people. As God's chosen people they carried a burden of responsibility: they were to make God known to all peoples (in every other language, tribe, and ethnic group) by living lives that were in harmony with God. To be *Hebrew* was to be the same as being a worshipper of God.

Jesus, a descendant of Abraham, told His followers to go all over the world and tell people about Him. That became the Christian movement and it is fulfilling God's promise to Abraham that his descendants would be a blessing to all the earth. It is being accomplished by those who believe in Jesus, most of whom by now are not literal *Hebrews*. The Bible says that all believers in Jesus are descendents of Abraham or *Hebrews,* by faith (Galatians 3:7).

Hebrews (or Jews) today, for the most part, do not follow or believe in Jesus. The earliest Christians were mostly *Hebrews;* but soon the faith began to spread to non-*Hebrews* (*Gentiles) and there came to be a division between Jews and Christians. Sadly, that division eventually resulted in a lot of hatred and severe persecution of the Jews in the centuries that followed, the Nazi holocaust being only a part of it.

Christians and *Hebrews* believe in the same God, in fact use the same Bible except for the New Testament (the part written after the time of Jesus). *Hebrew* Bibles (which they call the Torah) do not contain the New Testament, since they do not believe that Jesus is the *Messiah (the one appointed by God and sent to make the world right again, and to restore the relationship between God and man). Jews are still waiting for the Messiah to come. Expectation of a coming Messiah was originally a Jewish idea that originated in their Bible. *Hebrews* who do become Christians don't change their religion, they call themselves "completed Jews" as they come to see that Jesus is the Messiah as prophesied in their Bible, the Torah.

Hell: a place of eternal torment in the spiritual realm, the eventual destination of all who do not believe in Jesus, and the predicted destination of the devil. Christians believe that *hell* is the place where people go when they die if they do not choose to believe in Jesus. Jesus talked about it a lot: it is a place of "weeping and gnashing of teeth" (Matthew 13:41-42). It is a place where the "worm does not die, and the fire is not quenched" (Mark 9:48). *Hell* is as eternal as heaven, but it is the complete opposite of heaven. Instead of comfort there will be torment, instead of pleasure there will be pain, instead of God's presence there will be the absence of God. That is probably the best definition of *hell:* "the absence of God." God is the source of everything good: love, gladness, peace, joy. None of these things exist in His absence, in *hell*.

To explain a little more about the Christian understanding of the idea of *hell*, consider the story of the flood in the time of Noah. In Noah's time all people were at risk to drown in the flood that God predicted. But God provided a boat, built by Noah, to spare the life of anyone who wanted to get on board. Noah spent decades building the boat and telling people what it was for, inviting them to get on board to be saved from the flood (1 Peter 3:20). No one except Noah and his family believed enough (had faith) to get on board.

In the same way, all people now are at risk of going to *hell*, however God has provided a way to be saved from *hell*, and that way is to believe in Jesus. "Whoever will call on the name of the Lord will be saved" (Romans 10:13).

Why are all people at risk of going to *hell*? In Christian understanding, it is because mankind is *fallen, that is, no longer in God's favor, no longer in cooperation with and dependence upon God. All mankind inherited the consequences of Adam's failure to follow God's directions (Genesis 3). Man has gone his own way; man has done what the devil wanted man to do (deny the need for God). Man's personal pride has eliminated the possibility of oneness with God. Man who rejects God in this life receives the consequences: God's absence, *hell*, in life after death.

One of the central messages of Christianity is that the only rescue from this risk of *hell* is through faith in Jesus. Jesus' life comes into a person through believing in His role as the one who saves from *hell* and brings people into relationship with God. Only then can one stop going his own way, and go God's way instead. By believing in Jesus, one may set aside personal pride for a humble life in Christ. One can stop rejecting Him, find oneness with Him, and find His presence for eternity (see *heaven).

Holy / Holiness: pure, unstained, completely clean and beautiful, perfect, good, sacred. God is *holy*. The Bible says that God dwells in unapproachable light, a *holiness* that cannot be approached uninvited. But the Bible invites those who have faith in Jesus to "enter the *holy* place [the place of God's presence] and draw near with a sincere heart in full assurance of faith, having our hearts sprinkled clean" (Hebrews 10:19-22). God's intention for mankind is to make men and women *holy* and acceptable in His presence. That has been made possible through faith in Jesus (Ephesians 1:3-4). Faith in Jesus makes one *holy*. To a Christian, *holiness* is the ideal standard for human behavior.

Bible teachers make clear the difference between positional *holiness* and practical *holiness*. Positional *holiness* is how God sees believers. God declares man to be *holy*, that is, acceptable in the presence of God because of faith in Jesus and association with Jesus, even though still flawed in this material world. Practical *holiness* is the lived-out, day-to-day behavior which becomes increasingly *holy* as the believer matures.

The *holiness* of God is not just something about Him, but entirely who He is. The *Holiness* that surrounds God is so completely different from what is experienced at the human level, that people who touch the *holiness* of God are either made *holy*, or are destroyed. Leviticus 10:1-3 is the story of two men who approached the *holiness* of God in a disrespectful manner and died. Christians are made *holy* by their association with Jesus. *Holiness* of God is often associated with fire. John the Baptist declared that Jesus would baptize people in the *Holy* Spirit and fire in Matthew 3:11. Fire, which purifies, is associated with *holiness*. Moses first met God when He visibly appeared in a burning bush in Exodus 3:1-6, and Moses was required to take off his sandals because the ground was *holy*.

Nobody is perfect, but God is completely *holy*, completely perfect. Jesus, who is the Son of God, is the only human being who has ever lived a completely *holy* life. He lived in a manner that was full of love and forgiveness, helpful, considerate of others, bringing healing, full of compassion, and bringing freedom. What He taught was *holy* living, that is, He taught people about living in a *holy* manner. He never disregarded God, never lied, stole, murdered. He was never unfaithful, lusted after a woman, disrespected His parents, or even envied someone for what they had. It was just not in Him. He was *holy*.

For the rest of mankind, *holiness* is always lived out at a level somewhere below God's *holiness*. However, *holiness* is always something that is improving in a Christian.

The basic principle for gaining *holiness* is that people become like that which they worship. A Christian who worships God discovers more of His character, and as a result, learns more about who he, the Christian, is in the eyes of God. The real person he is, as created by God, the holy person, gradually emerges. Worship and adoration towards God actually results in *holiness* in the people of God, not by extreme effort (although believers are commanded to work at behaving in a *holy* manner), but through relationship with God. If one worships Jesus, the *holiest* man ever, then there is a corresponding gentle influence from God on one's life, in the direction of *holiness*. Because of Jesus' indwelling presence in the Christian's life, the believer recognizes wrong and decides, "I don't want to do that anymore." The power of temptation is broken by *holiness*.

To Christians, the ultimate promise of knowing Jesus is that when they get to heaven they will be *holy*, just like Jesus. There is no wrongdoing in heaven. Everything will be bathed in perfect love and the purity of God.

One mistake a lot of people make is in thinking that they have to be *holy* <u>before</u> they can come to Jesus. On the contrary, people can come to God full of guilt and out of control, giving in to every temptation, but then deciding to ask God for forgiveness and help. God alone can make a person truly *holy*. Christians believe that any form of *holiness* that a person creates apart from God, actually just stinks because it is done out of pride; it is done out of self-sufficiency instead of God-dependency. The pattern of every high-profile believer who ever lived is God-dependency and *holiness*.

Holy Spirit: one of the names of God. Usually God is invisible, and that is the *Holy Spirit*. God is visible in the Bible at times as "the Angel of the Lord," and He is seen as fire or smoke sometimes, and He is seen in the person of Jesus, but most of the work of God is done as the invisible *Holy Spirit*.

Jesus spoke of the invisible work of God as being like the wind; one can see the evidence of His presence, but He is invisible (John 3:8). He is a *Spirit* of purity and power. Christians experience the *Holy Spirit*, the invisible presence, help, and power of God. Christians call the *Holy Spirit* the "third person of the *trinity" (Father, Son, and *Holy Spirit*, not three Gods, but One. See *trinity). Christians have a relationship with the *Holy Spirit* as God because He is a person, not just an idea, not a ghost (although He is called the Holy Ghost by many Christians). Christians believe they have the *Holy Spirit* dwelling within them (1 Corinthians 3:16, and 2 Timothy 1:14). He is sent to believers by Jesus and by God the Father to be the helper, comforter, and teacher. Jesus promised His disciples that when He was no longer with them, they would receive the *Holy Spirit* in a much greater level than had ever before been the experience of believers (John 14:16-17, John 14:25-26, John 16:7-15, Acts 1:8).

He is *Spirit*, not body. He moves into the place of spiritual leadership in a Christian's life only when He is invited. He begins to influence a person toward right living and purity (*holiness) by granting power over temptations, by changing attitudes towards things so that temptations lose their power. He warns Christians when they do wrong. His influence brings awareness of having done wrong. His influence also inspires believers to do good at a supernatural level (for example, working in a clinic for lepers because Jesus loves them). One of the main jobs that the Bible says the *Holy Spirit* does is to glorify Jesus, that is, to make Jesus look good, and to bring people to a level of adoration for God and reverence for God that is called *worship.

The *Holy Spirit* dwelling within a believer is spiritual power. Those committed to God's service are empowered by the *Holy Spirit* to meet the need of the moment. The power of the *Holy Spirit* is the power to be Jesus' witnesses, that is, the power to do the works of Jesus in healing and teaching, and to tell people in a convincing way about Jesus.

Most Christians are Christians because someone told them about Jesus, and they came to believe because the *Holy Spirit* gave power to the spoken words that drew them to God and gave them faith.

All Christians believe that they have the *Holy Spirit* living in their hearts. That is clearly taught in the Bible. In Acts 2:38, Peter preaches that believers will all receive the "gift of the Holy Spirit," and Paul says much the same thing in Ephesians 1:13-14, also stating that the giving of the *Holy Spirit* is a down payment, or pledge, of much more to come from God in glorious blessing for the believer.

There is some disagreement among Christians about the "*baptism of the *Holy Spirit*," which is a Biblical concept originally stated by John the Baptist in Matthew 3:11 where he says that he, John, baptizes in water, but that Jesus will baptize in the *Holy Spirit* and in fire. This is spoken of later by Jesus in Acts 1:5, and it actually happened the first time in Acts chapter 2.

In very general terms, this "baptism of the *Holy Spirit*" is what happens to a believer when the Holy Spirit fills, surrounds, washes, or renews that person in a life-changing way. Exactly what the experience is, this "baptism of the *Holy Spirit*," is what the disagreement is about.

Some Christians insist that when one becomes a Christian, one automatically receives all of the *Holy Spirit* (a baptism of the *Holy Spirit*) and the Bible verse about that is 1 Corinthians 12:13 which says, "by one Spirit we were all baptized into one body…we were all made to drink of one Spirit."

Others insist that the baptism of the *Holy Spirit* is a second experience after the experience of becoming a Christian, and there are some scriptures that seem to indicate that (Acts 19:1-7).

One person's experience with God is not the same as another's, and it is difficult to explain each person's experience biblically.

Furthermore, the examples in the Bible happened at a time of general change in the understanding of the *Holy Spirit*, so they don't really apply as rigid directions for today. What is clear is that God has abundant spiritual power for people who believe in Him; power to live a life that is strikingly different from "normal," a life that can be an inspiration for others to come to believe in God. Spiritual power from the *Holy Spirit* is necessary to live in this manner.

It is impossible for a person to love his or her enemies or turn the other cheek (things that Jesus taught) without the *Holy Spirit's* power at work inside that person. It is impossible to convince skeptical people to become believers without the *Holy Spirit's* power, and it is impossible to work a miracle of any kind without the power of the *Holy Spirit*. All this and much more is possible by the power of the *Holy Spirit*.

Homosexuality: any sexual activity between people of the same gender. This is defined in the Bible several times as wrong-doing (sin). It is listed along with being a drunkard or being covetous or a liar (1 Corinthians 6:9-10, 1 Timothy 1:10). It is called an abomination in Leviticus 18:22, and is called degrading and indecent in Romans 1:26-27. 1 Corinthians 6:9-11 goes on to say, "such were some of you [*homosexuals*, drunkards or covetous] but you were washed, but you were sanctified, but you were justified in the name of the Lord Jesus Christ and in the Spirit of our God."

God has dealt with all wrong-doing (sin) in the same way: by the work of Jesus Christ on the cross, and by faith in that accomplishment. Those who believe in Jesus receive His forgiveness, and are "washed, sanctified and justified." And just as the one who was a liar and has become a believer is expected to find his new life free from lying, the *homosexual* is expected to find his or her new life free from *homosexual* behavior. This is the most basic stance of Christians on the subject, although one can always find those who have differing opinions one way or the other.

Hope: a combination of longing and expectation, with confidence, for something not yet seen. To Christians, *hope* is a much different concept than to unbelievers. To the unbeliever, *hope* means "maybe" or even "probably not, but it's better to *hope* than to give up." To Christians *hope* is certainty, because God gives *hope*. The only reason it is still called *hope* instead of certainty is because that which is *hoped* for is not yet seen. Romans 8:24-25 says, "For in *hope* we have been saved, but *hope* that is seen is not *hope*; for who *hopes* for what he already sees? But if we *hope* for what we do not see, with perseverance we eagerly wait for it." Christians *hope* for *salvation itself, which is promised by God, and they *hope*, often against all logic or evidence. ("I have been a scoundrel, but I *hope* for and have confidence in my salvation.) Believers *hope*, not knowing everything about how the promise will be fulfilled or how much difficulty lies between now and its fulfillment, but knowing that God is faithful. That is Christian *hope*. All of this is by *faith, that is, just because they believe God is faithful and good. By faith, believing God's promises and faithfulness, *hope* replaces doubt and fear and, of course, hopelessness, which is an impossible way to live.

God promises many things. He promises *salvation (Romans 1:16). He promises a good plan for the believer's life (Jeremiah 29:11, Ephesians 2:10, Psalm 139:16). He promises that He will not leave His children (Hebrews 13:5). He promises that He loves those who believe in Him (1 John 4:16-19). He promises forgiveness of sin (1 John 1:9). He promises righteousness (Philippians 3:9, Romans 9:30). He promises protection (Psalm 91: 11-16). He promises provision (Philippians 4:19). He promises heaven (Philippians 3:20, Colossians 1:3-5). And He promises many other things in the Bible, most of which have no visible form. Christians *hope* for these things, but with a certainty that these things <u>will be</u>, rather than being doubtful or afraid.

Humble: the personal character trait of modesty, submission, meekness, and lowliness. Jesus says, when invited to a banquet, it is best to take the less important seat (further from the host) and perhaps be called to come to a higher seat, "For everyone who exalts himself will be *humbled*, and he who *humbles* himself will be exalted" (Luke 14:7-11).

In Romans 12:3, Paul writes that one is "not to think more highly of himself than he ought." In a passage of instruction to Christians about being *humble*, Philippians 2:3-10 says, "with *humility* of mind regard one another as more important than yourselves." And, "[Jesus] *humbled* Himself by becoming obedient to the point of death." Peter writes in 1 Peter 5:5-6, "clothe yourselves with *humility* toward one another, for God is opposed to the proud, but gives grace to the *humble*. Therefore *humble* yourselves under the mighty hand of God, that He may exalt you at the proper time." Mother Theresa said that one learns to be *humble* by being *humiliated*. Well-known Christian teacher Anthony Campolo jokes that he wants to write a book titled *Humility and How I Achieved It!*

Since Jesus was *humble*, it is a quality that is important to Christians and clear instruction is given in the Bible. One of the most often quoted is above, saying, "God gives grace to the *humble*." (Grace is God's help to be more Christ-like.) Christians want to be *humble*, which primarily means avoiding being proud. Sometimes there is a false *humility* when one tries to appear *humble* but deep inside feels better than others, and it shows. Jesus, in the passage above, seems to be saying that it is a good thing to be exalted, but not a good thing to exalt oneself. Andrew Murray in his classic book *Humility*, defines pride as the loss of *humility*. Another good book is *Humility:True Greatness* by C. J. Mahaney.

Hypocrite / hypocrisy: a person who claims to be living by a high moral standard of behavior, but who actually behaves immorally. The *hypocrite* breaks the rules he says he keeps.

In a Christian context, the *hypocrite* is saying, "I am a Christian," but living in a way that is not different in behavior from all the people who say, "I'm not a Christian."

So, if a person says he is a Christian but fails to be perfect, is he a *hypocrite*? Not necessarily. Christians are often accused of *hypocrisy* because they aren't perfect. Non-Christians often know the standards of Christian behavior, and if Christians fall short of the standard, they are accused of *hypocrisy* (by non-Christians who have no intention of living by the standard to which they hold Christians). This is an interesting part of *hypocrisy*. It is unacceptable even among people who have no standards at all.

Hypocrisy is universally disgusting to all peoples and in all religions. People, even children, can see it easily and don't like it. There is no question that *hypocrites* damage the reputation of Christianity, because when people see *hypocrites*, they automatically tend to assume that what they see in one *hypocrite* must be representative of how all Christians live. *Hypocrisy* is a bad example, and biblical usage of the word includes the warning that it can lead people astray, towards wrongdoing.

Christians are aware of what they have done, because the Holy Spirit points it out to them. Christians *confess to God and to others what they have done wrong and are praying for help to do better (James 5:16). Christians are *repentant, that is, turning away from wrong behavior and turning towards right. And Christians know that they are forgiven (1 John 1:9). Trusting Jesus, being aware of wrongs done, confession, and turning away from wrong behavior frees a person from ever being a *hypocrite*.

Idol: a small "g" god which takes the place of the God of creation; it may be a statue, a creature, a river, the sun, etc. Many religions today and throughout history have included the worship of *idols,* usually a statue of some kind, or a feature in nature. Worship is offered to the *idol*, that is, people bow down to the *idol* as a god.

Often gifts are brought to the *idol*: fruit, candy, rice, etc., or sacrifices are made to the *idol*: a chicken or a goat or something is killed, and the blood or other portions are given to the *idol*. Historically even children or other humans have been sacrificed to *idols*.

Christians remember the *Ten Commandments (God's first guidelines given to His people). The second commandment is, (paraphrased) "Don't make *idols* and worship them." God prohibits *idolatry* (Exodus 20:4-5). Christians sometimes make statues of Jesus, but they are not supposed to worship the statue; it is only used as a reminder of whom they really worship in spirit and in truth. Christians are not limited to worshiping at any specific place or before a figure of any kind. There is no power in the figure.

In the *New Testament (the part of the Bible that was written after Jesus) *idolatry* is spoken of often. Romans 1:22-25 says that those who worship idols "serve the creature rather than the Creator." 1 John 5:21 says, "children, guard yourselves from idols." *Idolatry* was the practice of the religions of many people in biblical times, as it is today.

Do these people who literally worship *idols* get any benefit from it? *Idols* do have power sometimes, but that power is not the power of God, according to 1 Corinthians 10:19. It is the power that Satan gives to the *idol*, just enough to distract the worshiper from actually worshiping the one true God. Animism is the name given to religions that worship certain places and objects. Satan "animates" or gives liveliness to the things that people worship. So if a group of people worship a certain tree, unexplainable things may begin to happen for those worshipers, convincing them of the "tree god's" power, and *idolatry* around that tree continues.

Christians are at risk of making an *idol* out of money, car, boyfriend, girlfriend, career, etc. Whatever Christians are giving all their time, attention and money to could be an *idol*, especially if no attention is given to God. *Idolatry*, for a Christian, distracts from the worship of God.

Inerrancy: free from errors, specifically in regard to the Bible. Christians talk about the *"inerrancy of the Bible,"* basically meaning that the Bible doesn't have any errors in it. That is, that there are no errors in the original writing. Christians believe that the original writer was directly inspired by God to write, therefore it was perfect. It is admitted that some minor errors may have been made in copying it over the centuries or in translation into any of the thousands of languages of the world, but those copies and translations have consistently been done with a strong intention <u>not</u> to change anything of the meaning because of the belief that the original was *inerrant*.

The Bible stands up well under the definition of *inerrancy*. It does not contradict itself. If it appears to, there is always an explanation, and the harmony throughout the Bible is quite remarkable. It does not say things that are not true. And even though it was written over a period of 2000 years by about 40 different authors, it presents a consistent idea of God's character, man's nature, and God's dealings with men over history.

Other so-called sacred writings in other religions do not stand up at all under the definition of *inerrancy*. They have been changed over the centuries so much that they hardly resemble the original, and they are full of contradictions and fantasy. Josh McDowell's book, *Evidence that Demands a Verdict*, provides details about the comparison of ancient religious books in regard to *inerrancy*.

Iniquity: one of the biblical words that refers to doing wrong. (Other words are *transgression, guilt, and sin.) Literally, the word which is translated as *"iniquity"* is more like "guilt." Guilt is the awareness that wrong has been done and usually is an uncomfortable emotion. When Christians talk about *iniquity*, they are talking about something wrong that has been done. Guilt, or *iniquity*, is removed by changing behavior, making amends, or by getting forgiven.

Christians are supposed to change from habitual doing of wrong to doing right, and God will help them if they will tell Him that they recognize that what they are doing is wrong (that's called *confession). And then they must tell God they don't want to do that anymore and ask for help (that is *repentance). Through confession and repentance, *iniquity* is done away with. Psalm 32 is written by King David, and it is an actual account of David's process of getting rid of *iniquity* before God.

Intercede: a special type of prayer that includes deep spiritual identification with the person or situation (not necessarily any physical involvement). In *intercession*, the spiritual participation in what is being prayed about actually engages the praying person in the struggle on behalf of the one being prayed for. The *intercessor* totally identifies with the situation and those involved. The point of *interceding* is to add strength where needed. Therefore the *intercessor* must be able to add strength and be helpful, sometimes simply achieved by having more *intercessors* praying, strength in numbers. Christians ask their friends to pray for them. Churches have prayer chains, lists of people who will pray for any given situation.

Jesus is the supreme example of *interceding*. Hebrews 7:25 says that Jesus "always lives to make *intercession* for them" (for those who have faith). Jesus totally identified with mankind. Jesus put Himself directly in the place of sinful man (man having done wrong in the eyes of God) and in doing so, Jesus experienced the result of man's sin. Sin results in death. Jesus experienced death because He *interceded* for mankind, stood in the place of mankind. He also experienced resurrection (being raised from the dead) because the other part of His *intercession* is His own perfection: He won the struggle over sin and death because He came from a place of perfect strength. He was stronger than mankind and was able to win where man could not.

People who believe in Jesus receive resurrection and also get to win the struggle with sin because of Jesus' *intercession*. Christians live holy lives that inherit all that Jesus gave by *interceding* for mankind. Jesus died for the sin of all people so that they don't have to die for their own sin.

In the Old Testament, God calls out for someone to *intercede,* literally for someone to "stand in the gap" for the nation of God's people (Ezekiel 22:30). "Stand in the gap" refers to what happens when a walled city is attacked. If the wall is broken down in one area, defenders are needed to stand in that gap in the wall to keep the enemy from over-running the city. That is a picture of what *interceding* is: to be so involved, so committed to the protection of someone from danger, that the praying person would stand and be a wall of defense against the enemy on behalf of the person who was really in danger or in need. Clearly the intercessor must be coming from a place of great purity and strength. Beni Johnson wrote *The Happy Intercessor*, "Insights and experiences...born out of the desire just to know and love God with every possible breath." James Goll wrote *The Lost Art of Intercession.* The classic book on *intercession* is *Rees Howells, Intercessor.*

Israel: the name of a man, the name of an ethnic group descended from that man, and the name of a nation established by those people. (Also see *Hebrew) *Israel* is the present-day democratically governed nation. The man's name was originally Jacob before it was changed by God to *Israel.* God changed his name to *Israel* when Jacob learned some hard lessons from God. It is an interesting story in Genesis, the first book of the Bible (Genesis 25:19 through chapter 33).

For our purposes, just remember that *Israel* (Jacob) was a grandson of Abraham and *Israel* was the father of the famous 12 sons who produced the 12 tribes of Israel. Later, Israel became the name of the nation as well as the name of the ethnic group of people who are also known as Jews, Hebrews, or the children of *Israel.*

See *Hebrew to find out what it is that sets this people group apart from other peoples in the world.

The nation of *Israel* in current history seems to be important in the world scene. It is puzzling since it is geographically small and has a small economic influence, but it is a hotbed of issues not the least of which is how hated it is by many of its neighboring nations, some of which threaten to destroy it as a nation. *Israel*, at least as a people group, is still important to God. Romans 11:25-27 promises that "all *Israel* will be saved," although relatively few *Israelites* are Christians at this time. Psalm 122 says, "Pray for the peace of Jerusalem," which is the most famous city in *Israel*. In that Psalm, God expresses His desire to not only give peace, but also prosperity and goodness to *Israel* and all who love *Israel*.

Jacob: a man whose name was changed to *Israel; he was the son of Isaac, who was Abraham's only son. Abraham, Isaac, and *Jacob*, these three men are called the "patriarchs," or the fathers of the Jewish people, the Hebrews, the Israelites, all names for the same people. *Jacob* and his people the Jews are important to Christians because Christianity is born out of the Jewish faith in God. The Jewish people are all descended from Abraham, Isaac, and *Jacob*, so he is an important historical person in the Bible. This name, *Jacob*, is used often in the Bible to mean the entire race of people (Jews) descended from *Jacob*.

He is also important for the spiritual lessons he had to learn (the hard way) just like most people do. See his story in Genesis, the first book of the Bible (Genesis 25:19 through chapter 33). It includes many lessons from his life, for example, not to cheat, or be selfish, that God will bless the smallest amount of faith, that God will fulfill His promises, and that He will direct the life of one who depends on Him.

Jacob started out as a young person who would trick people to get what he wanted. His name *Jacob* meant "heel catcher." But God worked in his life and he gradually became a more righteous person. Finally, God changed his name to Israel which means "he who strives with God."

Jacob came to a personal faith in God because God was so good to him. When he first encountered God and saw what is referred to as "*Jacob's* ladder," in a dream, he knew he had met God and he addressed God as, "God, the God of my fathers." He continued to call Him that for the next 21 years, until he finally submitted himself personally to God and began to call God, "God, the God of Israel" (or, God, my God). Christians often go through a similar process of gradually developing a relationship with God. Growing up, at first faith is just part of being in the family, or being in a church, but later, one must develop one's own personal relationship with God. It is a progression much like *Jacob's*, growing from merely getting what he wanted from God to becoming a person who desired to love God, seek God, and be in His presence.

Jerusalem: a famous city in the country of Israel, originally established by King David as the center of worship and a place for the presence of God about 1000 years before Jesus. To Christians, *Jerusalem* is important for three reasons. First: it is a present-day city in the country of Israel, with thousands of years of Biblical history. In many Christians' minds is the belief that *Jerusalem* still has a major historical role to play in the future. Many future events which are written about in the Bible in the book of *Revelation will take place in *Jerusalem*.

Second: *Jerusalem* is called the "Holy City" for several reasons. Jesus spent a lot of time there, was crucified and resurrected there, and it is the birthplace of Christianity. For hundreds of years before Jesus, *Jerusalem* was clearly the place that God chose to dwell among men. He set up His presence there in the temple, and for hundreds of years it was the place where believers went to worship and serve God. The temple was destroyed 1900 years ago. (See *temple to get more details.) Many Christians believe that the temple must be rebuilt in *Jerusalem* before Jesus' *second coming, based on a verse that seems to imply a modern-day rebuilding of the temple (2 Thessalonians 2:1-4).

Another religion, Islam (the Muslims) built their own important place of worship called the Dome of the Rock on the very site of the temple about 1300 years ago. That complicates things for any potential rebuilding of the temple.

In eternity, in heaven, God <u>will</u> dwell among men with or without a literal temple building (Revelation 21:3). It has always been God's goal to have a close daily relationship with His people, and He will fulfill that desire in the end.

Third: *Jerusalem* has taken on a symbolic importance to Christians. The hearts of those who believe in Jesus are now the dwelling place of God and they have therefore taken the place of literal *Jerusalem*. Many Christian teachers believe that any rebuilt temple referred to in the Bible is therefore a spiritual temple made without hands, which is the body of Christian believers worldwide. Peter wrote about this in 1 Peter 2:5.

"*Jerusalem*" in many places in the Bible now represents the church, the believers around the world. So, for example, Christians reading Psalm 48:12-13 are encouraged as it says, to "Walk about Zion [*Jerusalem*] ...count her towers, consider her ramparts, go through her palaces...." These verses are seen by today's Christian as being about the wonderful features of the Church, but originally they were about the splendor of *Jerusalem*. So *Jerusalem* is near and dear to the hearts of Christians, and Psalm 122 encourages continued concern for her well-being. Furthermore, in Revelation 21, there is a detailed description of the "new *Jerusalem*" which is also called the "*bride of Christ." The "bride of Christ" means all those throughout history who have come to believe in Jesus. In the prophesied future era after Jesus' return, this new *Jerusalem* will be the dwelling place of both believers and God; a place of sinless peace, joy, light, and love.

Jesus: Christianity's most important person, historically and spiritually for eternity. To Christians, *Jesus* is absolutely central to everything else. *Jesus* is God and Christians worship Him as God.

There is no wavering on this for Christians, no question; the Bible is clear. There are many false-Christian religious groups, or non-Christians, who say *Jesus* is just a good man or a prophet, or an important spiritual figure in history, but that He was not God. The Bible makes it clear *Jesus* is God; He Himself claimed to be God (Mark 14:61-62). That's one of the reasons He was murdered. For someone to claim he was God in those days in Israel was a crime called *blasphemy, that carried the death penalty.

Jesus is also known as the Son of God. The Bible is very clear on this too. Believing that *Jesus* is the Son of God is the foundation of the Christian faith. 1 John 5:4-5 makes it clear that believing in *Jesus* as the Son of God is the powerful point-of-entry into the new life possible in *Jesus*. He was born from a virgin, a young girl, Mary, who had not had sexual relations with a man. *Jesus* was conceived in her womb because the Holy Spirit of God overshadowed her and the boy was conceived. (This story is in Luke 1:26-35.) Therefore *Jesus'* Father was truly God, not Joseph, the man to whom Mary was engaged. In further regard to *Jesus* as the son of God, see the "*Trinity."

Jesus is also a man, fully human, and as a man He is a *savior (one who saves people from condemnation). *Jesus* is the English pronunciation of "Joshua" or "Yeshua," as it is pronounced in the Hebrew language, and it means savior. Many children were named *Jesus* (Yeshua) at the time of *Jesus'* birth because everyone hoped that their son would be the predicted savior. But God sent the Angel Gabriel to tell Mary, *Jesus'* mother, to name Him *Jesus* because He really was the savior, the Son of God; God in human body on earth (Luke 1:31).

Jesus is also known by many titles and names, such as; the Lamb of God, Lord, the Bright Morning Star, the Son of Man, the Lion of Judah, the Messiah (the anointed one or the deliverer), the Rock of our Salvation, the Rock of Ages, and many others.

Jesus was born as a human baby although He exists in all eternity (existed in eternity before He was born as a baby and He exists now as the resurrected Son of God in heaven). *Jesus* lived a perfectly good human life (no sin, no wrong doing). He loves mankind. He healed the sick and fed the hungry. He got rid of demons that tormented people, demonstrating that He has all power in the spiritual realm. He spoke truths that were so profound that all who heard Him were changed forever.

Jesus was arrested by His enemies, those envious of Him, and they killed Him by nailing Him to a *cross. His dead body was put in a stone cave tomb and on the third day He came back to life (was *resurrected). He appeared to up to 500 people for the next 40 days and then was seen ascending into *heaven.

As God in heaven now He is able to be present anywhere and everywhere at any time. From Heaven He is now praying for all His people to do well during their time on earth and to eventually be there with Him. Christians believe that He is the only way to heaven, the eternal home where there is no more darkness, no more pain, no more tears, no more crying. All who believe in Him will join Him in heaven. Many books have been written about *Jesus*. One very complete and studious textbook is *The Words and Works of Jesus Christ* by J. Dwight Pentecost. Another more recent is, *Who is Jesus?* Video series produced by TrueU.

Jesus' name: names carry authority; *Jesus' name* carries His authority. Christians usually end a prayer with, "in *Jesus' name*." What this means is that Christians come to God in prayer and ask for things as a representative of Jesus (in His *name*) or in the same authority as Jesus (as if He were asking). It is as if God handed Christians a checkbook and said, "You can write checks and sign My name." The early disciples had seen Jesus' authority and had that authority given to them to heal and set people free. When Jesus told them they could ask for anything in His *name*, they got it (John 16:23-27).

All Christians have permission to ask God for anything in *Jesus' name*.

Consider this example: an Ambassador from the United States goes to a foreign country as a representative of the United States. That Ambassador has a lot of authority to ask for things "in the name of the United States," as if the President were there. Similarly, Christians have been given permission to use *Jesus' name* and authority so that God's influence can be requested to make things right, just like Jesus did. When Jesus prayed, things were made right, sickness was healed and demons were defeated. When Christians pray in *Jesus' name*, the same results can happen.

"In *Jesus' name*" is not a magic formula, not a set of words that have power when spoken like a lucky charm. "In *Jesus' name*," if spoken by a person, will only have an effect if that person has a relationship of faith in Jesus, just like that Ambassador must have a relationship of faith in the President. (The Ambassador was appointed by the President as someone trusted and faithful to represent the United States.) There is an interesting and amusing story in Acts 19:11-17 about people praying in *Jesus' name* without the relationship, and it did not turn out well.

The following passages are some of the places in the Bible where Jesus gives believers permission to use His name to validly represent Him or speak in His authority: John 14:12-14, John 15:16, Luke 10:17-19.

Jew: a certain race of people, like the Italians or Japanese. They are also called Hebrews, Israelites, or the children of Israel. See the definition of *Hebrew to see what really makes these people different from all other peoples.

Biblically, the *Jews* were a group of people set apart by God for the purpose of making God known to all the world. They are descendents of a man named Abraham, who was chosen by God to know God, experience God, and represent God to the rest of the world.

However, Abraham's descendants often chose to copy the religions of surrounding nations and began to worship idols, so they failed to represent God as they were assigned to. They gradually learned over hundreds of years that idolatry was not good and they became loyal to God. By the time of Jesus they had made it a point to completely separate themselves from other peoples and refused to have any relationship with them, when in actuality, they were supposed to have their relationship with God open for all other peoples and nations to see.

Jews worship the same God as Christians, however *Jews* do not believe that Jesus is the anointed one, the expected one, the *Messiah. They are still waiting for the Messiah. They have believed for centuries, long before Christ, that the Messiah was coming, promised by God. When Jesus came, He fulfilled the descriptions in their religious book the Torah (which Christians call the Old Testament) about the coming Messiah, and many *Jews* of Jesus' time came to believe that He was the Messiah. These believers were the earliest Christians, and at first Christians were a sub-group within the *Jews*. But eventually it became clear that the *gospel, the good news of Jesus, was not only for the *Jews* but for the whole world. It grew to be a worldwide religion without regard to race language or culture. Jesus Himself said, "salvation is from the Jews" (John 4:22). Today, only a small percentage of *Jews* believe in Jesus as the Messiah. Those who do, call themselves "completed *Jews*" or "messianic *Jews*" (or Christians) because they don't change whom they worship, they just realize Jesus is the Son of God, the *Messiah.

There has been a long history of terrible persecution of the *Jews* all over the world. They have been hated by many groups for various reasons. They tend to live together in a certain part of their cities (the word "ghetto" originally meant a district of a city where the Jews lived). Jews keep certain *Jewish* holidays, most notably *Passover (see definition) and the *Sabbath (Saturday as a holy day of rest and worship).

All of these things make them different, which of course makes certain people fear them or hate them. In the dark ages and during the *Reformation, even Christians promoted hatred for *Jews* because they blamed the *Jews* for killing Jesus. (*Jews* asked for His death. Jesus Himself was a *Jew*, but it was the Romans that actually crucified Him.) And furthermore, Jesus said, "I lay down My life so that I may take it again. No one has taken it away from Me, but I lay it down on My own initiative." (John 10:14-18). In contemporary Christianity, the vast majority do not discriminate against *Jews*, rather are thankful to them for the legacy of history, faith, and the Bible.

Judge: to pass a moral evaluation upon another person or on his or her behavior. One of the common questions among both Christians and non-Christians is about *judging* one another. Many people know Jesus' famous words, "Do not *judge* so that you will not be *judged*. For in the way you *judge*, you will be *judged*" (Matthew 7:1-2). People quote that verse because they do not like to be *judged* by others.

It is sometimes a confusing issue, but there are some biblical guidelines for *judging*. First, based on a problem presented in 1 Corinthians 5, in chapter 6 it says that Christians are the ones who are supposed to *judge* other Christians, and that Christians are subject to the *judgment* of fellow Christians. Christians are to go to one another to resolve a dispute rather than take it to an unbelieving worldly judge.

Furthermore, biblical limitations are set about the sorts of things about which Christians may be *judgmental*. Romans 14:10-13 says that, in regard to biblical restrictions about food and other minor matters, Christians should <u>not</u> *judge* one another, but give understanding and mercy to one another, knowing that all will stand before the judgment seat of God.

God will ultimately judge everyone (see the next definition) and Christians are <u>not</u> supposed to *judge* unbelievers for their behaviors.

Pastor Kristopher Dahir says, "It shouldn't surprise us when non-Christians behave like the world." There is no point in passing *judgment* upon them.

Christians in general are hesitant to *judge* anyone and would rather give grace and forgiveness. However, there are certain situations in which not *judging* a fellow Christian would perhaps be seen as giving permission for him or her to continue in wrong-doing, or could be seen as allowing a bad example to have influence in a group of believers. That was definitely the context in 1 Corinthians 5 and 6 where Paul instructs Christians to *judge* one another.

In John 3:17-19, Jesus says that He did not come to *judge* the world. *Judgment* eventually will come because all were given a choice, and each person will be *judged* upon the choice he or she has made. The choice is between light and darkness, or between believing in Jesus and refusing to believe. Refusing the light condemns one to darkness. Refusing Jesus condemns one to an eternal existence in the absence of all that He gives.

Judgment: the verdict from God as judge. God is the judge of every person individually, and there is also the final *judgment*, the time at which God will end things as they are on earth and establish His Kingdom. (See the *Day of the Lord.) *Judgment* day is understood in all religions to be that time when the bad news comes from God about everything done wrong. It is a day that is feared. Most cultures and religions believe that God is going to judge each person's life, <u>and</u> there is going to be a final day of *judgment* for the world, the end of the world, and a determination about who goes to *hell. (Hell is generally seen as the destiny for "bad people.") Often included in these belief systems are hopes of some reward for "good people," a heaven, nirvana, or a life after death.

Christianity has very clear definitions for these *judgments*. Christians believe in both God's individual *judgment* and in a final day of *judgment*. Christians accept that God has provided a way, through Jesus, and it is the only way of escape from a bad *judgment* as an individual.

Christians also believe that the only escape from a bad *judgment* at the end of the world is by believing in Jesus.

Christians actually view *judgment* from God as a good thing because of their confidence that the *judgment* for them will be good. Psalm 98:8-9 says, "Let the rivers clap their hands, let the mountains sing together for joy before the Lord, for He is coming to *judge* the earth; and the peoples with equity."

Christians have confidence that God has forgiven all the wrongs that might make them deserving of punishment. For Christians, God's *judgment* is always linked to His mercy and to His grace. To believers, *judgment* is still a future event which will be the final declaration of the mercy of God towards them. *Judgment* is still going to happen but it is going to be good (Revelation 20:11-13).

Christians will not undergo a *judgment* that determines whether they go to heaven or hell. That is already decided by their faith. They are going to heaven. Christians, by believing in Jesus, have escaped the *judgment* that would condemn them to eternal punishment (hell). Christians believe that God's *judgment* to condemnation, that is, God's decision to send a person to hell, may be avoided by believing in Jesus, by gaining the forgiveness He provides as revealed in the Bible.

Christians <u>will</u> be *judged* by God in a *judgment* apart from the consideration of heaven or hell. Christians will experience *judgment* as individuals for how they lived as believers and will be rewarded or suffer loss according to how they spent their lives (2 Corinthians 5:10). 1 Corinthians 3:13-15 says that meaningless things will be burned up on that day, but the believer will be saved. Those who have worked diligently to do God's will and serve Him will be rewarded. See *crowns.

Justified: personally made to be as though one had never done anything wrong. Christian teacher Derek Prince defined it this way; *justified* means, "just as if I'd never sinned." This is an important concept to Christians.

Justified in the non-Christian use of the word is an explanation or a rationalization for behavior that is actually wrong, but one is *justifying* that behavior because of special circumstances. For example: "I stole the medicine because my mom was sick and I didn't have the money, so that *justifies* why I stole medicine" (though it is still recognized as wrong).

Christians say, "I am *justified* through Christ," based on many Bible passages, among them is Romans 5:1: "Therefore, having been justified by faith, we have peace with God through our Lord Jesus Christ."

What *justified* means in Christianese is that the believer has been declared by God to be free from guilt of any wrong, and is completely innocent. It is God's statement about the believer. So it is <u>more</u> than forgiven. God is able to completely remove the believer's wrongdoing so that he or she can approach God in the same purity as Jesus, as if he or she had never done anything wrong. That is *justified*.

How does one get *justification*? Christians believe one is *justified* by faith, by believing that Jesus made a way for a person to be seen by God as innocent of all wrongdoing. Romans 3:24 says that believers are "*justified* as a gift by His *grace." (Grace means the influence of God to make believers holy like Jesus.) Justified is how God sees Christians. Christians are in Christ and Christ is in them; that's all God sees.

Christians, however, are granted *justification* in which they become people who never did anything wrong at all in God's eyes, because of their faith in Christ. That is *justified* to the Christian.

King James Version: one of the early translations of the Bible into English, also known as the Authorized Version. There are many types of Bibles in English today, but there were no Bibles in English until John Wycliffe, an English college professor, translated and, with the help of many scribes, hand-copied dozens of Bibles into English in 1380 A.D.

This displeased the established religious authorities of the time (who only read the Bible in Latin) and most of the copies were confiscated and burned. Later, in 1525, William Tyndale was the first to print an English Bible. (The printing press had been invented by then.) His translation was printed by the thousands for the common man. Many of these were also destroyed by religious authorities.

In 1612, King James of England commissioned 50 scholars to do a new translation in English. That is the Bible that became known as the *King James Bible* or the *King James Version*, or KJV, or the 1612 Authorized Version. It became the standard of English Bibles for hundreds of years, and there are those who still insist it is the most accurate, but that is a debate that will not be settled in these pages. It is most recognizable now by its use of old-English wording.

The New *King James Version* (NKJV) has more modern language but is translated from the same original texts from which the KJV was translated in 1612.

Reading a Bible in one's own language is recognized as essential to building faith. The Bible has been translated into thousands of languages for this reason, and thousands more are being worked on today to reach every language group in the world with their own Bible. The *King James Version* was the first Bible widely distributed in the common man's language and the impact of that on the English-speaking world has been a deep and lasting and on-going transformation of the entire culture.

Kingdom of God: the place of the dominion of the King, Jesus; wherever God rules, also known as the *kingdom of heaven*. One of the first declarations Jesus made was that, "the *kingdom of heaven* is at hand" (Matthew 4:17 and 5:3-20). Jesus instructed His disciples to go into a house and "heal those in it who are sick, and say to them, 'The *kingdom of God* has come near to you'" (Luke 10:9). Just like any kingdom, the *kingdom of heaven* is the place where the King (Jesus) has total rulership; everything is done His way.

This *kingdom* is a place where there is no sickness (Jesus didn't put up with it when He was here on earth because it does not exist in heaven) and there is no evil, and no sorrow. There is joy, love, peace and *holiness.

When a person submits to Jesus as King (or as Lord), the dominion of the King begins in that person's life. The *Kingdom of God* is <u>now</u> for the believer, not some future hoped-for development. That believer is submitted to God's instructions. However, the *devil is called the "ruler of this world" in the Bible (John 12:31). The devil promotes pride, selfishness, and greed as a lifestyle. When Jesus takes the position of King over a person's life, pride and greed are replaced because Jesus promotes love, humility, serving others, and giving. Colossians 1:13 says, "For He [God] rescued us from the domain of darkness, and transferred us to the *kingdom* of His beloved Son [Jesus]." Being transferred to the *kingdom of God* is the invisible but central effect of the believer's faith.

Prayer brings the *kingdom of God* to earth instead of the rulership of the devil. In the *Lord's prayer, Christians pray, "Your *kingdom* come, Your will be done on earth as it is in heaven" (Matthew 6:10). Presently, the *kingdom of God* is total only over heaven, but bringing the influence of *God's kingdom* on earth is the primary assignment of Christians. God's will for earth is always for love to have dominion, for wholeness to be the standard, and for light and truth to prevail. Christians can pray for healing and see it happen, can forgive when they are hurt instead of hurting back, and they can show kindness and generosity even to their enemies. That is the *kingdom of God*. Faith in Jesus brings this *kingdom*, this influence of the King, into this world and overthrows the rulership of the devil.

Lake of fire: a clear word picture of the place of eternal torment for the devil and all his followers. This lake of fire is mentioned in the book of Revelation in the Bible.

Obviously this is a burning lava-like pool of all-consuming fire. It is the final destination for Satan and all who follow him. Even death and Hades (hell) will be thrown into the *lake of fire* (Revelation 20:14). It is the final and most severe *judgment. It is a place of torment day and night forever (Revelation 20:10). It is also called the "second death" (Revelation 20:14). It is where every individual whose name is not found in the "Lamb's book of life" will be destined to go. (This is a book in heaven recording all who have faith in Jesus, according to Revelation 21:27.)

Lamb: figuratively Jesus, who lived out the role of the sacrificial lamb, that which was sacrificed to take away sin. When Christians talk about the "*Lamb* of God," they are talking about Jesus. John the Baptist saw Jesus and said, "Behold the *Lamb* of God who takes away the sin of the world" (John 1:29). The reason John called Jesus a *lamb* is because, in John's mind, and in his experience in the Jewish religion, the way that sin is taken away is through sacrificing a *lamb*, or some other animal (see *blood). John the Baptist was given miracle ability from God to see in the future. (That's called *prophecy: the ability to see secrets of the future or to see invisible things in the present.) John apparently saw Jesus, like a *lamb* being sacrificed, taking away the sin of the world through his own death. So Jesus, through the sacrifice of Himself (Hebrews 9:26) gave mankind the possibility of forgiveness from God.

Later in the Bible, in Revelation 5:1-14, John the apostle writes that he saw Jesus as the "*Lamb* standing as if slain." Later in Revelation 13:8 and 21:27 is a mention of the "book of life of the *Lamb*," a book in which one's name must be written to be sure of acceptance by God. John the apostle in Revelation uses "the *Lamb*" about 30 times as synonymous with the name "Jesus."

Interestingly, another animal that is used as symbolic of Jesus is the lion, or the "*lion of Judah." So Jesus is both like a lion and like a *lamb*.

Law: specifically the first five books of the Bible, and generally all the *laws* that God commands. "The *Law*" is the general term that Christians use to mean all the rules of God, for example things like "You shall not murder" or "You shall not steal." The Bible itself has many references to "the *Law*," and it is generally referring to the *Law* that was given to Moses for the people of God (the first five books of the Bible). John 1:17 says, "For the *Law* was given through Moses; grace and truth were realized through Jesus Christ." This is one of the big differences between the part of the Bible before Jesus (the Old Testament) and the part that was written after Jesus (the New Testament). The Old Testament focused on the *Law* as the way to please God. Obedience to the *Law* is the proper response to the *Law* and brings blessing from God. ("The *law* of the Lord is perfect, restoring the soul" Psalm19:7.) That is still true even though the New Testament focuses on faith to please God ("without faith it is impossible to please [God]" Hebrews 11:6). Taken together, the whole message of the Bible is that it was never the purpose of the *Law* to make people right with God, because it is impossible to be perfect in obedience to it. The *law* was given to teach the right ways of God. Galatians 3:21 says, "For if a *law* had been given which was able to impart life, then righteousness would indeed have been based on *law*." The *Law* in itself is not able to change the human heart. Only Jesus can change a heart from having the natural tendency to do wrong to become one who does right. In the New Testament it is explained that Christ comes to live in the heart of the believer, and that indwelling Jesus does change the heart.

According to Romans 7:6, Christians "have been released from the *Law*." That does not mean that Christians get to ignore God's rules. It does mean that connecting with God, being right with God, is no longer centered upon obedience to the *Law*. It is more importantly a relationship of love. Furthermore, the New Testament message is that the *Law* no longer condemns Christians if they fail to obey it perfectly.

Romans 8:2 says, "the *law* of the Spirit of life in Christ Jesus has set you free from the *law* of sin and of death." The *Law* (the *law* of sin and of death) says, basically, "If you sin, you die." (That is the Old Testament message.) The "*law* of the Spirit of life" says, basically, "If you believe in Jesus, eternal life and Christ-likeness is yours." (That is the New Testament message.)

God's set of rules, the *Law*, is still to be obeyed, but to be a Christian, to be forgiven all wrong-doing and to be accepted by God does not require perfect keeping of the *Law*. Christians believe that they are saved by *Christ alone (no other savior) through *grace alone (only as a gift of God's love) and through *faith alone (not by keeping the *Law*). Romans 3:28 says, "For we maintain that a man is justified by faith apart from works of the *Law*."

<u>Legalism:</u> a belief that obedience to God's law is necessary for right relationship with God. In Christian society, a *legalist* (one who practices *legalism*) is a person who requires people to meet certain standards in order to be a "real" Christian. *Legalists* focus on certain behaviors that they believe are against the law of God and will disqualify a person as a Christian, for example, smoking, drinking, gambling, homosexuality, lying, stealing, or getting a tattoo. *Legalists* would say, "He/she cannot do that and be a Christian." They say, "Yes you have to believe in Jesus, but <u>also</u> you must obey God's written requirements."

It sounds good, and the intent is honorable, but it is not in agreement with the good news (the gospel) of Jesus. It is the opposite of grace which is at the center of Christianity and explained in the next two paragraphs. *Legalism* actually <u>denies</u> that Jesus has really done away with all wrong-doing. Christians believe that Jesus took care of sin: the record of it, the guilt of it, and the nature from which that wrong-doing comes. Christians believe that they are made right with God by believing in Jesus Christ plus <u>nothing</u>.

Legalists think that, besides believing in Jesus, certain laws must be upheld also in order to be really saved (accepted by God).

The New Testament *gospel (good news) is clear: *Grace (God's generous enabling power to make people like Christ) is greater than the *legal* requirements of the Old Testament (the part of the Bible that was written before Jesus). The grace of God is the basis of the new agreement between God and man. The old agreement between God and man was more dependent upon obedience to the law (the *legal* requirements of the Bible.) The law did generate a relationship with God. In the Old Testament, obedience to the law was the means by which one entered into relationship with God. In the New Testament (written after Jesus' death and resurrection) the way one enters into relationship with God is by believing in Jesus (Ephesians 2:8). *Legalists* want to keep the Old Testament in effect even though it has been made obsolete by the New Testament (Hebrews 8:13).

*Grace, briefly, is God's forgiveness given without cost, without being required to <u>do</u> anything to deserve it; only believe in Jesus as the Son of God (Romans 3:24, Ephesians 2:8). Grace also includes the enabling presence of God to make people more like Jesus. God knows that people who have no intention of stopping their wrong doing will step into Christian churches for any number of reasons. *Legalism* seeks to ensure that these people do stop their bad behavior, and look like real Christians, but God's method of changing people is different. God knows that when He, by grace, lifts the burden of sin from the sinners' shoulders, and when He transfers undeserving believers from the dominion of darkness to the kingdom of light, and when He pours out His love on them, the dullest heart, the most craven soul, will be overthrown, and a remarkable turning against sin and selfishness will take place in those hearts, and a new rulership of the love of God will take over. Christians call this being *born again by grace.

Legalism seems more logical to a lot of people than grace. *Legalism* says, "If one performs at a high enough standard, then one is qualified to get God's favor. One must earn what one gets from God." (Earning God's favor is the message of all the world religions.) However, Jesus routinely gave grace and forgiveness to people who had done nothing to be deserving of it. The woman caught in adultery (John 8:3-11) was forgiven in spite of the clear law requiring her punishment. Zacheus, although he was a scoundrel, was forgiven, and Jesus gave him favor (Luke 19:1-10). The criminal on the cross (Luke 23:39-43) knew he deserved no forgiveness, yet he believed in Jesus as the Son of God and Jesus said, "today you will be with Me in Paradise." Jesus declared this criminal to be worthy of going to heaven by God's generosity because the man believed in Jesus, not by keeping the law. A *legalist* would have said, "Sorry, you don't get to go to heaven because you have not been performing well enough to get into heaven."

Legalism condemns imperfect behavior and requires people to keep the *legal* requirements of the Bible. Jesus forgives imperfections and invites people to accept God's love. Jesus forgave all sin, so the *legalist* has no biblical grounds to condemn people for what Jesus has already forgiven. (Hebrews 1:3, 1 John 2:1-2, 1 John 4:14).

Lion of Judah: one of the names or descriptive titles of Jesus. In Revelation 5:5 Jesus is described as "the *lion* that is from the tribe of Judah." Jesus is from that family known as the tribe of Judah. There are 12 tribes or families of the Jews because *Jacob had 12 sons and the Jews are the descendants of those twelve sons. One of the sons was named Judah, and Jesus is a descendant from him; He is of the tribe of Judah. Jacob made predictions for all 12 of his sons before he died (Genesis 49), and Judah he declared to be a *lion's* cub, the one who would hold leadership. Judah's leadership first emerged about 500 years later.

David, who was of the family of Judah became the King and his descendants were kings, and ultimately a descendant of David, Jesus, is the "King of Kings and Lord of Lords," (Revelation 19:16). Jesus, from the tribe of Judah, is called the *Lion of Judah*.

Lord: a title for God. *Lord* means God from the mouth of a Christian, in any of the ways a Christian might be talking about God (as Father, Son, or Holy Spirit). In the Old Testament, because of difficulties in translation from Hebrew, the English Bible often reads *LORD* (all caps) which means that the name of God there in the original writing, is the most sacred name of God, the unpronounceable YHWH (Yahweh or Jehovah). In other places in English Bibles there is also, *Lord* (capital L, but lower case for the rest) which is a less sacred word in the original language, Greek or Hebrew, basically meaning Master. It also usually refers to God, but can mean a human *lord* too. Christians who say they know Jesus as *Lord* mean that they know Jesus as God. He is not just a historical man anymore to them, He is the *Lord*, and they acknowledge Him as such, their *Lord*.

Lord's Prayer: a model prayer given by Jesus, also known as the "our Father." Jesus instructed his disciples to pray in Matthew 6:5-15 and in Luke 11:1-13. In both passages He gave them a basic outline for prayer which has come to be known as the *Lord's Prayer*. This prayer has become familiar to anyone raised in a Christian culture: "Our Father who is in heaven, hallowed [holy] be Your name. Your kingdom come. Your will be done, on earth as it is in heaven. Give us this day our daily bread. And forgive us our debts [sins, wrongs] as we also have forgiven our debtors [those who have done wrong to us]. And do not lead us into temptation but deliver us from evil. For Yours is the kingdom, and the power, and the glory, forever. Amen." This prayer is not magic in its wording. It is not intended to be prayed over and over as a formula to getting what is wanted from God (Matthew 6:7).

The *Lord's Prayer* is an outline. It's intended to highlight the issues that are most important in prayer, who God is, and what we are to expect from Him, and to give to him. Believers are to know God is the heavenly Father. They are to worship Him, remember His holiness, and submit to becoming like Him in holiness. They are to pray for the *Kingdom of Heaven to come to earth. They are to ask for provision, daily bread instead of presuming that they will be able to get it without God's help. They are to move into the forgiveness God gives; receive it and be a forgiver. They are to pray for protection from temptation, and pray to be delivered from all evil.

Remembering and declaring God's kingdom, power and glory are traditionally part of the prayer, although scholars say that the last line of this prayer was not in the original oldest manuscripts, so it may not have been included in Jesus' original instruction. Used as a format for prayer, the *Lord's Prayer* focuses on recognizing and worshipping God, on submission to God, on relying on God as provider, on being forgiven, on being like Him in forgiveness, and on thanksgiving.

Lord's Supper: the occasion in which Jesus had His last meal with His friends and He instituted the ritual of *Communion. "The Last Supper" is the title of the famous Leonardo da Vinci painting of the last meal that Jesus ate with his disciples before He was betrayed, captured, and crucified. During this meal, He declared that one of His friends would betray Him, which happened later that night. During this meal, Jesus instituted the Christian ritual of *communion, saying that eating bread and drinking wine would be the way they would remember His death on the cross to forgive all sins (wrong doing) of mankind. (*Communion is the same as the *Lord's Supper*.) To Christians, the meaning of the bread is that it represents Jesus' body, and the wine or juice represents Jesus' *blood. For a deeper understanding of the meaning of it, read about the *cross and about the *blood, and about *communion.

Lost: the state of not knowing the way and not knowing about Jesus. *Lost* is the term Christians often use to mean people who have not come to believe in Jesus. In Luke 15, Jesus told three stories about finding important things that were *lost:* a *lost* sheep, a *lost* coin, and the *lost* son (the *prodigal son). He told these stories to reveal how very important it is to Him to find people who are *lost,* those who don't know the way to God. Jesus' point in telling those stories is to say that all people are valuable to God, and much effort must be made to help them find their way to God. This is one of the reasons that Christians all over the world are often the only ones that care for the diseased, the poor, the homeless, the alcoholic, drug addict, or the criminal.

"I once was *lost* but now I'm found," the famous line from the song "Amazing Grace," sprang from the heart of John Newton when he was led to understand Jesus. The *lost* spend their lives trying to find the way to happiness, to love, to peace, and to hope, but being *lost,* the only roads they try are money, sex, fame, power and pleasure. Those roads only lead to getting more *lost.* God's narrow road is faith in Jesus; it is surrender; it is humility; it is faith, the belief that God loves and looks to receive the *lost.*

Love: that which motivates God to pursue mankind, and that which He commands mankind to employ in all relationships, including the relationship with Him. Most Christians, when asked about *love,* will point to 1 Corinthians 13 in the Bible. That passage is a very clear description of *love* at its most ideal, in the way that God *loves.* In part it reads: "*Love* is patient, *love* is kind and is not jealous; *love* does not brag and is not arrogant, does not act unbecomingly; it does not seek its own, is not provoked, does not take into account a wrong suffered, does not rejoice in unrighteousness, but rejoices with the truth; [*love*] bears all things, believes all things, hopes all things, endures all things. *Love* never fails [never falls down or stops]." Christians call this unconditional *love.*

Unconditional *love* is the kind of *love* that God gives; *love* without conditions. One does not have to perform to receive it; one does not have to be strong, good-looking, smart, or capable, and even if one does something bad, wrong, or out of line, that unconditional *love* is still there. There is nothing a person can do that will make God *love* him more, and there is nothing he can do to make God *love* him less. It is the way that Christians understand God's *love*. In the Greek language (the language in which most of the New Testament was originally written) God's *love* is called "agape." It is the very best kind of *love*, the *love* that 1 Corinthians 13 is talking about, and the kind of *love* that makes no sense to a performance-based culture (a culture in which only the athletic, the rich, the beautiful, and the clever are *loved*). It is the kind of *love* that Jesus teaches people to give. Turning the other cheek (Matthew 5:39) is one of the extreme examples of unconditional *love* that Jesus taught; even if slapped in the face by someone, keep *loving*.

In another *love* passage, 1 John 4:7-21, the word "*love*" is used 27 times. And in that passage, twice, it says, "God is *love*." Because of that, Christians find *love* in everything that God does. "God is *love*," however, does not mean that *love* is God. God is *love*, but He is also unimaginably more than *love*. *Love* alone does not cover all that truly is God.

There is a little book called *If* by a missionary to India, Amy Carmichael, that is all about *love*. She calls it "Calvary *love*," the *love* that Jesus exhibited on the cross while He was dying in order to give mankind the possibility of the mercy of God. She says that Calvary *love*, when experienced by believers, is *love* that can "so charge a moment that it seems to open the Eternal to us." It is the *love* of Jesus, that which motivated Him to give up His life for His friends.

Manna: miraculous food that God provided for His people while they were going through the desert. *Manna* was the name given to the food from God that came down from heaven and appeared daily.

Manna was found on the ground every morning to give the traveling Israelites something to eat in the desert. When God took the Jews from slavery in Egypt to freedom in the land that He had promised to give to them, they went through the desert where there was no food, so He miraculously fed them each day. Each day there was plenty for everyone, and every day they had to go out and gather enough for the day. Exodus Chapter 16 tells about the *manna*.

Manna has come to represent, for today's Christian, the word of God, the Bible, miraculously nourishing every day because Christians are taught to read the Bible every day to feed their souls. This is also called daily *devotions, or quiet time. The Bible is seen to be nourishment for the spirit; just what one needs for today, every day, coming from heaven, food for the soul. It is miraculous; it is nutritious, predictable, reliable, and sufficient, just like *manna*.

Jesus was questioned about the *manna*, and He said in John 6:33, "For the bread of God is that which comes down out of heaven and gives life to the world." Then He said, "I am the bread of life." Jesus is often the fulfillment of stories that were written in the Bible long before He was born. Here, He is more than food for a day. He is the true *manna*, the bread from heaven, the bread for eternal life (John 6:30-59).

In Revelation 2:17 there is also a mysterious promise that Jesus will give some of the "hidden *manna*" to the one who overcomes in times of difficulty. One can presume that means there is a storehouse hidden in the spiritual realm, a storehouse of the kind of nourishment for strength that one will need in times of trial, and God will give that to those who stand firm in His truth.

Mantle: a cape or cloak which figuratively represents the God-given role and abilities that are displayed in a servant of God. The word is only used in the Old Testament (written before Jesus) but the principle of the *mantle* continues into New Testament (Christian) thinking. In the Bible, the clearest picture of this is in the story of a prophet named Elijah.

Elijah literally passed his *mantle* (both his cloth cape and the role he had received from God) to his student, Elisha. Elisha then picked up both the cloth *mantle* and the role from God and started where his teacher left off carrying on the work with the same role and same God-given abilities (2 Kings 2).

This example of godly leadership and other similar stories in the Bible teach that the role of leadership (having a *mantle* of leadership) requires great sacrifice. For Christians, it is the cost of leading like Jesus to the point of entering into suffering for the sake of those who are being served. Philippians 3:10-11 is the Apostle Paul's personal account of entering into "the fellowship of His [Jesus'] sufferings, being conformed to His death," which was the God-given role that Jesus assigned to Paul. In Acts 9:1-15 is the account of how Paul (then called Saul) met Jesus and what Jesus said about what He would have Paul do.

Jesus grants Christians certain *mantles*, certain roles in life that require much sacrifice but result in much gain for the purposes of God. Sometimes Christians will speak of a believer's *mantle*, meaning the authority and God-given abilities upon that person to carry out what it is that God has called him or her to do.

Martyr: someone who has been killed because of his or her belief in Jesus. Christians in many places around the world will be killed today, yes today, (and yesterday and tomorrow) just because they are believers in Jesus. It is very dangerous to become a Christian in many places around the world. Jesus told His disciples (those who were learning from Him) that they might be in great danger (Matthew 10:16-39).

A famous *missionary, Jim Elliot, said, "He is no fool who gives what he cannot keep to gain what he cannot lose." In other words, if one gives up this temporary life on earth in the service of helping others gain eternal life, that's not foolish. To believers, this is a good summary of the ultimate life as a Christian, laying down all personal ambition.

Giving up ambition does not necessarily mean becoming a *martyr*, although that possibility is always real, but to be a Christian, one must, must give up on all that the world says is good (fame, money, pleasure, long life) and look first to what God's Kingdom might require.

Jim Elliot and four other men of the same mind were killed, *martyred*, by the primitive tribesmen to whom they were beginning to speak about Jesus. Jesus said, "he who has lost his life for My sake will find it" (Matthew 10:39).

In Revelation 6:9-11, John sees in heaven those who have been killed throughout history because of their faith, and reveals that there are still those who will yet be killed, *martyred*, because they will testify that Jesus is the Son of God, and refuse to worship another, but there will be a time when all of the killing will stop and there will be no more *martyrs*; their number will be completed.

Mercy seat: the sacred place where the presence of God rested, in the most holy part of the place of worship (the Tabernacle or the Temple). This was not really a place to sit, at least not for a human being. The *mercy seat* was the lid of the *Ark of the Covenant, the box that God instructed to be hand-crafted and put into the *Tabernacle (the place of worship) as the very place where His glory would rest. It is described quite exactly in Exodus 25:17-22, and in Numbers 7:89 it says that Moses went into that holy place and heard the voice of God speaking to him from above the *mercy seat*. Sometimes God's glory appeared on or above the *mercy seat* as a cloud, the actual visible presence of His being (1 Kings 8:10-11).

A more accurate translation of the original Hebrew name for it, rather than "*mercy seat*," would be "a propitiatory place" or a place where *propitiation takes place. Propitiation means to regain favor. The *mercy seat* was the place where all the people of Israel could regain favor with God, no matter what things they had done wrong. This was accomplished by one priest one time a year as a representative for the entire nation, coming before the *mercy seat*.

That is how sacred the *mercy seat* was: it was only visited once a year by one priest and the entire population's wrongs were forgiven for the entire past year. Leviticus 16:3-31 is a detailed account of exactly how this day of forgiveness began and was to take place each year. To Christians, the *mercy seat* pointed to Jesus. He was the final forgiveness, the final propitiation for sin, once for all. God's very real presence has always been about forgiveness.

Read more about the *Ark and the *Tabernacle and the *Temple, where the *mercy seat* was kept. Apparently the Ark, or the *mercy seat*, was destroyed or stolen by the invading Babylonian army in 586 B.C. No further record of it is in the Bible. Many speculations exist, some based on the non-biblical writing of Maccabees 2:4-8 which says that the prophet Jeremiah hid the Ark in a cave.

Messiah: the one who is expected to come and make everything right. It seems to be a basic expectation of mankind that some kind of leader will emerge, someday, like Neo in the movie, *The Matrix*, who will have the miraculous ability (the *anointing) to set everything right. Everything is clearly not right at this time. There is a *messianic* expectation among Buddhists, Muslims, Hindus, Indonesians, and some Native American tribes, specifically the Hopi and Sioux, as well as among modern day *Jews, the people of Israel. A *Messiah* had been expected for hundreds of years by the Jews at the time of Jesus' birth, and the excitement was growing and widespread. Daniel 9:25-26 speaks clearly of the coming *Messiah*. Isaiah 52:13 through 53:12 also speaks of the *Messiah,* but not by the name or title *Messiah*, but by the things He would accomplish. There are hundreds of *messianic* passages in the Old Testament that foretell the coming *Messiah*. Jesus fulfilled everything in all of those passages.

Messiah in Hebrew, or Christ in Greek, both mean "the anointed one." Being anointed means having been given power and/or authority. Jesus used one of the *messianic* passages, Isaiah 61:1-2, to declare that He was the *Messiah*.

He read, "The Spirit of the Lord is upon Me, because He anointed Me preach the gospel to the poor. He has sent Me to proclaim release to the captives, and recovery of sight to the blind, to set free those who are oppressed, to proclaim the favorable year of the Lord." The story of Jesus reading that in public is in Luke 4:18-19 (it reads a little differently in Isaiah).

To Christians, the *Messiah* has come; Jesus is the *Messiah*. He stated it Himself very clearly at His trial, and that was the basis of His conviction (Mark 14:61-62). He was sentenced to death for saying He was the *Messiah* (see *blasphemy). There is no need of another *Messiah*. Christians don't have an expectation of a future *Messiah*, but they have thankfulness that they know the *Messiah*, Jesus. And Jesus is using His people all over the world to complete the work He began as *Messiah*, bringing the impact of God's Kingdom to all of the world's problems.

Millennium: the thousand year reign of Christ when He returns. (See also "*end times.") A *millennium* is a thousand years. Christians speak of the *millennium*, meaning a time predicted in Revelation 20:1-7, when Satan will be imprisoned for a thousand years. During this time the first resurrection will take place. (There are going to be two times of resurrection of the dead, Revelation 20:4-5 and verses 12-13.) In this first resurrection, Christians who have already died will be resurrected and will reign with Christ for that thousand years. Then Satan will be released for a short time before he is thrown into the *lake of fire.

This thousand year reign is only mentioned that one time in the Bible. There is disagreement among some Christians about exactly when it will take place, about whether it is a literal thousand years, and about what will take place just before or just after it. For most Christians, it is a biblical concept that does not impact their daily lives, and they trust God to sort out how all the events at the end of the world will happen.

Minister: anyone who is a representative of Jesus or the church, bringing love, help, generosity, comfort, etc. A *minister*, to a Christian is usually a *Pastor, or a leader of a church, however, it can mean any person who helps others in Christian circles. This is anyone who is serving God by doing whatever it is they are good at or whatever is needed. So a *minister* can have a bathroom-cleaning *ministry*, or a preaching *ministry*, or anything in between (*ministers* of worship, *ministry* to welcome people, food bank *ministry*, Sunday school teaching *ministry*, etc.). Christians talking to one another may say, "that really *ministered* to me," meaning that whatever the other person did or said was a touch or a word that seemed to have the influence of God upon it. It just means that the *minister* has been an effective servant of God, carrying out the purpose of God in what the *minister* was assigned to do.

Sometimes *minister* is a title for an appointed position in the church. There are *ordained *ministers* who have some sort of credentials (ordination) from an organization that affirms that this person is indeed smart enough and experienced enough to *minister*. *Pastors, *deacons, *elders, *priests, are all positions of *ministry* in some churches, some are ordained and some are not.

Christians depend on their *ministers*. Those who *minister* can expect to be called upon in their area of *ministry* quite regularly. Being a Christian *minister* on almost any level can be quite demanding. Christians often go to college to be in the *ministry*, and desire to give their lives to serving the church, the believers, in one way or another.

Miracle: anything that appears to be scientifically unexplainable. Christians say, "It's a *miracle*!" What they mean is that they believe that God was involved; God made it happen. It may be the birth of a baby, the healing of cancer, or finding a job. "It's a *miracle*" means God did it. Christians are excited to give God credit for whatever good thing has taken place, and it is often credited as a *miracle*.

Sometimes, what Christians call a *miracle*, non-believers may explain away as a natural occurrence, but no matter, Christians will recognize the *miraculous* and give God the credit.

Jesus did many *miracles* as recorded in the Gospels (Matthew, Mark, Luke, John). He healed the sick, delivered people from demonic possession, raised the dead back to life; food was multiplied; the blind saw; the lame walked; the deaf heard. Wherever Jesus was, He prayed, and *miracles* happened. His disciples continued, after Jesus went to heaven, to do similar things as is recorded in the book of Acts in the Bible. Furthermore, Christian history up to the present is littered with notable *miracles* that have happened when Christians prayed. Jesus promised that people who believe in Him would go on to do even greater works (*miracles*) than He did (John 14:11-14).

The *New Testament was originally written in Greek, and the word that is sometimes translated as "*miracle*" is "dunamis," in Greek, which is translated in other places as "power." Jesus promised to give His followers "dunamis," or power, or *miracle*, when the Holy Spirit came upon them (Acts 1:8). This power of the Holy Spirit came upon them a few days later as recorded in Acts 2, and from then on, the *miracles* were happening wherever Christians were. God's power is "dunamis," and by His power in Christians He works *miracles*. *Miracles* are the result of faith in God, a God of power and love. *Miracles* are not the result of some special words, some magical incantation, or some kind of formula by some special person. *Miracles* happen when people believe that God is good enough and loving enough, and powerful enough to intervene and bring about change (a *miracle*). Jonathan Welton tells the story of an uneducated, illiterate "Untouchable," (according to the caste system of India) Christian woman who has raised more than a dozen people from the dead by her faith in Jesus. (The book, *Normal Christianity*.)

Missionary: a person who crosses over into an unfamiliar culture to take the message of Jesus to the people of that culture. (See *great commission) Christian *missionaries* have gone all over the world ever since the time of Christ. Jesus commanded His followers to go to all the world and preach the gospel (Matthew 28:18-20, Mark 16:15, Luke 24:46-47, John 20:21). *Missionaries* are those who go specifically to a culture different from their own, possibly learn a new language, and a new lifestyle, in order to make "Jesus" a household name in a place where there was little or no knowledge of Jesus before the *missionary* arrived. *Missionaries* have translated the Bible or portions of it, into thousands of languages. Christian churches have become commonplace in many countries all over the world where there were no Christians before. Many *missionaries* have been *martyred (killed because they represented Jesus). Many more have died of strange diseases or just because of the hardship of a life in a primitive culture. A few famous *missionaries* are: Paul the apostle and Polycarp to the Roman empire, Francis Xavier to Japan, Adoniram Judson to Burma, Hudson Taylor to China, Dr. David Livingstone to Africa, William Carey to India, David Brainerd to the American Indians, Las Casas to Central America, and more recently, Bruce Olson to jungles of Colombia, and Jackie Pullinger to Hong Kong, just to mention a few. Books are written about all of these *missionaries*. There is a book of *missionary* biographies by Ruth Tucker, entitled *From Jerusalem to Irian Jaya,* that gives an eloquent history of *missionary* activity from the time of Christ to the 1980's.

    The world today is a very different place than it was 2000 years ago because of the influence of Christ in nations where *missionaries* have gone. Women have a role in many societies where it was not so 2000 years ago. Human sacrifice was commonplace in many non-Christian cultures, but now it is fairly rare and banned in places where it used to be practiced. Shamans, witch-doctors, and other *occult practitioners are much less common.

Missionaries continue today to go out from their own countries, not just from the U.S. and Europe, but from China, Korea, India, South America, Australia, and Africa. They often go to "Hidden People Groups," a term coined by the U.S. Center for World Mission. Hidden People Groups are people who are remote from Christians either geographically, or by language or culture. There are many possible reasons they have never heard of Jesus. *Missionaries* go to them, work to fit in, to become as close to being one of those people culturally as they can in order to communicate with them about the "good news," the *gospel of Jesus. It is the heart of God to speak in an understandable way about His love to every person in his or her own language. Adoniram Judson stated that, "The motto of every *missionary*, whether preacher, printer, or schoolmaster, ought to be, 'Devoted for life.'"

Mount Sinai: the mountain where God appeared to Moses and to the people Moses was leading out of slavery. See *Sinai* for the full definition. Just briefly, it is the mountain to which the Jews went as they left Egypt on the *exodus. It was where they first experienced God's holy and frightening presence (Exodus 19:17-20), where Moses got the Ten Commandments (Exodus 20:1-17), and it was there where they built the *Tabernacle, a place to worship God and the place where His very real presence could dwell (Exodus 40). The actual location of *Mount Sinai* is not certain today. The important thing is that God made an appointment to meet with His people, and He met them there, and that encounter has significantly impacted human history ever since.

Mount Zion: a small mountain chosen by God as central to His worship. (See *Zion*) Just briefly, it is the mountain on which *Jerusalem and the *Temple of God were built. It is mentioned in the Psalms often as *Zion*, and it usually means the place of God, or the place of God's people, and Christians understand that they may now substitute "the church" for "*Zion*" whenever it appears in the Bible.

The reason this substitution can happen is that God's intention through the church is very similar to what his intention was in establishing His presence on *Mount Zion*. His intention was always to become known in all the earth, beginning with Jerusalem (*Zion*). Today He is becoming well-known through the church around the world.

Natural man: the nature of man before entering into a relationship of love and trust with God. Christians will often talk about the changes that happened in their lives when they came to believe in Jesus. They talk about their "old man," or "*natural man;*" some Bibles say "the old self," the person they were before they were changed by Jesus love. In Ephesians 4:20-24 the Bible talks about the *natural* or "old" man as compared to the new man. The new man is the changed person that one becomes after giving one's life to Jesus. Generally the change is something like this: the *natural man* was selfish, enjoyed *sin and liked the darkness of wrong-doing. John 3:19-21 says that people whose lives are evil prefer to live in darkness, either literally dark, or intentionally avoiding the influence of Jesus. The *natural man* was often very angry or depressed, was not a good parent or employee, maybe drank too much or used drugs. The new man, the new self, "in the likeness of God has been created in righteousness and holiness" (Ephesians 4:24). The new man, under the influence of Jesus, avoids sin (no longer wants to do those wrong things), prefers the light (is not living a secret life hidden in the dark somewhere), is no longer angry or depressed, is a better parent or employee, and lives a clean and sober life.

These changes are not just the result of strong willpower, but because of the presence of God in his or her life. Biblical teaching on this is that the *natural man* or the old man <u>dies</u> when a person surrenders to Jesus, and the new man is resurrected, brought to life (Roman 6:3-9). It is a resurrected life that the Christian is living, a life that is supernatural, heavenly, and changed. (See *resurrection.)

New Age: a spiritual view that believes man is basically good, as long as he finds "light," a connection to the spiritual realm which may include a wide variety of pursuits, almost anything <u>except</u> traditional Christianity. Christians see themselves as very different from those with a *New Age* view. *New Age* is a philosophy, a way of thinking, not really a religion.

People with that mindset are called *New Age* because they emerged as a group when some of the leading personalities among them declared that mankind was entering a *new age* in the late 1970s because of the aligning of the planets. They see this *New Age* as a spiritual era, and they welcome every imaginable spiritual perspective as part of the big picture. So they often (not always) include Jesus as one of their avatars, along with Buddha, Krishna, etc.

The perspective of Christians is quite different. Christians see Jesus' work as purification and forgiveness of sin (wrong-doing). Christians are interested in *salvation from the effects of sin and receiving eternal life (heaven) through faith in Christ alone.

New Age people, though they may admire Jesus, aren't really centered on purification of sin. They may not even believe there is such a thing as sin. They are focused on enlightenment, wisdom, love, and self-actualization. The *new age* view also doesn't agree that there is only one way to heaven (through Jesus). In fact, there is usually a refusal to acknowledge that there is any universal truth or any clearly defined universal code of behavior outlining what can be called "good" or "wrong." They look to the universe as the voice of guidance and the power for direction in life.

Christians see the position of the *new age* person as good in that they are hungry for spiritual help (so many people do not even acknowledge the spiritual realm), and Jesus is very willing to love and come alongside anyone seeking spiritual truth.

New man: new personhood that is experienced after coming to faith in Jesus. A *new man* is what one becomes when one begins to trust in Jesus. It is a biblical concept of the new self versus the old self (Ephesians 4:20-24), and it only really makes sense if one understands the idea of the *natural man, or the old self. See the definition of *natural man.

This idea of the *new man* is very important to the Christian's thinking about who he is. Romans 6 outlines that the old sinful self has died through *baptism (the ritual bathing in water that signifies becoming a Christian), and the *new man* has been raised from the dead, no longer a slave to sin and very much alive to God and walking in the newness of life. This change is so complete that Jesus calls it being "*born again." It is not a make-over or a determination to try to be better. Christians universally experience a newness of life and become a *new man* in many observable ways. Christians talk about their "identity in Christ" as distinct from their old identity based on how they look or what they have done. The *new man* is defined by his relationship with Jesus.

New Testament: the part of the Bible written after Jesus' life, death, and resurrection. This is the second of two parts of the Bible. The first part, that Christians call the Old Testament, was about God's dealings with man before Jesus was born. The *New Testament* is about the good news (the *gospel) of Jesus. It is about His birth, what that meant, what He taught, the things He did, and the new possibilities He brought to the manner in which God deals with man. Several authors contributed to the *New Testament*, offering a broad view of the profound differences that Jesus brought not only to the Jewish religion, but to the world.

"Testament" means agreement (or *covenant). So there is the old agreement between God and man (the Old Testament) and the new agreement between God and man (the *New Testament*). God had perfect love and trust with Adam and Eve, the first created people.

Although God loved and was deeply related to them, Adam and Eve were deceived by the devil and came to believe that the relationship God established was somehow not enough, or was too restrictive, and Adam and Eve disobeyed the original guidelines that God had provided. Those guidelines were the very first agreement between God and man, and man broke the agreement. After that, a series of agreements were made by God (and broken by man) through the history of God's dealing with people. All are included in the Old Testament, along with predictions that a *New Testament* was coming (Jeremiah 31:31-34).

The *New Testament*, Christians believe, is the final agreement; it cannot be broken because it depends on God's strength, not man's. It can't be added to; it is lacking nothing, nor can anything be taken away from it. The *New Testament* brings men into joyful, holy and complete relationship with God, an eternal love relationship beyond the capacity of man to generate on his own.

There are big differences between the Old and *New Testaments*. In the Old Testament, relationship with God was established by obedience to God's requirements and by observation of certain rituals and traditions. In the *New Testament*, God relates to man on the basis of man's faith in Jesus, plus nothing else. In this agreement, Jesus Christ lives in the heart of the believer, which was not part of the Old Testament at all. "Christ in you" is often repeated in the *New Testament* because this indwelling presence of God changes everything. God sees Christians as forgiven. He does not remember any wrongs or hold them guilty any more. They are acceptable into heaven because all wrongs and guilt have been erased by Jesus and by faith in what He did. God loves the believer, and God's one command in the *New Testament* to the believers is to love one another (John 15:12).

In the *New Testament* God brings the *gospel, the good news through Jesus to the poor (every imaginable variety of poverty), and freedom to captives (every kind of captivity).

God gives sight to the blind (all forms of blindness), freedom to the oppressed (all of the down-trodden), and the general favor of God (Luke 4:16-21) in the *New Testament*. In the Old Testament, all of these blessings were only available to those who met certain conditions or had waited until the appointed time. The requirement for personal performance is eliminated in the *New Testament*, the good news is for all.

Occult: any religious system that is distinctly opposed to Jesus and/or prefers the devil. There are several religions or spiritual pathways that Christians would define as *occult*. *Occult* religions usually have ancient roots, often back to pre-Christian times, and often include worship of the devil, sometimes use curses and spells, and generally reject, ignore, or even directly oppose anything about Jesus. These days, some of the *occult* practices that one might encounter are Wicca, Voodoo, Odinism, Druids, and Satan worship. Babylonian religions, idol worship (worshiping statues or pictures), animistic religions (those that use feathers, charms, crystals, or worship rocks and trees), witchcraft and shamanism, all of these still exist, and have been around for thousands of years, and are defined by Christians as *occult*. Christians see the *occult* as the opposite of Christianity: as darkness rather than light, as devilish rather than godly.

Old man: the person before being changed by faith in Jesus. That old way of being is replaced by a new way of being, the new man, when one drops self reliance and begins to believe in Jesus and rely on God's all-sufficiency. See *natural man.

Old Testament: the first three quarters of the Bible, all written before the birth of Jesus. Read about *New Testament to understand why there is a New and an *Old Testament*. About 4000 years ago the record of God's dealings with man began to be written down and put together. These writings by different authors and in different times of history were collected and preserved until the time of Jesus. This is the *Old Testament*.

This book, or collection of books, became the primary religious book of the people called Jews or Hebrews, and they still use it today in their worship and in their study of how to please God and receive His favor. The Jewish version has the various parts in a different order than the Christian version. Jews call it the Torah, and if one goes to a Synagogue (a Jewish place of worship), and experiences that way of worshiping God, there is often a ceremonial copy of the Torah, usually a huge scroll, carried around the room, celebrated with songs and shouts and tears, people reaching out to touch it with a handkerchief (it is regarded as too holy to touch). And the Rabbi (the Teacher) will read and preach from the Torah, what Christians call the *Old Testament*.

It is the record of all of the history of God's dealings with mankind up to the time of Jesus. It contains writings by those who had a deep reverence for God and a longing to know Him more and follow Him better. Much of it is historical accounts of what God has done and what happened to God's people. The prophets who wrote in the *Old Testament* had messages from God that they were required to proclaim and to record. Testament means agreement, and the *Old Testament* contains, woven into the history and the prophecy, the various agreements that God made with man (all of which man failed to keep) up to the time of Christ.

Ordain: to give credentials that verify the education and experience of anyone who works in any capacity in the church, but especially for those who are Pastors (the senior leader of the church). Some Christian leaders in a church are called *ordained* ministers. It is a certification. This means that they are trained and experienced enough that their group of churches, or their *denomination, knows them well, and includes them as a part of their Christian movement. It means that they are part of a bigger team, not just working solo. It means that their representation of God is basically the same as others in that association of church leaders.

Ordained ministers are *ordained* to serve as a part of that association and all agree as to the key interpretations of the Bible and central ideas about who Jesus is, and so forth. Each group will have slightly different requirements for *ordination*.

In many churches, the celebration of *ordination* is also believed to be an occasion upon which a real impartation of power and authority is given from God to the one who is to work in the church in order to enable him or her to carry out the work. *Ordination* has its roots originally in Leviticus chapter 8, in the story of how Aaron, the brother of Moses, and his sons were *ordained* as priests. For them it was a seven-day process (verse 33) and it says literally that God "filled their hands" for those seven days. This work of being a representative for God requires that the worker have God-given tools, wisdom, and understanding to help others come to God and to be the representative of God to mankind. *Ordination* means that a group of associates have agreed that this worker has those tools and abilities and may be *ordained*.

Original sin: the original offense that man committed against God. Christians and non-Christians will use this term when they talk about the event that caused the first problems between God and man. So what was it? The full account is in Genesis chapters one through three (the first book of the Bible). A quick summary: God created Adam and Eve, the first humans, and gave them some guidelines of how to live in the Garden of Eden which He had planted for them. They were permitted by God to eat anything that grew in the garden except the fruit from one of the trees, the "tree of the knowledge of good and evil." A serpent, who was the devil, persuaded Eve that it would be good to eat the forbidden fruit, so she did, and she gave some to Adam and he ate it. That was the *original sin*, the first time that humans forgot the priority of loving God, and wanted something besides what God had provided, and that pattern has been happening ever since.

Original sin changed man from knowing only the holy and innocent ways of life in love with God, to knowing the ways of evil (lying, stealing, killing, envy, and ignoring God). It resulted in man being forced out of the Garden of Eden to make a difficult living cultivating food by the sweat of his brow. Everything in creation changed. As theologian Mike Webster says, "Even the dirt changed," so it brought forth useless weeds instead of food or fruit.

God's plan is to restore man to perfect relationship with Him again, because He loves mankind. Christians believe that Jesus has made a way for anyone who believes in Him to be restored to that perfect loving relationship. To understand that more fully, read about *salvation and about the *Cross. God finally will accomplish this goal as told in Revelation 21 and 22, the last chapters of the Bible. In that account, God sets up a new Kingdom in which He makes all things new; all is love, beauty, and splendor between God and man again, and man has eternal life. The negative effect of *original sin* is no more.

Orthodox: a branch of the Christian church that split off from the *Catholic Church in 1054 AD. The split was mostly because of disagreements over some of the finer points of "Christology," that is, the exact way in which God became a man in Jesus Christ, and His nature, as such. There was also disagreement with the Catholic structure of the Church which is under the leadership of the Pope. The *Orthodox* Church has no leader over the whole organization, but each church has its own leadership team, or "synod." They have remained a separate sect of Christianity, and form the majority of Christians in Greece, Turkey, and in Russia.

Overcomer: one who is not able to be pressured into doing wrong things and is able to live above the ways of the world. In a Christian view of the world, there are many things that must be *overcome*. There are spiritual forces of wickedness that must be resisted and *overcome*. The media and culture bring temptations that many give in to, Christian or not.

Sex, drugs, and alcohol are notorious for dragging many lives down, but their influence must be *overcome*. Besides that, there is discouragement, despair, disillusionment, disappointment and depression, all of which need to be *overcome*. *Overcoming* for the Christian is the ability to remain in love and agreement with God, in spite of all that negativity.

The Christian's tools for being *overcomers* are Bible truths, prayer, thanksgiving, praise, and worship. These things bring the influence of the very presence of God. *Overcomers* are empowered by their knowledge of God and have become people who know that they are able to rise above the powerful effects of everyday life. John writes in 1 John 5:4-5 that someone who "*overcomes* the world" does so by simply believing that Jesus is the Son of God. Jesus made certain promises to *overcomers* in Revelation, chapters 2 and 3. He says repeatedly, "To him who *overcomes* I will give..." and then He names spiritual rewards that He has for *overcomers*. According to those passages *overcomers* may even have to die in the process of *overcoming* (Revelation 2:10), but death to a Christian doesn't mean one has lost the battle. The battle is not about life and death; it is about keeping faith in God in the face of severe opposition. If one dies in faith, then one has *overcome* by entering into eternal life. Christian *overcomers* can walk through life as strangers in a strange land, immune to influences that might cause others to stray from their values, in fact, *overcomers* will influence others to rise above the ways of the world and the devil.

Pagan: people who do not believe in God as revealed in the Bible. Maybe they never heard about God or Jesus and the Holy Spirit. Maybe they heard but decided not to believe. In any case, they live their lives according to *pagan* practices including whatever religion it is that they have chosen. All non-Christian religions are considered *pagan* religions by Christians except for Judaism, the religion of the Jews.

Christians don't call Jews *pagans*, because they worship the God of the Bible. They differ in that they do not believe in Jesus as the son of God, the Messiah. *Pagans*, on the other hand, do not live at all in submission to the God of the Bible. They may be very much in submission to fear or superstition about other "gods" or spirits. They may in fact be very religious. But not being followers of Jesus defines them, to Christians, as *pagans*.

Parable: a story or word-picture Jesus used to teach those who really wanted to learn. Jesus taught using a lot of *parables* to teach about the kingdom of God on earth. The *parable* of the wheat and the tares (weeds) is one such *parable* (Matthew 13:24-30). It teaches how the good and bad grow up together and their fates are not decided until the end, the harvest.

Parables are not myths or fantasies. They may be fiction or non-fiction, but they are everyday-life stories and certainly could be true. People can relate to the principles of the *parables* if they have hearts open to the truth. Jesus said that He used the *parables*, oddly enough, to conceal the mysteries of the kingdom of God from the majority (Luke 8:10 and Mark 4:11-12). Those who are outside the Kingdom of God only heard the *parables* as undecipherable mysteries. Jesus taught that it was useless to "throw your pearls before swine." In other words, the pigs are not going to value the pearls, so Jesus presented His valuable spiritual truths to only those who had an interest in what He was bringing. To do this He used *parables*.

Passover: a Jewish holiday that remembers how the Jews were set free from slavery in Egypt. It falls usually around the time of the Christian holiday Easter. Christians are interested in this Jewish holiday because believers in Jesus see *Passover* as predicting Jesus. The holiday celebrates the liberation of the Jewish race of people from slavery, and Jesus liberated the entire human race from slavery to sin, for whoever will accept it. (The whole *Passover* story is in Exodus chapt. 1 through 12.)

Passover, the holiday, remembers an historical event 3500 years ago. God chose Moses at that time to lead the Jews out of slavery. As a part of the story, God sent 10 disasters, or plagues, to Egypt to convince the Pharaoh (the king) that the God of Moses really wanted Pharaoh to let the people go free. The last disaster was that, on a certain night in all of Egypt, the firstborn of man and animals would die. God told the Jews, through Moses, that if each family killed a lamb and put its blood on the doorpost of the house, the angel of destruction would <u>pass over</u> that house and the firstborn would not die there (Exodus 12:13). The Jews had enough faith in God to follow this instruction and were spared, but the Egyptians suffered the death of all of the first-born. After this, the Pharaoh relented and allowed the Jews to leave immediately. So it became a Jewish holiday, *Passover*, to remember how God delivered the Jews from slavery through the blood of the lamb, and allowed them to go to the land that God had promised to them, a good land, "flowing with milk and honey."

Christians say that the *Passover* lamb is symbolic of Jesus because they believe that Jesus' blood releases them from slavery to doing wrong (sin), because it forgives and cleanses their sin, protects them from God's judgment, and grants them access to the promised new life. (One of the names of Jesus is the "*Lamb of God.") Furthermore, most Bible scholars agree that Jesus actually died on the day of *Passover* and was crucified at the very hour that the Jewish priests began to kill the *Passover* lambs for the ceremony of *Passover*. There is also much symbolism in the traditional rituals of the *Passover* meal which point to Jesus, and Christians will sometimes celebrate *Passover* as a reminder of what Jesus has done for them.

Pastor: the leader of the church, the primary helper and teacher. In many churches there are several *pastors* leading various parts of the work, and usually one of them will be called the "senior *pastor*" or the "lead *pastor*."

Some churches include women as *pastors*, but most do not because the most common interpretations of the Bible prohibit having women as *pastors*. In today's American church, *pastor* is the term used most often meaning the leader of the church. Some churches use the terms *elder or *bishop instead of *pastor*, and having the same meaning as *pastor*, and many scholars use the three terms, elder, bishop or *pastor* interchangeably.

There is a list of five church leaders in Ephesians 4:11 which is generally recognized as the full combination of healthy church ministry. It is called the five-fold ministry, and includes; *apostles, *prophets, *evangelists, *pastors* and teachers. *Pastor* is included in this list and is generally understood to also include elder and bishop in its meaning. Many scholars combine *pastor* and teacher, saying that the *pastor* must also be a good teacher of the Bible. The contributions of the apostle, prophet, and evangelist are essential to a fully functional church as a world-changing influence.

Traditionally the *pastor's* duties are to preach on Sundays in the church and perhaps lead other times of gathering for Bible study or worship during the week. However, the much greater job for the *pastor* is caring for the people of his church. He is the "shepherd of the flock" in biblical terms (1 Peter 5:2-4). He is to find the lost, seek the young, care for the sick or wounded, and feed the hungry.

Pastors are usually wonderful, generous, loving people with whom everyone gets along, but if they make a mistake they can be the target of vicious attacks from those whom they have loved and served. Unfortunately, the job is loaded with potential for burn-out. *Pastors* often care too much, give too much, and finally run out of energy, sometimes never to recover. They usually need more help than they often get. They often do most of the work of the church: Sunday morning church services, funerals, weddings, replacing toilet paper in the bathroom, etc., too many expectations.

Pastors who succeed for the long term discover how to delegate much of the work to other willing hands (to *elders and *deacons and co-*pastors*). These *pastors* are able to intentionally set aside time and energy for themselves and their families.

Peace: the peace of God; an unshakable position of calm that keeps one above chaos and fear. Jesus is called the Prince of *Peace* in Isaiah 9:6. Ephesians 2:14 also says, "He [Jesus] himself is our *peace*." Jesus says that He gives *peace*, not as the world gives *peace* (John 14:27). In the natural world, *peace* is dependent upon circumstances. It is easy to feel *peace* when all is well. Jesus promises to give *peace* in every circumstance, even in distressing situations. Habbakuk 3:17-18 says that the followers of God know how to have *peace* and confidence in God even when "the fig tree should not blossom and there be no fruit on the vines...and the fields produce no food." In times of great distress, Habbakuk says "Yet I will exult in the Lord, I will rejoice in the God of my salvation." That is the *peace* of God. The famous Christian song, *It is Well with My Soul*, by H. G. Spafford declares peace in a similar way to Habbakuk, "Whatever my lot, Thou hast taught me to say, 'it is well, it is well with my soul.'"

Romans 14:17 says that the kingdom of God is righteousness, *peace*, and joy in the Holy Spirit. *Peace* is part of what is promised through faith in Christ. That is not a promise that life will no longer include situations which are disturbing, chaotic, or even dangerous and traumatic. It is a promise that the *peace* of God can attend a person in any situation. It is not a skill one learns through discipline and training, it is an impartation, a gift from God. Testimonies of Christians over the centuries demonstrate this truth. Christians executed by burning at the stake, in severe physical anguish, have been heard singing *peace*-filled praises to God until their death. A book titled *Fox's Book of Martyrs*, tells many of these stories of the *peace* from God that helps one rise above every circumstance.

Pentecostal: a branch of Christianity with more emphasis on the power of the Holy Spirit. *Pentecost* is a Jewish holiday, and on that day, ten days after Jesus went to heaven, the *Holy Spirit (the Spirit of God) visited a gathering of frightened, praying Christians and filled them with the miracle power of God to the extent that they all began to speak in languages that they had not spoken before (*tongues), and they were speaking of the mighty deeds of God (Acts 2:1-11). From that time forward, those Christians who had been frightened and hiding, went out boldly performing miracles of healing just as Jesus had done, and they were unafraid to tell everyone the good news (the *gospel) that Jesus was the Messiah and that there was forgiveness in His name and no other. The power of the Holy Spirit is what Jesus gave them to carry out His assignment (*great commission) to tell the whole world about Jesus.

Centuries later, that understanding about the power of the Holy Spirit had been largely forgotten, but in the early 1900's it began to be restored, including speaking in tongues. *Pentecostals* was the name given to the groups of Christians who began to believe that way and pursue God's miracle power. Pastors began teaching about the power of the Holy Spirit, and significant miracles and healings began to be much more commonplace among the *Pentecostals*. There was a more recent movement called the *Charismatic renewal which was very similar to the *Pentecostal* movement. Today something like one fourth of the world's Christians are *Pentecostal* or Charismatic. There are *Pentecostals* and Charismatics in virtually every area of Christianity and some entire denominations (divisions of the church) are *Pentecostal*.

Persecution: mistreatment or discrimination experienced on the basis of being a Christian. Many Christians in various places in the world routinely experience *persecution*. *Persecution* is the constant, hostile, harsh treatment given to people of a religion that is different from that of the attacker.

Jesus says it's a blessing to be *persecuted*. "When people insult you and *persecute* you and falsely say all kinds of evil against you because of Me. Rejoice and be glad for your reward in heaven is great" (Matthew 5:11-12).

Christians have been *persecuted* since the beginning. (Many peoples of many religions have been *persecuted*; it is not exclusively a Christian experience.) Jesus says, "If they *persecuted* Me, they will also *persecute* you" (John 15:20). And Jesus, when *persecuted*, did not take revenge or try to return insult for insult. 1 Peter 2:20-24 says Jesus was the example of how to respond to *persecution* and ill-treatment; He "kept entrusting himself to Him who judges righteously."

Pharisee: a small but influential religious group within Jewish culture at the time of Christ; ultra-strict about keeping the *Law of God. Pharisees believed that if everyone kept the Law of God given by Moses, then the Kingdom of God could be established over all nations (NLT Study Bible, notes on p.1581). This put them in stark contrast with Jesus whose goal was to establish God's kingdom by faith. Jesus did not oppose keeping the Law. He stated that "not the smallest letter or stroke shall pass from the Law until all is accomplished" (Mattew 5:18). But He opposed the *Pharisees'* position that strict keeping of the *Law was the only way to get right with God. The *Pharisees* opposed Jesus for what they held to be a disregard for God's requirements. He pointed out that the *Pharisees'* requirements were so burdensome that the *Pharisees* themselves could not keep them (Matthew 23:1-5). Jesus' main accusation against the *Pharisees* was that they made a show of being very pure, but inwardly they were corrupt. He called them *hypocrites.

Christians will use the label, *Pharisee*, for anyone today who puts unnecessary importance upon strict, unbending adherence to biblical guidelines and insists that those legal requirements should be followed by others. Jesus had a clear position against the *Pharisees'* view of Law-keeping.

Christians place the importance on *grace (the generous influence of God to make one pure) and *faith (believing that Jesus has provided a way to perfection apart from strict law-keeping). Christians get to eternal life, to heaven, to favor with God, by grace through faith, not by keeping a set of rules perfectly, not by being *Pharisees*.

Praise: the act of declaring God's goodness, singing or speaking about how wonderful He is, or any other expression of celebration around how good God is. Christians *praise* God. Pastor Bill Johnson says that *praise* sees the nature of God in every act He performs and responds accordingly. Praise searches out the ways of God's heart. It is a response to Him that is automatic because of His worthiness; there is no personality even close in comparison to God. *Praising* God places God in the most important place, above any other joy or sorrow that the believer is experiencing. *Praise* is an expression of how wonderful believers recognize Him to be. They tell it to Him and they declare it to all who are around. God is good and loving and those who know Him give Him *praise*.

Another reason Christians *praise* God is in order to intentionally put themselves spiritually in a different place. A Christian who is *praising* God, even when circumstances are going badly, lives in a much different place spiritually and emotionally than she would be without *praising*. That is, she is hopeful, joyful, and optimistic instead of woeful, depressed, and hopeless.

Merlyn Carothers wrote the classic book, *From Prison to Praise*. One of the main ideas of the book is that when Christians *praise* God, good things happen; things that wouldn't happen if they weren't *praising* God. *Praise* to God changes a person's expectations. *Praising* Him puts God's superior reality over every situation. Well-known pastor Kenneth Hagin says that *praising* God for what He has already accomplished, even before there is any physical evidence of it, brings the reality of God's intervention.

Praise agrees with how all of heaven is moving on behalf of the one *praising* God. So Christians *praise* intentionally, out of the fullness of their own hearts, a true expression of faith in God's goodness. *Praise* changes things. The Bible is full of *praise*, especially in the Psalms. Psalm 22:3 says that God is enthroned on the *praises* of His people; He is sitting right there when *praise* is given. "Hallelujah," which appears often in the Psalms means "*praise* the Lord." Psalm 148:13-14 says, "He has lifted up a horn for His people, *praise* for all His godly ones." It is His people who have the privilege of *praising* God, and in this verse, *praise* is called a horn, which is the symbol of strength and honor. The *praises* of God's people are honored by God and become strength for the people.

Prayer: communicating with God. *Prayer* is sometimes out loud, sometimes silently in thought, sometimes in an unknown language (see *tongues). Many Christians develop a habit of talking to God about everything. Talking to God includes listening to God; it is a conversation, and He can speak to the soul (one's mind, will, or emotions) and to the spirit of the *praying* one. This constant conversation between a person and God maintains a holy connection of input from God and submission to God's leading, resulting in a life that is strikingly different from a life led on the basis of only human wisdom, human strength, and finite personal resources. It grants the *praying* person the resources, encouragement, wisdom, and strength of all of heaven and of God Himself who is partnered, through *prayer,* with the one who *prays*.

Christians believe that *prayer* changes things. Jesus says, in one of His instructions about prayer, "Ask, and it will be given to you; seek, and you will find; knock, and it will be opened to you" (Matthew 7:7). He also used everyday stories to encourage His followers that "at all times they ought to *pray* and not to lose heart" (Luke 18:1-8). John Wesley, famous Christian from the 1700's, said, "God does nothing except in response to believing *prayer*."

Prayer is sometimes mistakenly seen as just a formality; only to be done by a professional, or something done before meals, or during church, or at bedtime. Sometimes *prayer* is seen as the last resort, a last-gasp effort when all else has failed. Many Christians, however, have learned that *prayer* is best as the first resort, the first response to every circumstance of life, the necessary ingredient to knowing how to live through everything, from the greatest success to the most terrible disaster. "*Pray* without ceasing," is the teaching of 1 Thessalonians 5:17. *Prayer*, for those who pray a lot, becomes a lifeline of strength and nourishment and encouragement. Pastor Linda Anderson, in her book, *Where Miracles Begin*, says, "*Prayer* is not a thing I do, it is a place I go." She doesn't mean a special room, although Jesus directs people to pray behind closed doors (Matt 6:5-6). She means an attitude, a spiritual position of submission, communion, and expectation before God. Helpful authors on *prayer*: E.M. Bounds, Beni Johnson, Bill Johnson, C. Peter Wagner, Dutch Sheets.

Preach: to speak publicly declaring and teaching Christian ideas and encouraging the listeners to live in harmony with God. Sometimes people talk about "the *preacher*" when they are talking about the Pastor or leader of the church. *Preaching* (speaking at Sunday morning church) is usually the most high-profile part of the Pastor's job.

Preaching is public speaking, promoting Christian views on topics of concern. The point of *preaching* is always to give something that the speaker believes is from God to the hearers. It may be dry and dusty truths that require a lot of mental effort from the audience to listen and learn, or it may be exciting declarations and encouragement which require a lot of work on the part of the *preacher* to deliver.

People come to listen to a *preacher* because they are hungry for the truth, or they come for the excitement and encouragement. Christians, having welcomed Jesus into their hearts, usually become the kind of people who are hungry to hear the truth, hungry to hear something helpful.

Preachers represent God. (Jesus was also a *preacher*.) Much of the work of God in the church is accomplished through good *preaching*. People will be inspired to greater faith, to carry on with courage, to pray, to take action, to seek the face of God for themselves, to speak what they have heard to others, to forgive, to bless, to love, to hope, and to expect good things from the hand of a loving God as declared by the *preacher*. *Preaching* is a strong part of what goes on in church, not the only thing of course, and not always the most important. There may be times when worship becomes the most important element of church gatherings, or times when it's all about prayer or just getting together. Along with all the rest, *preaching* can often be marvelously helpful and meaningful.

Predestination: the idea that one's ultimate end is destined before even being born. This is a biblical word from the New Testament. In its simplest terms it means that a person's destiny, that is, the ultimate destiny of whether a person becomes a Christian or remains an unbeliever, the ultimate destiny of heaven or hell, is pre-established, before birth. Some Christians believe that people are *predestined* in that way, and some reject the idea as inconsistent with the heart of God and the principles of *grace (God's generosity) and *free will (man's ability to choose). So there is a big debate over this concept in some Christian circles.

It exists as a concept because it appears as a word in two passages in the New Testament (Romans 8:29-30, and Ephesians 1:3-12). There is disagreement between Christian scholars about what this word really means and how to interpret these Bible references. What *predestination* means has been the question for hundreds of years as a general principle of Christian *theology (the study of God).

Predestination brings up several serious questions. It asks whether God gives every man the same opportunity to believe in Jesus and accept the truth about Jesus in order to receive eternal life and be saved from hell.

It asks whether a person becomes a believer because he or she makes a choice, or because God alone, through *predestination*, provides faith, the ability to believe in Jesus. It asks whether the grace of God which leads one to believe is a force that cannot be ignored or one that could be rejected. That leads to the question of *free will; has God given man the ability to make decisions that will affect his ultimate destiny, and can man resist God's leading, no matter how persuasive God might be? Another question is, just how lost is man? Is he so completely out of touch with God that he is incapable of even being involved in the choice to believe? *Predestination* asks whether Jesus really went to the cross for everyone or just for those who are *predestined* to believe.

Christians have widely differing answers to the above questions depending upon their views of *predestination*. And each one's answer is based on interpretations of Bible verses which others interpret differently. So it is a debate that will continue, and it will not be settled in this short paragraph. To some it is an important issue. To most Christians the concept of *predestination* doesn't affect their lifestyle as believers and doesn't affect their desire to tell others about Jesus. Most Christians are not thinking about it when they talk about Jesus. They don't wonder whether the person they are talking to is *predestined* or not, they just want everyone to know Jesus.

Pride: a tendency to want to promote oneself above others, and perhaps even above God. Christians avoid *pride*. The devil was *proud*. In Isaiah 14:13-15, in a passage that is usually understood to be about the devil, the devil bragged that he would raise his throne above the stars of God (that's *pride*), but in actuality, he will be thrust down to Sheol [the place of the dead]. Andrew Murray defines *pride* as the loss of humility. 1 Peter 5:5 says God is opposed to the *proud*. *Pride*, in this Christian understanding, is the mindset that says, "I am better than others; I don't need others' help; I don't need God's help, and my life is about me."

A *humble person says, "I am not the center of my life; I am equal with the poorest of the poor and ignorant; I can accept help from others, and I definitely need God's help." And God gives grace to the humble. Grace is the supernatural ability to be more like Jesus.

Pride is natural; it is part of the selfishness which Christians believe everyone is naturally born into. Christians believe they are dead to selfish *pride* and alive to the loving generous purposes of God. For that, they are learning to lay aside selfish *proud* desires through believing in and being devoted to Jesus, and they begin to live humbly as Jesus did, serving others no matter how deep the need. See *death to self.

Priest: one who is in the position of representing God to man. In all of human history there have been *priests* in all religions; people who are seen as representatives of God, those who help others find the way to God. In Christian churches, the principle is also true, however, most Christian groups do not call the leaders *priests*, but pastors, ministers, preachers, or reverends. The exceptions to that are Catholics, Episcopalians, and some Lutherans; these groups call their leaders *priests*.

One of the reasons that *priest* is not a common title among Christians is because, in the Bible, <u>all</u> Christians are called *priests* (1 Peter 2:9, "you are a royal *priesthood*"). What that means is that Christians, just like any *priest*, are to proclaim the excellencies of God to their fellow man. *Priests* go to God on behalf of their people (praying for them). And *priests* go to their people as God's representative (bringing the influence of God to them). A *priest* is God's representative on earth and man's representative in heaven, and the Bible makes it clear that all Christians are to represent Him in these ways (1 Peter 3:15-16, James 5:16-20). Christians are to be people who are available to establish or enrich people's relationships with God.

Jesus is referred to as the "great high *priest*" many times in Hebrews chapters 2 through 10.

He is the supreme example to all other *priests*, the believers. Jesus the high *priest* sends believers into all the world to continue to do what He began to do and teach.

Principality: a spiritual establishment of power designed to exercise the devil's influence over mankind. Christians sometimes talk about the *principality* that is over a certain city, or a certain place. This idea comes mostly from Ephesians 6:12 in the King James Version of the English Bible, which says that there is a battle between Christians and "*principalities*," which is translated "rulers" in the New American Standard Bible translation. It is a recognized principle in contemporary Christianity that there are *principalities*, that is, spiritual establishments of power that have been given influence in certain communities, or even entire countries, to stand against the knowledge of God. That rulership is placed there by the devil, but is also there by invitation or permission from key people who live there. It rules, in a spiritual way, to direct what is allowed among those people, either through the religion of the area or through a lifestyle. Also certain mountains, trees, or rocks can be a place of spiritual power, a place where a *principality* may dwell, may be accessed, or prayed to.

Christians believe that an evil *principality* in a place has influence to cause people in that place to behave in evil ways that they might not if they were not under the influence of that *principality*. Christians also believe that an evil *principality* can be replaced by the Holy Spirit and by angels; powers that influence people to behave in ways that are righteous and good. This replacement of a *principality* by the installation of the Spirit of God is accomplished, Christians believe, by their prayers, praise, worship, and invitation, by *witnessing (making Jesus a household name) and *evangelizing (helping people to become Christians), by loving and blessing everyone, and by spiritual *warfare destroying those establishments of power (2 Corinthians 10: 4-5).

Prodigal son: one who lives contrary to the Christian values he or she once knew. When Christians talk about someone being a *prodigal*, or *prodigal son*, they are talking about someone who has known the love of God, but has chosen to spend his or her life on wild living, being irresponsible, casting aside all morals and just living for pleasure. The idea of a *prodigal* comes from a story that Jesus told about such a person in Luke 15:11-32. The father of that young man in the story loved his son, and instead of turning against him for his lifestyle (leaving home and living wildly), he longed for his return. When the son came to his senses and came home, the father forgave him and restored him. It is a story that parallels God's way of forgiveness. So when Christians talk about someone who is a *prodigal*, included in the concept is the hope or assurance that this person will come to his or her senses, and return to the love of God. Christians know that God will forgive that *prodigal*, and they are planning to forgive the *prodigal* also. (Or it could be someone who has already returned and been forgiven, and he will be spoken of as having been a *prodigal* in the past.) Christians do not want to be like the *prodigal* son's brother, the good son who stayed home and was reliable, but who was unwilling to forgive his brother when he returned. Having generosity with forgiveness is part of what Christians take from the story.

Also, for Christians, this story that Jesus told teaches believers to expect that God is waiting for them with complete forgiveness, no matter what they have done. The principle is that God is eager to forgive, not eager to punish. God is eager to welcome people back into the kingdom, no matter how wayward they have been. Many of today's Christians were *prodigals* in the past.

Promised Land: the land that God promised to give to Abraham, His chosen representative, and it was inherited eventually by Abraham's descendants, the Jews. To Christians this can have several meanings.

The *promised land* may mean Israel, the country today, which is approximately the land that was promised to Abraham and his descendants, the Jews. Or it may mean heaven to Christians, which is a spiritual parallel to the physical land that God promised. It is the place God promises for those who have faith in Jesus. Christians may also use the term to talk about their own faith and hope that God is going to give them abundance in this life. When God began to talk about the *promised land*, He said it was, "a land flowing with milk and honey." That is quite a poetic picture of what most people hope for in life: plenty, and sweetness, and ease.

Originally, God spoke to Abraham about the *promised land* about 4000 years ago. (Full story is in Genesis chapter 12.) God told Abraham to leave his home and go to a new land. God promised to give that land to him, the *promised land*. Abraham went there and lived there, but never really possessed it. After he died, his descendants lived there also until a severe famine happened (no rain, no food). God provided them food in Egypt, so they all moved to Egypt. At that time, Abraham's family was about 75 persons, and they made their home in Egypt.

Abraham's descendants lived in Egypt for 400 years and became slaves to the Egyptians, but never forgot the *promised land*. God also did not forget the promise, and eventually God delivered them (that story is in Exodus) and led them, over a period of about forty years, and through many crises of faith, to the *promised land*. And once they got there they still had to fight for it to actually possess it.

One thing Christians learn from the story of the *promised land* is that, whether it's one's personal hopes, or a spiritual promise from God, the road there is not necessarily straight and simple. Pastor Kenneth Hagin points out that the *promised land* today includes all the rights and privileges in Christ for the believer, but it must be possessed, fought for, and for the Christian, that is done by faith.

Faith takes possession of what God has provided. God's promise is sure, but it is a process to get what is promised, often because the people receiving the promise have some things to learn along the way. The people involved are destined to learn and be transformed as they follow after the promises of God. All of this is in the story of the *promised land* in the Bible (in Genesis, Exodus, and Joshua).

Prophet: (also prophetic, prophesy, prophecy) A *prophet* is a person who can declare things by the inspiration of God. When God wants to speak clearly to His people, He uses a *prophet* to speak His message. A *prophet* is able to *prophesy*. *Prophesy* (prof-uh-sigh) is the action-word: meaning to declare by divine inspiration. *Prophecy* (prof-uh-see) is the ability given to the *prophet*, as in, "He has the gift of *prophecy*." Or *prophecy* can also be the statement itself, as in, "She gave me a word of *prophecy*." Sometimes *prophecy* is foretelling the future, but it can also be anything that God wants spoken to anyone. In 1 Corinthians 14:3, the definition of prophecy is: "one who prophesies speaks to men for edification and exhortation [earnest advice] and consolation."

Although the entire Bible is considered *prophetic*, certain books of the Bible are written predicting the future and stating why God was doing what He was doing. Those books are called books of *prophecy*. Some of the biblical *prophets* are Isaiah, Jeremiah, Ezekiel, and Daniel. In Biblical times, there were both male and female *prophets* and *prophetesses* (Deborah in Judges 4:4 and the four daughters of Philip in Acts 21:9). People who study the Bible talk about the Major *Prophets* (whose books in the Bible are long, like Isaiah and Ezekiel) and the Minor *Prophets* (short books, like Habakkuk and Zephaniah.)

Some Christians don't believe it is still possible to *prophesy* today. They interpret the Bible in a way that rules it out. Other Christians do believe in and practice *prophesying*, that is, they may have the gift of *prophecy* or be willing to receive *prophecy* from modern-day *prophets*.

A very good book on *prophecy* is *Translating God* by Shawn Bolz (pronounced "bolts"). Shawn, as a modern day prophet defines prophecy saying, "This is the goal of prophecy: to connect people to the empowering nature of God so they can become like Him and display His marvelous nature to all the earth." Shawn believes that prophecy is the means through which people can see themselves or others in the way God sees them, that is, restored to God's original intention when He created them, rather than as broken, damaged, flawed, or failing.

None of these *prophets*, among reliable mainstream Christianity, make any claim to be able to add to the Bible as God's *prophetic* word to mankind. The Bible stands complete, has been seen as complete by Christians for almost 2000 years. It is a *prophetic* book, inspired by God, or "God breathed," not to be added to (nothing is missing) nor is anything to be taken away (none of it is extra or unneeded).

Propitiation: regaining favor for someone else. An example with two people, Hank and Max: if Hank has deeply insulted Max, and a friend of Hank's goes to Max, and restores the friendship between Hank and Max, then that friend has made *propitiation*. The friend has satisfied, on Hank's behalf, whatever was required by Max for the friendship to be restored.

Propitiation is a word that gets used among Christians, but rarely elsewhere. Christians will say, "Jesus is our *propitiation*." (1 John 2:2, Hebrews 2:17). Theologian Mike Webster points out that *propitiation* means that Jesus satisfied all of God's requirements for people to get back into His favor in spite of the deep insult that mankind had given God. Restoration of that relationship would have been impossible without Jesus' *propitiation*. No amount of personal human effort could have satisfied God's requirements. Some definite measures had to be taken; some real problems had to be solved. *Propitiation* by someone else, (Jesus) was needed.

God had very solid reasons for ending the high-level trusting relationship that He had with Adam and Eve, the first-created people. (See *fallen.)

The things that God required in order to restore the relationship were, in short, (1) satisfying the demands of the law, (2) righteous obedience, (3) doing away with sin. Entire books have been written about all of these and how Jesus met those requirements on behalf of mankind. Briefly, let it be known that all the problems that needed to be solved, Jesus solved; all the measures that had to be taken to accomplish restoration of relationship, Jesus accomplished. And all that Jesus acquired for mankind is available to anyone who will believe in Him. Romans 8:3-4 says that Jesus "condemned sin in the flesh, so that the requirement of the Law might be fulfilled in us, who do not walk according to the flesh but according to the Spirit." Jesus is perfection for believers (Hebrews 10:14). God requires sin to be done away with and Jesus accomplished that for believers (Hebrews 1:3). There is no mark of sin on a believer in God's eyes (Ephesians 5:27 and Colossians 1:22).

Christians say that Jesus "identifies with us." Every hardship a Christian experiences is a hardship that Jesus has already carried for the believer who will welcome Jesus to come alongside. He lived a life of unimaginable difficulty and He did it with grace, beauty, and love. God the Father completely approved of His life. That life is then given to believers. Christians get to look like Jesus in the eyes of God, so all God's requirements are met by faith in Jesus.

Jesus did not convince God that mankind was going to be good now. Rather, He has <u>changed</u> believers one by one through faith into the image that God intended when He created them. That is how Jesus can be the *propitiation* for humanity.

Proselytize: to attempt to convince someone to change his religion (pronounced prah-sel-leh-tize). *Proselytizing* gets grouped in with criticizing and harassing.

Sometimes people will tell Christians, "don't *proselytize* me!" It means, "Don't try to talk me into becoming a Christian!" People who use the term *proselytize* like that, mean it as if it were a bad thing to do, an intrusion upon one's privacy. People who use the word *proselytize* are usually sick of Christians trying to get them to believe in Jesus.

Christians don't use the word usually. If Christians are trying to get people to believe in Jesus, they call it "*evangelism" or "*witnessing." It's just not a word they would use, partly because it is a word used in the Bible to describe a very different thing. *Proselytizing* actually refers to the efforts made by Jews to convince non-Jews (*Gentiles) to become Jewish. A *proselyte* is a Gentile who has agreed to become a Jew in religion and has submitted to all the required education and rituals and confessions necessary to become a Jew. Christians don't see that process as anything but an empty religious exercise because it doesn't lead to salvation (acceptance into God's presence). Agreeing to follow certain rituals does not win salvation for a person. True *salvation is forgiveness of sin, surrender to God, new life in Christ, and being filled with the Holy Spirit.

Evangelism or witnessing are the terms Christians would use to talk about bringing about all of the above. It is about a transformational connection between a repentant human being (someone really willing to change) and a loving God. *Proselytizing*, however, is the convincing of someone to engage in certain statements and rituals in order to be qualified for inclusion in the Jewish religion. So Christians don't *proselytize*, but they get accused of it when they witness or evangelize; trying to help people come to trust in Jesus.

Protestant: a Christian who is not *Catholic (one of the organized divisions of Christianity). There are two main divisions of Christians. Some Christians call themselves *Protestants*, some call themselves Catholics. There are definite differences between these two groups in what they believe and in their approach to God.

There are also wide and important points of agreement that keep them both within the definition of being Christian.

Historically, *Protestants* and Catholics divided hundreds of years ago over faith issues and became enemies. Before that, in early Christianity, there was really only the Catholic Church (catholic means universal), but much discontent began to arise with the way the Catholic Church represented God to man, and the things the Church required of people in order to qualify to approach God. The discontent was so serious that those who protested about the Catholic Church were willing to take a stand and die for the changes that they believed needed to take place. (Their protests earned them the label, *Protestants*.)

Among the earliest to take a public stance against the Catholic Church was John Haas (1319-1415 A.D), who had quite a following of believers at the time he was killed by Catholic authorities. Haas's influence did not stop when he was executed. Martin Luther called attention to some of the same ideas about a hundred years later. He and John Calvin were leaders in reforming the beliefs of Christians. These leaders and many others inspired a whole movement of believers, *Protestants*, away from the Catholic Church (now called the Roman Catholic Church) to a renewed form of faith.

This movement was historically called the *Protestant Reformation*. It resulted in a great split between Catholics and *Protestants* with actual battles and wars between the two sides. Over the centuries since then, the split has become much less serious in the view of most Catholics and *Protestants*. (There are still some on both sides who will deny that people on the other side are even Christians, but they are relatively few.)

Most *Protestants* and Catholics want to work at getting along. Consequently, the points of agreement are very important. Both *Protestants* and Catholics believe that Jesus is the Son of God, and one with God, and one with the Holy Spirit. (Not three Gods, but one God seen in those three ways. See *Trinity.)

Catholics and *Protestants* both believe that eternal life in heaven is only possible through faith in Jesus. Both groups believe that on the cross Jesus atoned for man's sin by the sacrifice of Himself, and that He was resurrected from death to live in heaven forever.

Quiet time: time spent daily in the disciplines of building faith. This is also known by Christians as "*devotions." Christians who are interested in keeping their faith strong and are interested in getting closer to God and studying the Bible, work to have a regular daily *quiet time* in which they do that. Many Christians read daily from a devotional book, or some other publication that has a paragraph or two that is inspiring, leading to some deeper thinking or prayer. Others may have a place, or several places, marked in their Bibles where they pick up and read each day, and maybe a journal to write down notes and prayers. Others find devotionals on-line, or listen to pod-casts, or Christian radio or TV.

The idea is that church attendance alone is not enough to keep a believer's faith strong. There is daily influence from secular radio, TV, and the world in general, every day all day, which can have a much greater impact than that of church attendance, just because it is so constant. Consequently, serious Christians make sure they spend some time each day in communication with God, making sure they hear from Him, reminding themselves of the truth, remembering the goodness of God, hearing again that God loves them, learning that God will protect, provide, encourage, and give wisdom. Well-known Pastor Bill Johnson says that people doing their *quiet time* simply need to read until they hear from God. One daily touch from God can overrule much of the influence from the world.

Rapture: a time in the future when all Christians will ascend into the air to meet Jesus. Strange as it sounds, "the *rapture*" of the Church is a biblical idea. (A description of the event is, in 1 Thessalonians 4:13-18.)

The common name for this event is "the *rapture* of the church." This idea of the sudden disappearance into the air by thousands of people obviously generates a fair amount of curiosity, excitement, and anticipation, but it is far from clear biblically, exactly <u>when</u> this will happen.

It is commonly believed by a American Christians that the *rapture* will happen before a time of extreme hardship that will come upon the whole world, known as "the *great tribulation," and all believers will escape the hardship. Christians in countries outside of the U.S. largely believe that the event written about in 1 Thessalonians will happen when Jesus returns to establish His Kingdom, which will be after the great tribulation, and Christians will have to go through the hardship. Christians in cultures and nations outside of the U.S. have a very different understanding about hardship (see the definition of *tribulation, and also *millennium).

All of this is much debated among Christians who study eschatology, that is, the study of what will happen on earth at the end of the world. It is by no means an exact science, this business of figuring out what is predicted to happen and when it is going to occur. Some books (notably the *Left Behind* series) and some groups of churches will present the *rapture* from a single view, as if there were only one way to understand what is written in the Bible about that, but there are many unknowns that make exact predictions about the *rapture*, the *second coming of Jesus, the *tribulation, or the*millennium quite impossible. Christians believe all of these things will happen, but no agreement exists on exactly how and when, simply because no single interpretation is clearly presented in the Bible. Many Christian teachers say that God keeps the future veiled for the good of the believers; that knowing too much would be harmful to the ultimate purpose that God has for believers in the earth.

<u>Reconcile</u>: to make up after a fight, to restore friendship. If friends argue and split up for a while, when they make up and decide to be friends again, that's *reconciliation*.

When Christians talk about being *reconciled,* they are talking about what happened between them and God when they came to believe in Jesus. *Reconciled* means they are friends again. (The well-known Christmas carol says "God and sinner *reconciled.*") There is a need for *reconciliation* between God and man. God loves all mankind, and always has, but mankind disobeyed and turned against God. That's where the break in friendship started (see *fall). There is a standing break between each individual and God. There is a need to be *reconciled,* and Jesus provided the way for *reconciliation* to take place.

Reconciled with God, to a Christian means a renewal of friendship with God. Friendship with God is a much more significant friendship than any other. Deeply meaningful friendship with God is possible through *reconciliation.* Christians say that they did not know how distant they were from God until they were *reconciled.* Then it became clear how lost and blind they really were. They have had the experience of regaining a friend Who was there all along, but they never were aware of His presence.

To fully understand how that was made possible by Jesus, read about the *Cross, *atonement, and *propitiation. Also read about *reconciliation* in 2 Corinthians 5:18-21 which says that "God was in Christ *reconciling* the world to Himself, not counting their trespasses against them, and He has committed to us the word of *reconciliation.*" Christians have carried that "word of *reconciliation*" around the world, inviting unbelievers to be *reconciled* to God.

Redeemed: bought back with a price. Christians believe that they have been *redeemed.* They use this word to describe one specific aspect of their relationship with God. Think about *redeemed* this way: if a man puts his guitar in a pawn shop, then later goes back for it, he has to pay a high price to get it back, and he says he has *redeemed* his guitar. *Redemption* requires that a high price be paid.

Redemption also means that the man really wanted that guitar back; to him it was worth the high price. So Christians use this word to understand that God paid a high price to *redeem* them. They were worth it to God. He very much wanted them back in His family. (The price that He paid was to give His Son, Jesus, according to John 3:16.) God bought the Christians out of the place where they were, locked up in guilt and shame because of wrong things they have done. They were of no good to anyone in that place. Jesus had to *redeem* them. There was nothing that the Christian could have done to get out of there. The Bible uses this word to describe how God delivered the believer from a very bad situation into a very good situation. Acts 26:18 says that Christians have been able to "turn from darkness to light and from the dominion of Satan to God." Jesus is humanity's ultimate and final *redeemer*; there is no further *redemption* necessary. It is a wonderful thing to be *redeemed*. Like the example of the guitar, people are created for something truly beautiful, but before *redemption* they were locked in a dark place, not able to function to glorify God. Jesus' *redemption* restores people to their original created purpose; to know Him, love Him, love others, and to bring heaven's reality to earth, inviting the miracle interventions of God.

Another way Christians use this word is to describe how God so often brings good out of bad situations. For example, God *redeems* a situation in which someone gets mugged, by having the victim then visit the mugger in jail and forgive him and help the mugger to come to believe in Jesus, which changes his life, so he never steals again. So God had a *redemptive* effect on the bad event, and used it to change the mugger's life. That's the *redemptive* effect God often has on bad situations. God doesn't make the mugger so desperate or immoral that he would steal. God doesn't put the believer in his path as a victim. Bad things happen to good people, but God always has *redemptive* work that He does to miraculously bring good out of bad.

Reformation: a historical era during which Christian thinking was greatly changed (reformed). This was a time in Christian history (roughly 1300 to 1500 AD) when the Christian Church rediscovered its original foundations. Originally, the earliest Christians became Christians by believing that Jesus was the Savior, the Son of God. There were no other requirements: no money to be paid, no rituals to perform, no certain prayers to be said in a certain way to certain people, and no required church membership. There were only two rituals that Jesus gave to Christians: *baptism and *communion and even those were not originally seen as requirements for becoming Christians. Later that changed.

Over the first thousand years of Christianity, that simplicity was gradually lost and it began to be taught by the Catholic Church that certain rules, and requirements, and church membership, and baptism, and giving of money, etc., were necessary requirements to become a Christian and to be acceptable to God. A small group of people began to protest against these religious requirements and call for a return to faith alone as the basis for becoming a Christian. (These people became known as *Protestants or *reformers*.) That small group became a movement as thousands of people returned to the origins of Christianity. It also included a renewed interest in theology (the study of God and His interactions with mankind), and much was written during this time in history which became known as the Protestant *Reformation*.

Four names are particularly important in the *Reformation* although many more people were contributors in the movement. John Wycliffe is called by some the "morning star of the *Reformation*." He first translated the Bible into English, against the wishes of the Church which only allowed the Bible to be written in Latin, a language that very few people besides the priests could read or understand. Another well-known man, John Huss, was burned at the stake for preaching in agreement with John Wycliffe's teachings against the authority of the Pope.

About a hundred years later, Martin Luther became perhaps the most famous for his boldness in protesting that a person is a Christian and saved from hell by faith, not by the Church (not Church membership, not Church rituals, not giving money to the Church, not by the authority of the Church leaders).

John Calvin is also well-known because he was a writer and intellect, writing out *reformed* thinking on Christianity (theology). Calvin's books are still read and studied today, particularly by those were interested in what is called *reformed* theology. *Reformed* theology has become one of many schools of thought about understanding God, and some of its central beliefs are not widely accepted but continue to be debated in Christianity.

Religion: a man-made belief-system to get in touch with God. When Christians talk about *"religion,"* the word will have a different meaning than in general usage. Christians have a motto: "Christianity is not a *religion*, it is a relationship" (a relationship with God). Christianity is a belief-system that originated with God; it was not something that man came up with. Christianity reveals that man may accept God's invitation to relationship through Jesus Christ.

Religion operates on the assumption that God is distant and unwilling to be involved with man and something must be done to earn His attention. But Christianity sees man as the one who is lost, in the dark, distant from God, and God is the One who is near, is light and loves mankind. *Religions* are man-made belief-systems that usually attempt to get man to the place of <u>deserving</u> God's attention through doing religious feats of strength (severe treatment of the body, poverty, fasting, solitude, or abstinence).

One of the reasons that Christians separate their belief-system from being a *religion* is because the centerpiece of any *religion* is that it has a set of rules and requirements. The only requirement of Christianity is a faith relationship with Jesus.

There is nothing one has to accomplish, nothing one can accomplish to earn that relationship with God. It is a family relationship; a believer becomes a member of God's family, adopted into the family as a child of God.

Another reason that the word *religion* is avoided by Christians is that during times that Christianity operated as a *religion* (Christians have always been at risk of falling into *religious* efforts to impress God), many wicked things were done, things that were entirely *religious* (man-made) rather than God's will. *Religious* Christians have killed Jews, Muslims and others. *Religions* in general do that sort of thing. Muslims, out of *religious* duty, have killed Hindus and Christians; Hindus in turn have killed Muslims and Christians, and these days, Shiites kill Sunnis and vice-versa, and the list goes on. Christians don't want to be associated with that kind of *religion*. Ideally, Christians want to love God and love people. They want to love people even if those people don't agree with them, even if those people hate them, even if those people are trying to kill them. When Christians lose sight of love, they become Christian in name only. They become *religious* Christians, focused on *religious* duty, *religious* views, *religious* standards, self-preservation and pride, instead of a relationship of faith, unquestionably trusting Jesus. It is that relationship of love that is the substance of Christianity.

Remission: pardoned, completely forgiven. Christians say that Jesus died for the *remission* of sins (forgiveness of everything done wrong). *Remission* means that God pardoned those sins; God completely forgave them. Many religions seek *remission* of sin. The Hindus in India wash in the Ganges River to wash away sin, or they perform long difficult painful pilgrimages in hopes of getting their sins forgiven. Muslims believe that when they die, sin is weighed by God against the good that they have done. They hope that the good outweighs the bad, but there is no offer of *remission* in that belief-system.

Some religions offer sacrifices to the gods in hopes of *remission*, but there is no promise of it, no assurance of *remission* because the gods are fickle and unpredictable. Judaism, the religion of the Jews, promises *remission* of sin in the Old Testament (the part of the Bible that was written before Jesus) but it was based on obedience (Isaiah 1:18-20) and sacrifice. Christianity stands alone in the way Jesus offers *remission* of sin by faith in Him. See *cross for a full explanation of how that *remission* has been accomplished.

Remnant: a small portion left to work with. To Christians, the *remnant* means the few believers who are left after most have been lost to unbelief or removed by the Lord. Isaiah 10:20-23 foretells a time when God would remove all those who were not generous to the poor, were unjust, and worshipped idols. Isaiah predicted that they would be defeated by enemy nations and carried away as slaves. Isaiah goes on to say that when the time of captivity was over, a "*remnant* will return...to the mighty God." The *remnant* was the group of people whom God used at that time in history to start over.

Or, the *remnant* may also be those who, after all the rest have fallen away from the faith, God gathers together to lead them into new life (Micah 2:12). Either way, the *remnant* is that small select group of true believers whom God then uses to rebuild the community of faith-filled people.

One of the themes of the book of Isaiah is that, although God was going to bring disastrous judgment on His people for being unfaithful, there would be a *remnant* that would return. Isaiah even named one of his sons Shear-jashub, which means, "a *remnant* shall return." Romans 11:5 says that there is "at the present time a *remnant* according to God's choice of grace." Those who chose to follow Jesus were the *remnant*. Jesus was never wildly popular, but persecuted and rejected in the end. There were a fairly small number of people who followed Jesus. God has always kept a *remnant* of people who were close to Him and could represent the Kingdom of God.

Repent: to change one's thinking, to have a change of heart; recognizing wrong, turning away from that, and turning towards God. This is an important Christian word because *repentance* is necessary in coming into the new life that Jesus promises. Both John the Baptist and Jesus began their work of preaching saying, "*Repent, for the kingdom of heaven is at hand*" (Matthew 3:1-2, Matthew 4:17). What they were saying was, "Change your way of thinking, change your heart; turn from wrong to right." In the words of Jesus, it could be understood to mean "recognize that the way you have been living is not what God wants, and choose to live in the way God does want...for the kingdom of heaven is at hand" (the kingdom of heaven is approaching). In 2 Timothy 2:24-25 Paul writes that God may grant *repentance* to people if Timothy will just be gentle with them, which indicates that *repenting* is partly a gift from God. Graham Cooke, Pastor and teacher, says that *repentance* makes the statement; "I am no longer that person, because I have newness of life."

Repentance is a turn-around; a person is going south, for example, but turns around 180° and begins going north. King David in the Bible writes about two of these occasions in his own life in Psalm 32 and Psalm 51. Such a change requires a change of mind, a *repentance*, a decision to take a different direction in life, God's way, not the selfish hurtful way anymore. *Repentance* is not a promise never to do wrong again, but it is a resolve that says, "I don't ever want to do that again." If a Christian makes a mistake and does the wrong thing again, it does not mean that the *repentance* did not work. That *repentant* person can still count on God's help in overcoming temptation. Sometimes coming to *repentance* is the final end of the behavior. Sometimes the struggle continues for a while, however, *repentance* does not permit one to do wrong presuming God will forgive. That is not *repentance*. Bible verses about that are in Romans 3:8 and 6:1-2.

In Christian thinking, one is led to the point of *repentance* by God's kindness (Romans 2:4).

In other words, God's kindness comes first, then comes faith, that realizes, "Oh, God really is good; God is real; God is helping; God loves me; the Bible must be true; Jesus died for my sins." Pastor Graham Cooke teaches that only a repentance that is motivated by positive influence (love and encouragement) will last. If it is motivated by negativity (judgment and condemnation) it won't last long; it is forced. Stopping the wrong behavior that once was a lifestyle is the *repentance* part. It is like waving the white flag in surrender, "I'm not fighting you anymore God; I surrender." Changing the way one lives is not easy, but *repentance* makes it possible. God grants forgiveness to the genuinely *repentant* one; He is the One enabling real and lasting change. God enables purity through *repentance* (Acts 5:31, Acts 11:18). Purity is not achieved by trying harder for the Christian. Purity is accessed only through *repentance*.

Resurrection: coming back to life after being dead. The most important *resurrection* is Jesus' *resurrection*. He was left for dead in a tomb but came back to life. If Jesus had not raised from the dead, He would be just another famous dead person. Jesus predicted in John 14:20, "[When I am raised to life again,] you will know that I am in my Father, and you are in me, and I am in you." Jesus being raised from the dead revealed a whole new picture for believers about who Jesus is and how they would be in union with Him for eternity.

To the Christian, Jesus' *resurrection* says many things. Most importantly, it imparts to the believer a life that makes death irrelevant. Jesus has conquered death, it is no longer to be feared (Hebrews 2:14-15). Also, Christ died for man's sins and was *resurrected* because He had restored all who believe to a right relationship with God. He *justified them, just as if they had never sinned (Romans 4:25). Furthermore, Christians see themselves as having died to the old way of life and living a *resurrected* life now in the power of Jesus' *resurrection* (Romans 6:1-11, Galatians 2:20).

Well-known pastor Jack Hayford from Van Nuys, CA, talks a lot about living the *"resurrection* life" that Jesus gives to believers. Christian life is not a make-over or a touch-up; it is a death and a *resurrection*. *Resurrection* life allows one to view everything in life from the spiritual reality of heaven.

So the concept of *resurrection* is central to Christian thinking because anything good that is experienced after giving one's life to Jesus is credited to the new, *resurrection* life, and everything bad in the past is considered part of the old life that has died, no longer having the power to create an ugly present or a frightening future.

Jesus Himself taught the skeptics about resurrection (Mark 12:24-27). Looking ahead, the Bible talks about the future *resurrections* of all the dead of all the earth for all time. Revelation 20:4-5 says that the first *resurrection* will be a *resurrection* of people who have been killed for believing in Jesus (*martyrs) and it will occur just before the *millennium, that is, the 1000 year reign of Christ. Christ will reign for a thousand years and Satan will be bound in the Abyss for that time. Sometime after that, there will be the second *resurrection* when everyone else will be *resurrected* to face the judgment of God. If their names are not found in the book of life at that time, they will be thrown into the lake of fire with the devil; this is called the *second death (Revelation 20:13-14). Revelation 3:5 says that those who are overcomers will not have their names erased from the book of life. The Prophets Isaiah and Daniel were among the first to receive understanding of the *resurrection*: Isaiah promises *resurrection* (Isaiah 26:19), and Daniel writes about the dead rising, some to "disgrace and everlasting contempt," and others to "everlasting life" (Daniel 12:2).

Revelation (the book): the last book in the Bible. This final book of the Bible, and probably the last one written, is the exclamation point at the end of the whole Bible. It deserves special mention in *Christianese* because it contains important prophecies, and is understood in so many different ways.

According to Pastors Wesley and Stacy Campbell, *Revelation* is "the supernatural unveiling of the splendor of the Son of God to His Bride to awaken her heart in love; the great gift of God to the Church through the ages; the displaying of His Son." They present this view in a CD called *The Bride's Anthem* at revivalnow.com. Some Bible scholars see *Revelation* as a great book of encouragement to the believers to let them know that there is victory in the end, and all the suffering of this life serves a greater purpose, the victory of the Kingdom of God. Others see it as the prediction of many yet-future events. Still others avoid it altogether because they find it confusing and frightening.

It is important to know that *Revelation* probably was not written as a prediction of a set of events that are going to happen in the order in which they are written (several scholars agree on this, including Christian statesman and Pastor, Jack Hayford). It is definitely an account of things God has done, some that He is doing now, and some that He is going to do in the future. There is disagreement on what has already happened and what is still to come. It is an account of the spiritual realms in which spiritual battles take place that have consequences for all people on the earth, past, present and future. It is also a display of the splendor of the Son of God Jesus and the incredible relationship between Him and His bride (the church). It is an explanation of how God is going to use believers to ultimately do away with the devil, his demons, and his followers, and it is the clearest picture of the end of the age in the Bible. It explains the establishing of the Kingdom of God, the fate of mankind, and of heaven and hell. There is a popular bumper-sticker that says, "I've read the end of the Book, and God wins!" That's about the Bible, and about the end of the Book, the *Revelation*.

<u>Revelation (the experience)</u>: having a hidden thing revealed, or coming to understand something that was not understood. Christians talk about "getting a *revelation*." What they usually are implying is that God communicated to them.

Perhaps it was while reading the Bible, or He visited them in a time of prayer, or intruded into their daily thoughts, and suddenly there was a clarified understanding of something about God's nature that was previously unknown to them. With *revelation*, confusion is gone, and there is usually the ability to explain the *revelation* to others.

For example, Peter in Acts 9 had an experience of God dropping in on him with a vision that gave him this *revelation*: "I should not call any man unholy or unclean." Prior to that, Peter thought Gentiles (non-Jews) were unholy and unclean, and he wouldn't even associate with them. He was confused about why God would call him to go talk to Gentiles, but once he got that *revelation* and understood God's mind about it, he was able to go and spend time with Gentiles and feel good about it. *Revelation* can be given in a vision like Peter's; it can jump off the words in a page of the Bible; it can be couched in the words of a friend, in an experience, a movie, a dream, or a *prophecy (communication from God). God can give *revelation* in any way He wants, and His timing is always perfect. Corey Russell, in his book, *The Glory Within*, says, "one of the Holy Spirit's main job descriptions is to search out the deep things of God (His mysteries) and make them known to the redeemed [to believers]." Christians pray for *revelation* and are excited to receive it. *Revelation*, that is, getting the mind of God, is always a life-changing experience because God-thoughts are so different from man-thoughts. And the Christian who wants to be "transformed by the renewing of [his or her] mind" welcomes God's renewing thoughts (Romans 12:2, Isaiah 55:9).

Revival: a time of intense, sweeping, individual and community-wide awareness of the reality of God and the influence of His presence upon people. Christians talk about *revival*: times past, present, or future, during which the invisible person of God is made crystal clear to everyone. God becomes as real during *revival* as the sunlight, apparent to everyone and more important than anything else.

There have been many of these times of *revival* during the history of the Church. Probably the most famous are the Welsh *revivals* in 1904-5 in Wales and the Azusa Street Revival in Los Angeles about the same time, but before that there was the "Great Awakening" in Europe and the American Colonies before the Revolutionary War. There was also a second, third, and fourth "Great Awakening" in the U.S., and more recently the Toronto *Revival*, in Canada.

Revival is a time when virtually everyone in a community recognizes, is drawn to, and excited about God, about the word of God, and preaching, and worship, about being holy, and about getting saved (making sure they are heaven-bound and right with God). During these *revival* times, many who don't know God suddenly are impressed with the need to give their lives to God, and/or many who are sick or have disabilities are healed, and/or many who have been lukewarm about God suddenly become passionate about their faith. During these times, churches fill up and bars, jails, and casinos empty out. During these times there is an easy acknowledgment of the awfulness of sin, and a happy receiving of God's forgiveness. Godliness is easy during *revival*, and worldliness is shunned, not even tempting any more.

Many *revivals* throughout history have been short-lived; a few months, or a few years, but there are *revivals* going on today that have gone on for many years, for example in South Korea, and Redding California. George Otis Jr. has done a lot of research into *revival* and has produced videos about communities that have been completely transformed by *revival*. His videos are called "Transformations" and are available from the Sentinel Group. George Otis has some theories about what needs to be done in order to begin and sustain a *revival* so that God can change a whole community. *Revivals* are most often the result of people praying fervently for the influence of God on the community, as in the classic book by Leonard Ravenhill, *Why Revival Tarries*.

Righteous: a standard of good behavior set by God. Even though *righteousness* is important, observing this standard of behavior does not make a person a Christian. Being *righteous* is not required before becoming a Christian. It is *faith (believing in Jesus) that makes the person a Christian, and the behavior only changes genuinely from unrighteous to *righteous* as a result of a new life of relationship to God, submitting to God and depending upon God. Internal purity from loving God results in external *righteousness*.

The Christian ideal (the example of *righteousness*) is to <u>think</u> in the right way, <u>behave</u> in the right way, and even <u>feel</u> right about it. For example, the Christian thinks, "I should help that homeless guy," (that would be the *righteous* thing to do), so the Christian buys him a hamburger and a Coke. But then, if the Christian resents having to spend the money, or is disgusted by the homeless person, that Christian will not consider himself truly *righteous* because he didn't <u>feel</u> good about it. Because of this inability to keep a pure heart about it, it soon becomes clear that these ideal Christian standards are humanly impossible. For another example, Jesus says, "love your enemy." Humans can imagine <u>pretending</u> to be nice to an enemy (and grumbling about it silently inside) but to truly love an enemy is beyond the *natural man's ability. CBN News has a video about a policeman, Officer Perez, who said "God bless you brother" to a desperate criminal who had just shot him twice, and it changed everything. That is a testimony of supernatural *righteousness*.

So here's the Christian secret. *Righteousness* is not something that is achieved by hard work. It is reached by relationship with God based on faith (trust and dependence upon God) and grace (as a gift from God). Paul writes in Philippians 3:9 that he, Paul, wants to be a person "not having a *righteousness* of my own derived from the Law [by keeping the rules] but that which is through faith in Christ, the *righteousness* which comes from God on the basis of faith."

So the Christian receives a deposit of *righteousness* straight from God as part of the new life that Jesus promises. By this deposit from God the Christian <u>really can</u> love his or her enemy, and feel good about it. This can happen immediately, as it did for Officer Perez (above), although sometimes there is a lengthy period of time in which the believer strives for *righteousness* and fails. That waiting time is not wasted; it is the deep process of coming to the end of self sufficiency. True goodness happens only when the believer realizes that he can only be *righteous* when he is dead to self effort (stops trying so hard) and becomes alive with faith that Jesus lives within him (Galatians 2:20). True *righteousness* is supernatural.

<u>Rock</u>: stone as a symbol of Jesus and of God's faithfulness to His people. There are many prominent *rocks* in the narrative of the Bible that point to Jesus and to God's faithfulness. For example, Moses encountered a *rock* in the desert which became a gushing spring when he struck it, and it supplied life-saving water for all the people whom Moses was leading (Exodus 17:2-6). Compare to Jesus, who said that people who drink from Him will get eternal life (John 4:14). Psalm 61:2 says "Lead me to the *rock* that is higher than I," which Christians automatically think of as Jesus, the *Rock* that is higher than I. Daniel and King Nebuchadnezzar saw a *rock* in the King's dream that smashed all other governments into dust and it grew to rule over the whole earth (Daniel 2:34-35 and 44-45). Daniel declared this rock to be the Kingdom of God (and Jesus is the King in the Kingdom of God). Psalm 118:22 (written long before Jesus) speaks of a *stone* that the builders rejected, but it became the most important *stone* in the building. Several writers after Jesus wrote that Jesus was that *rock*, rejected by national leaders, but becoming the foundation of life-changing faith in God (Ephesians 2:20).

Jesus re-named Simon, His disciple, and called him Peter ("Petros," *rock* in Greek), and He said, "you are Peter, and upon this *rock* I will build My church."

There has been much discussion about what that meant. Jesus the *Rock* was willing to call Simon a *rock* and to call him to a foundational role in the establishment of the church. The story of the early church as it unfolds in the book of Acts presents Peter as the undisputed leader, and his faith is looked up to even today.

Another *rock*, more difficult to understand, is written about in Romans 9:33. In that verse it says that God has placed Jesus as a *rock* to be either tripped over, or to be trusted in. Those who tripped over Him took offense at His teaching and His life. Those who trusted in Him, it says, will never be disgraced (put to shame). The idea was first prophesied (predicted) in Isaiah 8:14 and it shows up several times in other Bible passages written after Jesus, saying Jesus is that *Rock*. There is a very real danger of tripping on some of the radical things about Jesus. One of the things about Jesus is that He refuses to line up with people's expectations. Even John the Baptist came close to taking offense at Jesus because Jesus looked different than John had thought He would (Luke 7:18-23). People who want Jesus to only fit the picture of the Good Shepherd with the lamb over His shoulders get tripped up when He calls the Pharisees a brood of vipers (Matthew 12:34). People who want Him to condemn sinners get offended when He lets sinners off easy (John 8:3-11). Most believers have had the experience of being shocked or offended by something they read about Jesus, but trusting Jesus is the way to never be disgraced or put to shame (Romans 9:33). The *Rock* of Jesus will not stumble the one who trusts in Him.

Rocks are immovable and unchanging, steady, safe to build upon, strong, and sometimes *rocks* can be stumbled over, all ideas that clearly point to Jesus, "the *rock* of salvation."

Sabbath: a day to worship and rest. Christians who talk about, "keeping the *Sabbath*," are usually talking about attending church on Sunday, and not working on that day.

However, to be accurate, the *Sabbath* is not on Sunday, it is on Saturday. The *Sabbath* is a holy day that the Jewish religion has kept as a special day of the week for thousands of years, and it is on Saturday. In the Hebrew language, *Sabbath* (or "*shabat*") meant a required day of rest, worship, and dedication to God. It is one of the *Ten Commandments (God's first basic guidelines to His people) that worshippers must observe the *Sabbath*. It is a day when no work is to be done and there are certain rituals to be observed in prayer and worship to God. *Sabbath* in Jewish culture is from Friday evening at sundown until Saturday evening at sundown.

God commanded a day of rest and worship. It is a privilege for Christians and Jews to have a day of devotion to God instead of unceasing self-efforts. It is not meant to be an obligation or a requirement in order to gain God's favor. Christians see the day of rest as a God-blessed time no matter how it is actually done or which day of the week it is. The gathering together of the believers once a week is understood to be an important part of worship among Christians worldwide. Like-minded people get together to agree for God's blessing and declare His goodness.

Somehow, in the early days of Christianity, the traditional day of worship changed from Saturday to Sunday. Most early Christians were Jews, used to worshiping on Saturday, so there are two theories about why the Christian worship day moved to Sunday. One is that the Jews and Christians couldn't get along worshiping in the same place on the same day, so they chose to worship on different days but used the same building that the Jews had for worship, the Synagogue. The other theory is that Christians chose to worship on Sundays because that's the day Jesus rose from the grave.

There is one Christian group of churches (*denomination) that insists that Saturday is the day of worship and so they have their church on Saturday.

In other countries, the day of worship for Christians varies according to cultural norms, for example, in Nepal, Christians have Church on Saturday simply because that is the national day-off, and everyone goes back to work on Sunday (they work six days, not five, like Americans). Romans 14:5-8 (written in the early years of the church when this issue was probably still unsettled) says that some believers may think of one particular day as more holy, but other believers may consider every day alike, however the most important consideration is that, "not one of us lives for himself....we live for the Lord." Exactly which day is the day of worship is apparently not that important. Every day is to be a day of acknowledging God and living for God.

Saint: a person set apart to God, or "sanctified." In the Bible, all believers are called *saints*. The word *saint* just comes from another word "sanctified" which means consecrated, holy or guiltless, clean, and forgiven. All Christians, according to the Bible, are sanctified (1 Corinthians 6:11). In the eyes of God they <u>are</u> holy, and in life on earth, they are <u>being made</u> holy. Christians see themselves as made holy by faith in Jesus; they quit their unholy habits and begin to live by the strength which God supplies; and begin to clean up their lives or become sanctified. Christians don't believe they are perfect, but that they are in the process of continually getting better. Therefore they're called *saints,* not because they are perfect but because they are being made perfect by faith in Jesus.

The *Catholic view is that only certain believers who have done exceptional things and have been remarkably holy can be called *saints*. They are declared *saints* by the church if they meet certain qualifications. There is disagreement between Catholics and other Christians about this issue. However, even Catholics believe that believers are in the process of being sanctified.

Salt: a good thing in the earth, as a flavor and as a preservative, and believers are the "*salt* of the earth."

Salt in Bible times was used to give flavor, <u>and</u> to preserve food, keep things from spoiling. Jesus declares that Christians in the world have an influence that helps the lives of everyone be better, and keeps the world from going rotten. He encourages Christians to stay *salty*, not lose their flavor, lest they become useless (Matthew 5:13).

<u>Salvation</u>: the condition of life given by God to Christians, that begins with faith and results in eternal life with God in heaven. *Salvation* is a condition of life like being healthy is a condition of life, but *salvation* has to do with the spiritual areas of life rather than with the body. *Salvation* is the spiritual condition of having changed from unhealthy to healthy in the concerns of right and wrong, guilty and innocent, peace and torment. Christians say that *salvation* is that condition which Jesus makes possible by believing in Him, and it is the condition of having received the love and forgiveness of God, being adopted into the family of God, and being destined to eternal life in heaven with Jesus. People who have *salvation* can tell you when they "got saved," and exactly how it came to them. (Also see *saved, below, because *salvation*, to a Christian, is the condition of being saved.) *Salvation* is a large-scale change of direction which is begun by accepting that Jesus really is who the Bible says He is. (He is the Son of God. He is Savior because He died on the cross for all the sins of mankind. He did it because of His love, and is resurrected from death to live eternally praying for His people.)

Salvation is a change of direction from what has been normal to a "new normal." A person who does not have *salvation* is going along in his or her normal, natural direction, is not forgiven by God, is still guilty for every wrong done and doesn't care. This person considers it of no importance to be forgiven, considers God to be of no importance, perhaps believes God doesn't exist, perhaps believes that there is no wrong or right anyway, has no interest in eternal life, has no concern about hell, perhaps believes it doesn't exist, and sure doesn't have an idea of eternity in the *lake of fire (hell).

In *salvation*, there <u>will</u> be changes in life; changes in what is seen as fun, what is seen as important, how one spends time, how one spends money, who one wants to be with, and how one sees the future. So *salvation* is <u>not</u> just the thing to do to escape from hell, it is a life-transforming encounter with God that begins an eternity of friendship, partnership, and love between the saved one and the living God. In *salvation*, the Spirit of God takes up residence in the deep inner being of the believer; God moves in to stay.

Salvation is also a long-term process for the Christian. The Bible says the Christian is to be participating in the ongoing work of that salvation: "Work out your *salvation* with fear and trembling" (Philippians 2:12). It is God's ongoing work also; "for it is God who is at work in you both to will and to work for His good pleasure" (Philippians 2:13). Just like being a good athlete or a good student, it's going to take application and dedication to the task to maintain and improve the condition of *salvation*.

Sanctified:
set apart for the purposes of God, having been made holy, or made into a "*saint." (See holy) All Christians who have been well-taught, or who know the Bible, know that they have been *sanctified*, and that all Christians are "saints." That is the <u>position</u> of *sanctification*. 1 Corinthians 1:30 says, "by His [God's] doing you are in Christ Jesus who became to us wisdom from God, and righteousness, and *sanctification*, and redemption." This <u>position</u> of *sanctification* allows the believer to expect he or she is now destined for heaven without regard to performance on earth.

Beyond the <u>position</u> of *sanctification*, there is a <u>process</u> of *sanctification* (an inward purification) that takes place in the saint as a result of the Holy Spirit living in the believer and influencing the believer to move ever closer to being like Jesus. Christians differ some on this idea of the process of *sanctification*, the main question being whether one can be completely *sanctified* in this life. The majority of Christians do not believe that it is possible to achieve this on earth.

Christians see *sanctification* both as a declaration of God that makes them eligible for heaven (the position), <u>and</u> they see *sanctification* as ongoing in their lives; bringing a continual increase in actual holy behavior (the process). Romans 6:19 says, "present your members as slaves to righteousness, resulting in *sanctification*." Hebrews 12:14 says, "pursue peace with all men and the *sanctification* without which no one will see the Lord." *Sanctification* does include an actual impartation from God to be transformed, to be made better, more Christ-like. But also Christians apply themselves to becoming better people, more surrendered to Jesus in loving, forgiving and blessing others.

Satan: a spiritual being, a fallen angel, who stands in opposition to God and to man's relationship with God. (See devil.) *Satan* is the devil's name, like "Bob" or "Jane." That name means "adversary" or "opponent," so it's pretty clear what he is all about. His appearance as an adversary of God and man happens very early in the narrative of the Bible. In Genesis 3 he shows up as the serpent to trick Eve (the first-created woman) into disobeying God, and in the book of Job (possibly the earliest portion of the Bible that was written) he tries to crush Job's faith (and does not succeed).

Satan is portrayed as evil personified, as the source of wickedness in opposition to man and God. In keeping with that, usually any media presentation of *Satan* is quite frightening. However, *Satan* is not feared by Christians who know and believe that Jesus has given them authority over <u>all</u> the power of the enemy (Luke 10:19). *Satan* is powerful, but Christians also know the Bible says, "greater is He [Jesus] who is in you than he [*Satan*] who is in the world," (1 John 4:4).

Satan is also called, "the accuser of our brethren" (Revelation 12:10), "the father of lies" (John 8:44), the "prince of the power of the air" (Ephesians 2:2), and the "ruler of this world" (John 12:31). Satan is also called "Lucifer" in the King James Bible which means "shining one," or "star of the morning" (Isaiah 14:12).

He is a created being, created by God, beautiful and powerful, but his pride caused him to oppose God, and he was cast out of heaven (Isaiah 14:12-15). Jesus recalls this event in Luke 10:18, and in Revelation 12:3-4 is a scene of the devil sweeping a third of the stars from heaven to earth. Most interpret that to be the time at which Satan was removed from heaven, and he took a third of the angels with him who are now demons, serving *Satan's* purposes.

Christians believe that *Satan* was defeated by Jesus. In John 12:31 Jesus says, "now the ruler of this world [*Satan*] will be cast out." Colossians 2:15 says that Jesus, "disarmed the rulers and authorities" [the devil and his demons] and that Jesus, "made a public display of them having triumphed over them." Hebrews 2:14 says that Jesus was able to "render powerless him who had the power of death, that is the devil." 1 John 3:8 says, "The Son of God appeared for this purpose, to destroy the works of the devil." Christians do believe that there is an ongoing war between God's people and *Satan* (see *spiritual warfare) but it will not be an eternal on-going war; it will end, and the outcome of that war is not in question. *Satan* is like a serpent whose head is crushed, it is defeated, dead, but it can still writhe around, bite, and be dangerous to people. Christians exercise caution, but know that the final outcome has already been determined.

Saved: destined to go to heaven upon death, and enjoying loving God during the life that remains on earth. "Are you *saved*?" Christians will ask. What they are asking is, "Do you have a relationship with Jesus that started with believing in Him enough to entrust your life to Him?" *Saved* is a position of faith, the condition of being rescued. Being *saved* is being a Christian. People say they are *saved* in many ways: "I believe in Jesus." "I met Jesus." "I gave my life to Jesus." "I trust in Jesus." "Jesus has forgiven me." "Jesus is the Son of God." These are all shorthand for all that is included in being *saved*. Very often getting *saved* is a profoundly moving experience of being touched by God in some way.

However, a remarkable experience is not the necessary ingredient of getting *saved*. Many are left wondering if it "worked." But then their lives begin to change and the excitement begins to grow, and the condition of salvation begins to become more obvious.

Christians believe that *saved* people are *saved* (rescued) from going to hell when they die, and are given entrance to heaven and full welcome into the presence of God. *Saved* people are adopted into the family of God, are loved by God, have been forgiven of all wrong, have been given the ability to choose the right thing instead of living in slavery to doing wrong consistently. *Saved* people grow continuously in their excitement about their new life, and their relationship with God. Not all church attendees are *saved*. Attending church does not earn salvation. Not all people who say they are Christians are *saved*. And it is not the job of other Christians to determine who is *saved* and who is not; that is entirely God's determination. Christians who question people's salvation can do great harm. *Saved* people have encountered Jesus by faith and have surrendered to Him. God alone knows if that has really happened.

One who is *saved* has an awareness of wrong and right that wasn't there before. *Saved* people, Christians, often radically change their behavior. They sometimes begin to be able to love people in a way they found impossible before. *Saved* people are usually drawn to read, enjoy, and be fascinated with the Bible. *Saved* people, having experienced the presence of God, usually begin to be drawn to church, and often find that the Jesus Whom they have encountered deeply in private is very present when they go to church. *Saved* people have an ongoing conversation with God, a desire to worship God, know Him, be with Him, and be in love with Him.

Savior: one who has saved others from danger. Christians speak lovingly about "Jesus my *Savior*." A lifeguard who rescues someone is the *savior* of the challenged swimmer.

Jesus is the Christians' *savior*, having saved them from three things: *sin (wrong-doing, its record, its guilt, and its nature), and *death (not physical death, but spiritual death and fear of death), and *hell (the destination of all mankind apart from Jesus).

Jesus saved people from sin by forgiving them. Forgiven sin is nullified; there is no more guilt and no longer any record of it, and there is no longer the natural inclination to sin. It is no longer a reason for separation from God. Jesus has saved believers from what would have been an inevitable and eternal separation from the love of God because God cannot be in the presence of sin.

Jesus saves people from death by giving them *eternal life, so that the experience of physical death is a transition to a new and better realm, and not the dark, frightening specter that it can be without Jesus. Christians will experience a physical death, but their faith leads their *souls (the eternal part of life) into the presence of Jesus. 2 Corinthians 5:6-8 makes it clear that, for the Christian, to be absent from the body (having died) is to be present with the Lord Jesus in the spirit.

Jesus saves people from hell, which is the eternal place after death for those who refuse the *Savior*. Hell is no longer an ultimate destiny for those who have come to believe in Jesus. The *Savior* Jesus made it possible for people to experience the love of God and go to heaven when they die, even without having lived a perfect life. (Christians believe that Heaven is a place of tranquil eternal beauty and peace in the presence of God: no more tears, no more darkness, and no more shame.)

In Christianese, the *Savior* is also the One who came from God to save each person from living a messed-up life. A "messed-up life" is a life that is self-absorbed. Selfishness, in the extreme, results in having nothing to give, no legacy of generosity, and an empty existence that meant nothing to anyone.

Life is messed-up when one is unhappy while striving for happiness, lonely while desperate for love, confused while trying to understand it all. A messed-up life usually includes hurting others in the process of trying not to hurt so badly. Jesus, the *Savior*, gives the believer a new heart, a heart generous and full of love.

Christians have accepted Jesus as *Savior*. Of course, when a person accepts Jesus, that person is agreeing that his or her life needs a *Savior*. Each person must come to believe that he or she is not good enough, not perfect enough without Jesus' forgiveness to go to heaven and live in the presence of God for eternity. People who become Christians have believed that without a *Savior*, they would have been destined to live excluded from the love of God forever.

Scepter: a symbolic ornamental staff that a king would hold, an emblem of the king's authority. When the king holds out the *scepter*, whatever he declares becomes law, and it is carried out without question. This word, *scepter* is used in the Bible. God, the king of heaven, has a *scepter*. It is the scepter of uprightness (Psalm 45:6). Psalm 125:3 says that the *scepter* of wickedness will not rest upon the land of the righteous. In other words, there will not be any spiritual authority that rules wickedly over those who trust in the Lord. Jesus has a *scepter* that was predicted (*prophesied) way back 1800 years before He was born. That *scepter* is the symbol of His rulership (Genesis 49:10). Revelation 19:16 says that Jesus is the "King of Kings and Lord of Lords." So of course He has a *scepter* and the authority which it signifies.

Scripture: all that is written in the Bible. Christians use this term meaning the Bible. "According to *scripture*," means according to the Bible. Christians speak of *scripture* with the same reverence that they have when they speak of the Bible. And anything that can be found in the Bible is said to be *scriptural*. Anything that is put forward as truth, but is not, will be said by Christians to be <u>un</u>*scriptural*.

It is un*scriptural*, for example, that "God helps those who help themselves." Although that is a common saying, the Bible does not actually say that. It actually says that God helps those who admit that they cannot help themselves (Matthew 5:1-12). *Scriptural* also is used to mean accurate, because the Bible is viewed as completely accurate. (See also *inerrancy.)

Second coming: when Jesus comes back to earth the second time. To a Christian, this term always refers to that time when Jesus comes to earth again, which He promised He would do. Matthew 24:36 through 24:46 is the passage that most unquestionably applies to the second coming. In that section, He told five stories to give an idea of what is to be happening among His believers until His *second coming* and how it is going to happen. He said to His followers, "Be ready," because no one will know when He is coming back. Also in Revelation 22:12-20, Jesus gives one final reminder that He is coming back. John, the apostle writes, "The Spirit and the bride say, 'Come.' And let the one who hears say, 'Come.'" And in verse 20, the second to last verse in the Bible, he writes, "He [Jesus] who testifies to these things says, 'Yes, I am coming quickly.' Amen. Come, Lord Jesus." These passages plant seeds of expectation in the heart of every believer.

His first coming to earth of course was when He was born as a baby in Bethlehem, the story that Christians celebrate on the Christmas holiday. At that time, He lived, grew up, talked about the good news of how to be forgiven and restored to relationship with God. He began to establish the Kingdom of God, which is the place, spiritually, of God's dominion. He healed all manner of sickness, raised people from the dead, and set people free from evil spirits that were ruling their lives, and forgave sin. All this He did because in His Kingdom none of those things exist.

He was condemned as a criminal by those who envied Him, killed by being nailed to a cross, buried in a tomb. Three days later He was raised from the dead and appeared to many of His followers over a period of 40 days.

During that 40 days, He commissioned His disciples to go all over the world and tell everyone the good news (the *gospel), including the story of His death and resurrection. He promised that the Spirit of God would come to empower them for their work of telling the world about Him. Then, in Acts 1:10-11, when Jesus ascended into the sky, the angels which were present told His followers, "This Jesus who has been taken up from you into heaven, will come in just the same way as you have watched Him go into heaven." It is understood by Christians that Jesus will come in the sky again at the end of the age to bring closure to this era and fully establish His kingdom (1 Thessalonians 4:16). In Acts 2:32-36, Peter says that Jesus is sitting at the right hand of God until His enemies are made into a footstool for His feet. So Jesus is sitting on His throne in heaven watching His Kingdom increase as those who oppose Him fall one by one. Then He will come back.

So the *second coming* is very important in Christian thinking. It is much-anticipated, often-predicted despite Jesus' warning that no one knows when it will be, (Matthew 24:36-37). It is very much hoped-for because it means, for the Christian, an end to all wickedness, pain, and the heart-wrenching struggle that is so typical of human life and death.

Jesus' *second coming* is when the Christian expects to be united with Jesus in loving unity. There will be no more torment from the spiritual enemy, Satan. There will be no more death, no more temptation to do evil. Jesus will be there brilliantly in peace and the joy of His kingdom.

Christians expect that Jesus' *second coming* could happen at any time, but they are willing to wait because God is patient, "not wishing for any to perish but for all to come to repentance" (2 Peter 3:3-13). Peter also asks this question: "what sort of people ought you to be in holy conduct and godliness, looking for and hastening the coming of the day of God?" How Christians make the presence of God apparent to the world can hasten the timing of the *second coming*.

Second death: the final death of those who do not believe in Jesus. According to the Bible, some people will die twice. The reason that they will have to die twice is that <u>everyone</u> who has died will be resurrected, or brought back to physical life on the final day of judgment (see*Day of the Lord). When resurrected, all will face the judgment of God (God will give a verdict as judge). The books will be opened in heaven and everyone whose name is not found written in the book of life, will be thrown into the lake of fire, another name for hell. That is called the *second death*. And others (on the basis of faith in Jesus) will be found not guilty and will go to heaven. Those who go to heaven do not experience a *second death*. For the details of this idea, read Revelation Chapter 20, and 21:1-8. Also read about *resurrection.

Self: the lower nature of man, that which insists on "me first." Christians earnestly try not to be *self*-ish or full of themselves. They try to be generous and to consider others' needs as more important than their own (Philippians 2:3-8). Christians see *self*-ishness as the basis of all wrongdoing. The *self* is seen as out to get attention, or out to get rich or famous. The *self* is seen as driven by the desires of a spoiled child: doesn't want to share, wants the biggest piece of cake, wants it now, and whines when it doesn't get its way.

Christians refer to this *self* as the "old man" or the "*natural man," and they believe that when they become followers of Jesus, that the natural man died: those old desires no longer are the driving force of life. They call this "*death to self." They want to die to *self* and live to God. The old *self* is a major obstacle to doing or being anything in agreement with God, until that natural man dies, because the old *self*, the *natural man, the *flesh, always opposes the Spirit of God (Galatians 5:17, Romans 8:5-8).

Jesus is seen as totally un*selfish*. He gave Himself away: His time, His energy, and ultimately His life, He gave to others. However He took time alone to hear from God.

He didn't usually share those times with others. Those times were essential to taking care of Him*self*. Jesus' *self* was not polluted with the desires of a spoiled child. He just wanted to be in agreement with God. His need was to know what God wanted Him to do and to receive the strength to do it. Believers live in a newness of life which is the new *self*, patterned after Jesus' *self*, free from sin and full of the Holy Spirit. This is the Christian's ultimate goal: to be doing what God has directed with the strength that God supplies. Healthy *self* care (like Jesus did, alone-time with God) is important to this, which means that Christians must constantly remind themselves who they really are now in the eyes of God and in the new creation of God.

Seminary: a university that trains Christian leaders. A *seminary* is a college that one would go to in order to learn how to be a church leader, whether a Pastor or administrator or theologian (one who studies about God). Seminaries offer college degrees on all levels and all aspects of the knowledge of God and working in the Church. Seminaries differ widely in the approach that they take in teaching about God and His ways, depending on the *denomination (group of churches) they serve, or the key leaders who founded the seminary. Seminaries differ from Bible Colleges; in that many Bible Colleges are not accredited (do not offer an actual college degree).

Shechinah glory: the mysterious visible manifestation of God. This word is not a Biblical word, but Christians will use it because it is used in the Hebrew language to describe the visible presence of God. His presence was usually seen as a smoke and/or light, in Biblical times, and usually appearing at the tabernacle or in the temple, sometimes in the most holy recesses of the place of worship and sometimes out in the open for all to see. (See *glory) Here are a few passages that are about this appearance: Exodus 40:34-38, Numbers 9:15-17, 1 Kings 8:10-11, 2 Chronicles 7:1-3.

In Matthew 17:5 is a story in which the *shechinah glory* appeared around Jesus, and God spoke from the cloud, "This is my beloved Son, with whom I am well-pleased; listen to Him!"

Sheol: the term used (before the time of Jesus) for the place of the dead, the grave. (See *Hades) For thousands of years before Jesus was born it was believed that, when people died, the grave was a spiritual place called *sheol*. It wasn't thought of as either heaven or hell. It was just the place of the dead. There were no material human bodies there, and it was not thought to be a place of either punishment or reward.

When Jesus began to teach about the destiny of the dead, He taught about places of punishment and reward; heaven and hell. In the story of the rich man and the poor man Lazarus who both died (Luke 16:19-31), Jesus describes a place in *sheol* which He calls Abraham's Bosom, a place of reward and comfort. And He speaks of a place of punishment in *sheol*, which was described as very hot and waterless.

Sheol was not viewed as a very nice place. There was no joy, no worship or praise of God (Psalm 115:17). There were no memories, rewards, love, hate or zeal (Ecclesiastes 9: 3-6). However, it is clear that since the time of Jesus, for the believer, to be absent from the body (dead) is to be in the presence of the Lord (2 Corinthians 5:6-8). Luke 23:39-43 tells the story of a man who was crucified alongside Christ, and Jesus told him as soon as he died he would be with Jesus in "Paradise" (heaven). So at the moment of Jesus' sacrifice of Himself, *sheol* was no longer the destiny of believers. The faithful could go straight to heaven.

Sin: doing wrong in the eyes of God, which breaks relationship with God. Christians view things as *sin* if they are defined by God as wrong. *Sin* is something that would never enter into the heart of God; He does not do *sinful* things. God is holy, therefore not even able to be in the presence of *sin*. Man is *sinful* (because of the *fall, when man ignored God).

Mankind must have the *sin* removed to be able to relate to God or be in His presence. Jesus saved people from *sin*; He made a way for people to be *sin*-free and restored to relationship with God. Yet Christians sometimes still *sin*, so it is an important topic in the Bible and in Christian conversation. Many Bible portions are devoted to understanding how to walk in holiness. Much preaching is about how to carry on in relationship with God even though *sin* still happens. Understanding how to live in the newness of life and in a way that is alive to God becomes the focus rather than trying to resist sin.

Well-known Christian leader Bill Bright taught that *sin* is the bad news, and the good news is that God loves people and has a wonderful plan for every person's life. The bad news of *sin* is that one will not be able to enter into God's wonderful plan with unforgiven *sin*. When a person is guilty of *sin*, he or she cannot enter the presence of God to get that wonderful plan He has.

The good news (the *gospel) is that Jesus provides a way for that *sin* to be completely cancelled. That is how God's plan for anyone must begin. Pastor Bill Johnson says that Jesus has freed the believer from the guilt of *sin*, the record of *sin* and even the nature from which *sin* comes. The critical part of the good news is that one must believe it; one must have faith and trust in Jesus in order to receive that gift of forgiveness and all that goes with it; new life, righteousness, and heaven.

Romans 3:23 in the Bible says that, "all have *sinned* and fall short of the glory of God." *Sin* is falling short of perfect. Our culture tends to think of *sin* as something really bad, like murder, rape, or maybe lying and stealing, but the Bible includes everything that is outside of God's perfection as *sin*. So that includes pride, envy, wicked thoughts, bad words, and things done in secret that people are ashamed to tell others.

One of the words for *sin* is also translated, "miss the mark," because, if people aim at perfection and miss that target in thought or even the way they feel about it, that is *sin*.

Romans 14:23 says that, "whatever is not from faith is *sin*." (That passage is about feeling bad about what one eats.) Another word for *sin* is rebellion. Rebellion, disobedience, and unbelief (refusal to believe) are all *sin*. No one, no human being except for Jesus, ever lived without *sin*. Jesus' perfect freedom from *sin* was one of the things that qualified Him to forgive all *sin*. He is qualified to make believers holy (acceptable in God's presence) just as He is holy. And His life is available to believers now by faith. Believers do not have to *sin*. Believers do not have to live guilty of *sin*. Pastor/teacher Graham Cooke emphasizes that believers are no longer sinners, they are saints. Mistakes, relapses, sin, may happen because of the old sin habit, but the new life focus is living to God, not spending a lot of energy trying to make the old nature shape up.

Sin nature: man's normal way of living in wrongdoing. Christians believe that man is by nature a wrong-doer. Prior to knowing Jesus, man will always include wrongness (sin) in whatever he does. Man inherited this *sin nature* from Adam and Eve the first created people because they chose to do the wrong thing and rebel against God. Ever since then, mankind has universally followed that pattern (see *fallen). The Bible says that man is "sold into bondage to sin" (Romans 7:14). That means man <u>must</u> sin; it is impossible to <u>not</u> sin. However the good news of Jesus is that, by faith in Him, one can break from that bondage to sin and be free to choose to do right. Romans 6:14 says, "sin shall not be master over you, for you are not under law but under grace." Freedom from the *sin nature* is through faith in Jesus. Before Jesus, the *Law required obedience, but since Jesus, the *grace of God (His enabling presence) provides forgiveness to all who want to break free from the *sin nature*.

Sinai: the mountain upon which God spoke to Moses and gave him the Ten *Commandments and the *Law (Exodus 19 and 20.) "Mount *Sinai*" can be either symbolic or historical.

Historically, Mount *Sinai* was God's first public and personal encounter with the whole race of people, the Jews. It was also the first place that God called all of His people together to hear from God, which they found so distressing that they told Moses, "let not God speak to us lest we die." God established right then the *fear of God (Exodus 20:20) and very clear laws (commandments) to direct people into right behaviors. That happened at Mount *Sinai*, but no one knows for sure today which mountain it really is.

Symbolically, when Christians speak about a Mount *Sinai* experience, they may be talking about their own personal experience of being called up to meet God, or of being frightened by His glorious presence, or about how very difficult it is to learn the lessons that God wants to teach His people. The people of God, the Jews, although they received clear direction from God at Mount *Sinai*, always struggled with living out the instructions for life that God had given them there.

Soul: the eternal part of a human being, and that which really defines an individual. Christians think of a human life as having three components: body, *soul*, and spirit, interwoven and inseparable. Many portions of the Bible talk about these three. First Thessalonians 5:23 says, "may your spirit and *soul* and body be preserved complete without blame the coming of our Lord Jesus Christ." Most Christian scholars define the *soul* is the combination of a person's mind, will, and emotion. So, with that definition, the *soul* is the collection of what a person is thinking, doing (or wanting to do), and how he or she is feeling about it. The *soul* is a person's consciousness, what he or she is, and as philosophers would say, "the awareness of being."

Well-known author Andrew Murray defines the soul as "the meeting-place, the point of union between body and spirit." The body relates to the world around a person and the soul relates to the spiritual world, its life and its power.

The soul of a believer goes to heaven fully aware, able to think, and fully feeling everything, a complete being, just like on earth. The natural or perishable body of the believer is replaced with what the Bible calls a spiritual body or an imperishable body (1 Corinthians 15:42-44), often referred to as the glorified body. And the spirit of a person, which was dead before knowing Jesus, has come alive at the time of coming to faith, and is able to have relationship with God.

The body can be killed easily, but the *soul* departs elsewhere when one dies. Matthew 10:28 says, "Do not fear those who kill the body, but are unable to kill the soul; but rather fear Him who is able to destroy both soul and body in hell." Christians believe that the *soul* is eternal. In heaven the believer experiences life eternally, body *soul* and spirit. The *soul* in hell is understood to be undergoing eternal destruction, eternal fire, and eternal punishment (Matthew 25:46, 2 Thessalonians 1:9).

There are many accounts of people who have been to heaven and then come back to tell about it. (One of the most authentic and detailed is *"Scenes Beyond the Grave"* by Marietta Davis, and also *"Return from Tomorrow"* by George Ritchie.)

These are stories about people who experienced heaven in every aspect except for having a body. They went there in *soul* and spirit without the body. The *soul* and spirit are separate from the body but tightly linked to it as long as the body lives. And the *soul* is a distinction, separate from the spirit, by definition, but so intertwined as to make it difficult to define a division between the two. God can and does define a difference between the *soul* and the spirit, and is able to speak to either one by the living and active word of God, the Bible (Hebrews 4:12).

Spirit: three definitions: (1) the essence (all of the important qualities) of a human life as distinct from the body, (2) an essence without a body, a being that does not have a body but is only a *spirit*, (3) the Holy *Spirit* of God, the essence of God, *Spirit* with a capital "S."

(1) Human beings are seen by Christians as having a body, a soul, and *spirit* (1Thessalonians 5:23). When the body dies, the soul and *spirit* go to heaven with Jesus and the believer gets an imperishable body, that is, one that will not get sick and die (1 Corinthians 15:42-44). The *spirit* of a person is understood to have come from God originally with the creation of the individual. God gave His breath (*Spirit*) to Adam and he was created (Genesis 2:7). But that human *spirit* became unaware of the things of God because Adam was *fallen (he fell out of touch with God). When a person becomes a Christian, the Holy *Spirit* is welcomed back in to be the life of the human *spirit*. When that happens, the *spirit* of the person and the *Spirit* of God become the very source of everything new that is promised in the new life with Christ. People are *spiritual* beings who have a soul and live in a body. The *spirit* lives in and gives life to the physical body. The human *spirit* is given from God with purpose and individuality, and that human *spirit* is made alive by being *born again, meaning that a complete new beginning is given by the Holy *Spirit*. The *spirit* is invisible, but it is a real thing; it is as real as the body.

(2) Some beings created by God are *spirits* rather than embodied beings at all. Angels and demons are purely *spirit* beings (the purposes *angels and *demons are very different). A *spirit* is invisible most of the time, though sometimes may be made visible for the sake of the humans with whom they are communicating. A *spirit* is a being: it exists; it communicates, has purpose, does things, and is powerful at least in the spiritual realm. Jesus says that "God is *Spirit*" (not an embodied being). Jesus was an embodied being for 33 years as a human, that is, He had a body, soul, and *spirit*. It was His *Spirit* that made Him who He was, a man stunningly different from any other man, a miracle man, a loving man, a forgiver. Jesus had the *Spirit* of God, that which made Him unique as a human being, a man whose *Spirit* was completely submitted to the purposes of God.

(3) Christians also have the *Spirit* of God in their *spirits* (in their hearts), which makes them unique human beings. Romans 8:9 says, speaking to Christians, "you are not in the flesh but in the *Spirit*, if indeed the *Spirit* of God dwells in you. But if anyone does not have the *Spirit* of Christ, he does not belong to Him." Also notice that the believer has the *Spirit* of Christ and the *Spirit* of God dwelling within. That puts the believer in spiritual harmony with God. The *Spirit* makes all the difference. The believer has had a transformation within his or her *spirit*, because the *Spirit* has moved in and everything changed. He or she becomes a new person with a new life, and with the potential to be impressively Christ-like, depending on how yielded he or she is to the *Spirit*.

Notice that the "*Spirit* of God" is used interchangeably with the "*Spirit* of Christ [Jesus]". That is one of the ways it is seen that Jesus is indeed God the Son, and one with God. The *Spirit* of Jesus is mentioned specifically several times in the Bible (Luke 23:46, Acts 16:7, Philippians 1:19, 1 Peter 1:11).

Spiritual: having to do with the realm of the spirit rather than the body, and not limited by a body. In Christian thinking, there are two realms: the material realm, that is the visible realm of human bodies, houses, chairs, etc, and there is the *spiritual* realm; a mostly invisible realm of angels, demons, God, heaven, and the spirits of humans. Both the material and the spiritual realms are equally real. The *spiritual* realm has a definite influence on the material realm, often an unexplainable influence that usually gets put in the category of spooky, weird, or miraculous.

When Christians see someone who constantly sees things with eyes that include *spiritual* reality and the kingdom of God, they often say that person is a particularly *spiritual* person. Christian teacher Graham Cooke says that *spiritual* people "perceive, think, and speak from a radiant knowledge of who God is," and they are able to "spiritually appraise" everything, or evaluate it, coming from the viewpoint of God.

Truly *spiritual* people have an understanding of the *spiritual* realm and they declare it, pray it, and bring the influence of that *spiritual* realm into the material or natural realm, and things change: minds change, hearts change, diseases change, pain, sorrow and discouragement change. When the influence of the *spiritual* realm of God appears, hope rises, faith increases, healing happens, forgiveness is released, behavior turns away from evil and towards good. Generosity happens, mercy happens, kindness happens, and love rules. In short, the material reality is powerfully altered by the influence of the Christians' *spiritual* reality.

The *spiritual* person may be an effective teacher and can make things of the *spiritual* realm very clear. Perhaps he or she will always pray with great sincerity, or perhaps he or she is just excited about God all the time and it kind of spreads around to others. Perhaps that person will always know just the right Bible verse to apply to any given situation. Whatever form it may take, *spiritual* people are working intentionally to bring the influence of what Pastor Bill Johnson calls the superior *spiritual* reality into this inferior natural reality. 1 Corinthians 2:12-16 gives the biblical explanation of the differences between being *spiritual* and being natural.

Spiritual gift: an ability or talent given from God. God gives *gifts away to Christians. He is very generous. These gifts are from the spiritual realm, not from the material realm (no toys, money and watches). *Spiritual gifts* are unnatural (or super-natural) abilities given to believers that are very helpful to others or helpful to the believers themselves. God gives *gifts* that come from heaven and are given to Christians to break into this often-miserable material realm with the always-wonderful influence of God. See a more complete explanation of these *spiritual gifts* under "*gifts."

Spiritual warfare: the war between Christians and the forces of darkness (the devil and all his demonic powers) that seek to discourage or stop the advance of Christianity.

In the Bible, there is a passage that says, "the weapons of our *warfare* are not of the flesh, but divinely powerful for the destruction of fortresses" (2 Corinthians 10:4). Another passage instructs how to put on "the full armor of God," because there is a spiritual battle going on with "spiritual forces of wickedness," and the battle is against the "schemes of the devil" (Ephesians 6:11-20). The tactics of the devil's attack are primarily through fear, but also through discouragement, lies, defeat, weakness, depression, betrayal, loneliness, confusion, and exhaustion.

Paul Johansson of Elim Bible Institute says that Christians must realize that following Jesus is not a Caribbean cruise, it's more like being on a battleship, and the battle is mostly in the invisible spiritual realm. Believers are in the battle, whether they like it or not. This battle is engaged in by faith, prayer, praise, thanksgiving, worship, the Word of God (the Bible), righteousness, the Gospel (the good news of Jesus), mercy, love, forgiveness, hope, and perseverance. The war is against all of the tactics of the devil.

A direct confrontation with the devil is not necessary or productive, according to Beni Johnson, author of *The Happy Intercessor*. She writes, "Two elements in *warfare* that I feel are our greatest tools of intercession are worship and joy." Spending time focusing on the devil just takes the believer away from spending time with Jesus. The stance of the Christian is confidence in, and celebration of, the victory and the authority of Jesus.

So, for Christians, there always exists opposition from the devil and the real possibility of defeat if one does not have wisdom and weapons at hand. Defeat might just be losing faith or giving up going to church, and not carrying out the good things God had for that Christian to do. Defeat might also be as extreme as falling into an addiction to drugs and spending the rest of one's life in prison for actions done under the influence. It can get that serious. Satan really wants to immobilize Christians.

The devil knows that God is going to use believers to defeat him. "And they overcame him because of the blood of the Lamb and because of the word of their testimony, and they did not love their life even when faced with death" (Revelation 12:10-11). Engaging in *spiritual warfare* means picking up all those weapons listed (prayer, faith, worship and joy, etc.) and saying "no" to all the attacks of the devil, whatever form they take; they do not have to be accepted; they may be refused. Christians must be diligent in this, not giving up, because Christians know the final outcome of the battle is not in question; God has already won; God wins on behalf of the believer. Satan was defeated when Jesus died on the cross. For Christians, the *spiritual war* is mostly won by just staying close to God and being in agreement with Him.

<u>Stronghold</u>: a well-defended part of life either defended <u>against God</u>, or the defense of the believer <u>against an enemy</u>. God, for the believer, is a *stronghold* against the enemy the devil, or any other opposition. Psalm 59:17 says, "For God is my *stronghold*, the God who shows me lovingkindness." And there are many other references to God as the believer's *stronghold*.

Interestingly, David the king of Israel captured what was already a *stronghold*, a fortress that belonged to his enemies, and it became Jerusalem the city of God, the location of the presence of God. So what once was the enemy *stronghold* can become God's well defended *stronghold*.

On the other hand, a person may have something in his thinking or attitude that opposes God. Christians often use the word *stronghold* to mean such a place in a person's life, or in the life of the community, where the devil has a very firm place of rulership. For example, a city might have deeply entrenched criminal gang activity that would be called a *stronghold* in the community. Or an addiction in someone's life could be called a *stronghold* in his life. In these cases, the devil got into a city or into a person's life and created something of his rulership that is very hard to break in natural terms.

Enemy *strongholds* are not difficult to break when put under the authority of Jesus. God can break the enemy's *strongholds*; they are no problem for Him. Often the problem is getting the person or the community to come into agreement with God enough for the *stronghold* to be broken by God. People or communities must submit to God's influence to let that thing go, and let God break it. God allows men to have *free will; the independent choice to decide how to live. If they want to keep the *stronghold*, He will let them, until the side-effects or consequences of living with that *stronghold* become so severe that submitting to God doesn't look so bad anymore. Many people come to be believers by using up all their own resources first, then finally submitting to Jesus. Then He comes in and breaks the *strongholds*.

Tabernacle: the original tent which was built as a sanctuary for God's presence. The *tabernacle* was a very elaborate and beautiful tent. It was completely portable, and it was the place of worship at the time when the people of God were traveling from slavery in Egypt to their new home (see *Exodus). It was a place above which the visible presence of God remained, seen as a pillar of smoke by day and a column of fire by night.

The *tabernacle* contained several pieces of furniture which were essential to worship: a candle stand, an altar to burn incense, a table to offer bread to God, and, in a separate room in the back, behind a thick curtain, was the *ark. The ark, basically, was a box, and above it was the actual place of God's dwelling among the people, the place of His presence. Once a year one priest was allowed behind that curtain, to pray for forgiveness for all of the people, and he had to bring with him the blood of a sacrificed lamb.

This *tabernacle* remained the place of worship for the Jews' forty-year journey through the desert and then for many years after the people settled in their new land. King Solomon eventually built a permanent building, the *temple in Jerusalem as the place for God's presence to reside.

Several Christian principles are symbolized in the *tabernacle*. One principle is that it is God's desire to be available to His people. It also shows what is required to enter into close relationship with God is a sacrificial death, which was the lamb at the time of the *tabernacle*, and for Christians, the death of Jesus, the *lamb of God. It illustrates that an approach to God is not to be done casually, but is a very intentional and reverential matter of faith. Many other details of the *tabernacle* point to prayer, cleanliness, and reliance upon God alone for life and godliness.

Sometimes Christians will say something like, "God has *tabernacled* among us," just meaning that the presence of God has been evident. Also sometimes Christians will speak of themselves or their bodies as the *tabernacle* of the Holy Spirit because God now dwells in believers and brings His influence to the world in that way.

Tabernacle (or tent) of David: a different tabernacle than that built by Moses, and only used during David's reign as King. The story is that the *ark of God (a box that was the place of God's presence) had been stolen by enemies and when King David retrieved it, he did not return it to the original tabernacle (tent) which was in Gibeon, about six miles north of Jerusalem.

He put the ark in a tent that he set up in Jerusalem, the *tabernacle of David*, and instituted a system of constant worship before God in that tent with the ark and the presence of God (1 Chronicles 16). This was highly unconventional. (Compare the description of the tabernacle above.) David was able to go in and stand before God and pray whenever he desired (1 Chronicles 17:16). David is probably the first writer in the Bible to express how much he loved the blessing of just being in God's presence. He writes: "One thing I have asked from the Lord, that I shall seek; that I may dwell in the house of the Lord all the days of my life, to behold the beauty of the Lord…in the secret place of His tent He will hide me." (Psalm 27:4-5).

David inspires Christians to love God and seek His presence that way, which is entirely possible for Christians because there is no *veil for Christians (the curtain that hid the ark in the original tabernacle). Christians may approach the presence of God just as it was in the *tabernacle of David*.

Among today's Christians many believe that this first introduced the idea of God being accessible to worshipers all the time. Later, in the temple built by Solomon, the presence of God was put behind a curtain again and only seen once a year by one priest. However, that period of David's kingship and the *tabernacle of David* remained in the minds of the prophets as tremendously meaningful. Amos, who was a prophet two-hundred years later, prophesied that the *tabernacle of David* would be raised up again. After the time of Jesus, James, a leader of the Christian Church, quoted Amos' words linking that prophecy to what was happening in the church at the time: the church was no longer only Jewish, but was recognizing that God wanted to reach all peoples with His message of salvation (Amos 9:11 and Acts15:16-18). Today Christians know God is no longer behind a curtain. That *veil had been torn from top to bottom at the moment Jesus died on the cross (Matthew 27:50-51). Many scholars believe that the short time of the *tabernacle of David* indicated a future way of worshipping God that was realized when the Christian Church emerged, after Jesus death and resurrection. Christianity introduced an era in which there is unhindered access to God's presence.

Temple: the building that was the place of worship in Jerusalem. When most Christians talk about the *temple*, they are speaking of that building that was in Jerusalem, a place of worship. But you may also hear Christians talking about their own bodies as *temples*, dwelling places of God.

In regard to the building in Jerusalem; there have been three *temples* built and destroyed. There is no *temple* now. The first *temple* was inspired by King David about 1000 B.C. This was to be a permanent building, a place to worship God.

David had the idea, but did not get to build his *temple*. King Solomon, David's son did. It was completed in 960 B.C. (Full details in 1 Kings, Chapters 5 through 8.) When Solomon had completed the *temple* and dedicated it, the *glory of God (in the form of a cloud and an overwhelming awareness of God) appeared in the *temple*. God's presence remained there about 350 years, until the glory departed as described in Ezekiel chapters 8 through 11, about 592 B.C. God left the *temple* at that time because the people had been worshiping idols and behaving like people who didn't know God, without morals, without mercy to the poor, and worshiping many different false gods. Shortly after God's departure from the *temple* it was completely destroyed by a Babylonian king and his army, about 586 B.C.

About 70 years later, the temple was rebuilt in 516 B.C. The story is in Ezra Chapter 3 through 6, and in the books of Haggai and Zechariah. Ezekiel had prophesied that the glory of God (the presence of God) would return to the *temple* (Ezekiel 43:1-9). This rebuilt *temple* was not as fancy as Solomon's *temple*. Whether or not the visible presence of God appeared there is unrecorded, however, in Zechariah 2:10, God promises "I am coming and I will dwell in your midst." He makes that promise while the *temple* was being rebuilt.

Apparently the *ark (a box that was the location of God's presence) was not in the rebuilt *temple*, probably having been destroyed along with Solomon's *temple*. (Many theories exist as to whether the ark was taken somewhere for safety when Solomon's *temple* was destroyed. One such fictional story is told in "Raiders of the Lost Ark," the Indiana Jones movie.)

About 500 years later, just before the time of Christ, King Herod, an architect in his own right, spent a lot of money to tear down Ezra's rebuilt *temple* and reconstruct the *temple* again in the same scale and grandeur as Solomon's *temple*. It took thirty years to complete it. Herod's *temple* was magnificent and famous for its beauty.

However, it may be that the only times that the presence of God ever came to Herod's *temple* was when Jesus was there on the several occasions when He was there during His life. Herod's *temple* stood until 70 A.D. when the Roman army completely destroyed it, and no *temple* has ever been rebuilt.

Many Christians interpret a few verses of the Bible to indicate that the *temple* must be rebuilt before the *second coming of Jesus, however it is a matter of controversy whether an actual structure will be rebuilt or a spiritual building. The main verses that encourage belief an actual structure are 2 Thessalonians 2:1-4 (which predicts that an enemy of God's people will take his seat in the *temple*, but some say that may have already happened while the *temple* was still standing). Also there is Revelation 11:1-2, a vision in which John is instructed to measure the *temple*.

Verses that are used to promote the case for a spiritual building are from 1 Peter 2:4-8. There Peter describes the building of a spiritual house (a *temple*) in which Jesus is the cornerstone and Christians are the living stones that are built up together into that house where acceptable sacrifices may be offered up to God. This is a *temple*, but a Christian *temple* without any blood sacrifices because it is entirely based on Jesus' sacrifice of Himself.

In either case, what is clear is that God desires to be completely available to His people, and He will accomplish that in the end, according to the predictions of Revelation 21:2-3: "Behold, the tabernacle of God is among men, and He will dwell among them, and they shall be His people, and God Himself will be among them."

Another meaning of the *temple*, closely related to the idea of Christians being built <u>together</u> into a *temple*, is that each Christian <u>individually</u> is a *temple* of God. 1 Corinthians 3:16 says, "Do you not know that you are a *temple* of God and that the Spirit of God dwells in you?" Jesus promises this, that God will live in the believer (John 17:23).

That is part of the reason that Christians, when they first become Christians, often go through a big change in behavior and a change in motivations and values, because the powerful holy influence of God now lives inside of them. For this reason most Christians, to the level that they are aware of that principle, are careful not to bring insult to the indwelling life of God. They want God's nearness in that way, so they are careful to live lives that welcome God, and do not offend God. 1 Corinthians 6:19-20 says, "your body is a *temple* of the Holy Spirit who is in you…therefore glorify God in your body."

Temptation: a person's desire to do something that he knows is bad and that he has decided not to do, but part of him still wants to do. *Temptation* itself, even if one does not give in, can be a stressful experience for the serious Christian. Giving in to the *temptation* means disobeying God. Disobeying God means there will be *conviction (the sense of guilt for having done wrong) and the fear of possible bad consequences. God, like a good parent, will not necessarily shield the child of God from the consequences of disobedience (like getting arrested for stealing). God doesn't reject the believer who gives in to *temptation*. God has done away with the sin nature in the believer; it is dead. The Christian is at risk in times of *temptation* if he forgets who he really is: he is a new man. The new man is created in the image of Jesus and therefore victorious over *temptation*. A Christian who is not yet convinced that his new nature is "dead to sin" (Romans 6:11) will be at risk of giving in to *temptation*.

Most Christians know that being *tempted* is not wrong. Even Jesus was *tempted* by the devil (Matthew 4:1-11). Jesus was "*tempted* in all things as we are, yet without sin" (Hebrews 4:15). It is giving in to *temptation* that is sinful. Christians turn their attention to loving God rather than resisting *temptation* and find the power of *temptation* is not there anymore.

Ten Commandments: the well-known and earliest written standards of behavior given by God. (See *Commandments.) The *Ten Commandments* are ten rules of conduct that are in the Bible (Exodus 20), which were first given to the people of God as they traveled from Egypt to their new home (now the country of Israel). The Commandments define right and wrong. To ignore the commandments and follow one's impulses and desires is wrong. The *Ten Commandments* provide the guidelines for how to keep a good relationship with God and how to live in relationship with one another. Four of the *Ten Commandments* refer to how to stay in relationship with God and six Commandments are about how to do well with one another. (See *Commandments for a more complete overview.)

Testimony: two definitions: (1) a Christian's account of his or her experience of God, (2) a statement of truth that is held by faith.

(1) The most common way in which this word is used by Christians is when they want to tell their *testimony*, or their story of how God led them to believe. *Testimony* is a courtroom term. In a trial, witnesses give their *testimony*; their evidence about what happened. A Christian's *testimony* is <u>any evidence</u> of the goodness of God in the Christian's life. In cases where someone is thinking about whether to have faith in God, believe in Jesus, or believe for a miracle, the *testimony* of Christians is often helpful.

Pastor Bill Johnson says that a believer's *testimony* reveals the nature of God and creates a faith-filled expectation in the heart of the listener. In a broader sense, much of the Bible is *testimony* about what God has done, and the Bible itself refers to these *testimonies* as being essential to remember (Psalm 119:99).

(2) *Testimony* is the agreement of a Christian with the truths of the Bible. That is part of "keeping the *testimony*," which is Christianese for "sticking to the truth."

Keeping the *testimony* is of foundational importance (Revelation 1:2 and 6:9). The Bible declares that *testimony* is powerful to overcome the devil, the enemy of faith (Revelation 12:10-11). Truth overcomes lies; light overcomes darkness, and keeping the *testimony* shatters whatever the devil is trying to do. This idea of *testimony* means the stated truths that are held in the heart and by which the believer remains unshakeable, both from the Bible and the *testimonies* of the believers' own experiences.

An example: 1 John 5:4-5 says that the one who believes that Jesus is the son of God overcomes the world. Stating that as truth, or giving that *testimony* of Jesus as the Son of God, has overcoming power against all opposition to Christian faith. Revelation 19:10 says that "the *testimony* of Jesus is the spirit of *prophecy," which means it has the same spiritual power or influence on the listener as the prophetic words of God. Bill Johnson says that prophecy and *testimony* have creative power to bring what is declared into being. It can make the influence of God very real when it was not there before. So Christians place a high value on their *testimonies*, both their personal stories and the statements of what they believe, and many will work carefully to prepare a *testimony*, written or spoken, in order to be as clear and as brief as possible to anyone who is willing to listen. 1 Peter 3:15 says that Christians are to always be ready to give an account, a *testimony*, for the hope that resides within them.

Thanksgiving: the believer's response to the works of God. Being thankful holds a high priority in the Christian's life. It is a biblical principle, to be *thankful*. It is a theme throughout the Bible, both before and after the time of Jesus. Very early in history, God established certain holidays centered on giving *thanks*; for the harvest, for shelter and protection, for deliverance from slavery, and for forgiveness of sin. Psalm 50:14 says, "Offer to God a sacrifice of *thanksgiving*," and verse 23 says, "He who offers a sacrifice of *thanksgiving* honors Me [God]."

Christians who understand this principle *give thanks* both in the good times and in the times when it would appear that there is nothing to be *thankful* about. 1 Timothy 4:4-5 says that *giving thanks* for food, even unclean food, makes it into clean food. Pastor Bill Johnson points out that this principle "extends to every situation in [the believer's] life in which [the believer] finds other powers at work besides the power of God." Giving *thanks* in a situation that is brought about by bad circumstances can turn it around to God's purposes. *Thanksgiving* actually has that power.

Christians live in an atmosphere of *thanksgiving*. It is part of the fabric of their lives because they see life and breath itself as a gift from God. 1 Thessalonians 5:18 says, "in everything give *thanks*; for this is God's will for you in Christ Jesus." Ephesians 5:20 says that believers should be: "always giving *thanks* for all things... to God, even the Father." And Colossians 3:17 says, "Whatever you do in word or deed, do all in the name of the Lord Jesus, giving *thanks* through Him to God the Father."

Theology: the study of God. How does one study God who is invisible? Those who study God (theologians) have three sources from which to research and understand God: (1) the Bible, (2) concrete experiences with God, (3) visions and prophecy from God. (These are intuitive messages; things that cannot be seen, photographed, tracked, or recorded but are very real encounters.) Much of the Bible is from these kinds of experiences by the people of God.

Not surprisingly, theologians do not agree about the definitions of God. Most theologians rely heavily on the Bible: "If it's not in the Bible, then there is no foundation for believing it." (This is undoubtedly a good standard.) But most theologians will also include experiential evidence as part of their understanding of God, and will interpret what they read in the Bible based upon what they experience. (If they often see people healed by prayer to Jesus, then they will include healing in their *theology* as part of what God does today.

On the other hand, if they do not see miracles of healing, then they may conclude that God doesn't do that anymore, and teach that as part of their *theology*.)

Those *theologians* who include their own experiences of prophecy, visions, and other personal encounters with God in their *theology* usually support their ideas and their experiences with biblical and historical evidence too. Their conclusions must agree with the Bible or they will be called into question by mainstream *theological* thinking.

God is not really able to be contained in a book, defined by a *theologian*, or completely understood by any human being. That does not invalidate the attempt. *Theology* is seen as a very valuable part of Christianity. Every Christian has a *theology*: his or her understanding of who God is, what He can do, what He won't do, when He loves, when He punishes, etc. And everyone's *theology* is incomplete. Well-known Christian speaker Anthony Campolo states, "God is bigger than your *theology*."

Thorn: some kind of problem that God has placed in someone's life for the purpose of keeping him or her from being proud. The idea comes from a letter written by the early Christian leader, Paul, who writes about a *"thorn* in the flesh," something that God did in his life (2 Corinthians 12:7). He had had such supernatural experiences with God that he might have thought himself to be better than others. So Paul believed God gave him an affliction (a *thorn*) that kept him from bragging. (It is not clear what Paul's *thorn*, or affliction was.) It's not a general principle that shows up elsewhere in the Bible (that God would put something painful in the believer's life to keep him or her from becoming proud), but Christians will sometimes think, "Maybe that's what's happening to me," and they will talk about their *"thorn* in the flesh."

Tithe: a tenth of all of a believer's income which is set aside to be given to God. The Bible makes it clear that one of the ways to worship is to give part of one's income to God.

In the Bible, God promises to pour out a blessing of plenty of provision to those who will give that tenth, that *tithe*, by faith. And many Christians have stories about how true that is. It is a frightening thing to give away money when there doesn't seem to be enough to meet the needs anyway. Those who do *tithe* go ahead and give that money to God while believing that God will respond with a blessing of providing enough, no matter how bad the circumstances might be at the moment.

Actually, Bible scholars will point out, the *tithe* is not all that God asks for in the Bible. He asks for additional offerings above and beyond the *tithe*, money given to the poor, or for support of other special projects. In Bible times before Jesus, the actual percentage given to God was between 15% and 18%. In the teaching of parts of the Bible written after Jesus (the New Testament) radical generosity is more the norm, rather than the idea that one should give a certain percentage to meet an obligation or a requirement of God. Jesus observed a widow giving a very small amount of money, but it was all she had, and He said that she gave more than anyone (Mark 12:41-44). Jesus often broke the legal standard of what the religion of the day asked for, and that is the New Testament pattern.

There are stories about believers who have given 90% away, and lived on the 10%, or have chosen to live on a very small fixed amount, and everything else that comes in is given to the work of the kingdom of God. So giving a *tithe* is more of an Old Testament (before Christ) idea. In the New Testament, giving cheerfully, generously, and consistently is more the idea that is promoted among Christians. The *tithe*, or the tenth, is only a standard, or a minimum.

Tongues: miraculous language. *Tongues* means languages (for example, "His mother *tongue* was Japanese"). *Tongues* in biblical use means the miracle of being able to speak a language without having to study it and learn it. In the Bible, the first occurrence of this was in Acts 2:4-12.

It happened at a time when the influence of God came so powerfully upon the gathered friends of Jesus (after He had departed) that they all miraculously, without any coaching or preparation, began to speak in the various *tongues,* or languages of that part of the world, and they were "speaking of the mighty deeds of God." This ability is one of the *spiritual gifts, or supernatural abilities, or miracles that God makes happen through His people.

Tongues today is somewhat of a controversy among Christians. There is debate about whether *tongues* or any other miracles happen anymore; however, people keep spontaneously receiving this ability, this gift of *tongues*. Many church leaders do believe that God gives all of the spiritual gifts today just as he did in the beginning, including *tongues,* and in these churches many people have received this gift, as well as other miraculous capabilities.

Biblical teaching and explanation of the gift can be found in 1 Corinthians 12:1 through 14:28, and some further stories about how people came to have the gift of *tongues* are in Acts 10:44-48, and in Acts 19:1-7.

According to this Biblical teaching, there are two kinds of languages that are spoken in *tongues*: languages of man, and languages of angels. In either case, the one speaking the language does not understand what is being said, "in his spirit he speaks mysteries" (1Corinthians 14:2), but the spirit of the person speaking is being strengthened from the speaking (1 Corinthians 14:4).

Tongues are most commonly used by the believer as a "prayer language," in which the believer prays without knowing what is being spoken, but things are happening because of the prayers. Another use of *tongues* is when, in a gathering of believers, one person speaks out-loud in a *tongue,* and then someone interprets the message for everyone else to understand. This is called "*tongues* and interpretation" and it happens commonly in some churches. It is one of the means used by God to deliver His messages to believers.

Transgression: the breaking of a rule or law of God. *Transgression* is one of several words used to talk about the broad category of wrongdoing, or *sin. A definite line has been crossed if there is a *transgression*. For example, if the rule is: "don't steal," and one does steal, that is *transgression*.

Transgression is not any different from other forms of wrongdoing. All wrong is potentially grounds for condemnation from God if it remains unforgiven. But all *transgression* is able to be forgiven by God: Jesus made it possible for anyone, no matter what foul things they have done, to come to God, believing in Jesus, and be forgiven. Rule breaking (*transgression*) can be forgiven by faith in Jesus, believing in His offer of forgiveness.

Tribulation: being afflicted by difficulties or abuse. In the Bible, this word shows up in a couple of different ways. The word means affliction. If one is in real trouble, it's going to hurt in some way; that is *tribulation*. Jesus says, in John 16:33, "In the world you have *tribulation*, but take courage, I have overcome the world." Christians know that faith in Jesus doesn't excuse them from experiencing the trouble and pain of life in this world, but they have the assurance that Jesus' presence will influence them in His beautiful supernatural response to the *tribulation* instead of a natural vengeful or defeated reaction. Jesus went through the *tribulation* of being crucified, but did not get angry, bitter, or defeated through it. That is what He promises when He says, "I have overcome the world." The pain He went through did not alter who He is; He overcame it.

The other meaning of the word is when Christians talk about "<u>the</u> *tribulation*." (The great *tribulation* is in the Bible; Matthew 24:21, Revelation 7:14). This is a time in history that is predicted in the Bible, as a time in which severe persecution against Christians as well as food shortages, hardships, and other difficult circumstances will take place. American Christians typically believe this is a yet future event.

In much of the rest of the world, however, the *tribulation* is seen as a present on-going reality. Christians outside of America and Europe have experienced *tribulation* throughout history. Life for them has been lived under oppressive governments, in deep poverty, with poor food, much sickness and disease, primitive living conditions, and a short difficult life span. Add to that, if one is a serious Christian, persecution and constant threat of death, torture, or imprisonment, and it is understandable for people who live that kind of life to have a view of the *tribulation* as the on-going and present-day condition. The important issue is Jesus' assurance that He has overcome the world, and that is ever so clear to these believers who have experienced so much pain.

Another group of scholars believe the great *tribulation* already happened in 70 AD when Jerusalem was destroyed by the Roman army and about a million Jews were killed and another 97,000 captured and enslaved after a long siege. Harold Eberle's book, *Victorious Eschatology* explains that idea.

Trinity: a Christian term for God, meaning all of God as expressed in three persons. *Trinity* is a common and important Christian word, however it is not found in the Bible. It is used among Christians to address a point of potential confusion that arises in the Bible. It is abundantly clear, when studying the Bible, that the Heavenly Father is God, and that Jesus is also God, and that the Holy Spirit too is God. Furthermore it is clear that there is only <u>one God.</u> This can be a problem to understand. Mark 1:9-11 tells about when Jesus was baptized: Jesus was there, and the Holy Spirit showed up in the form of a dove, and the voice of God the Father spoke out of heaven. All three are in the same place at the same time and yet it is accepted by Christians that they are One. (The event was of such importance that the full nature of God was perceptibly present, not just Jesus. See *baptism.) Christians don't worship three gods. They worship Jesus as one with the Father and showing up in the person of the Holy Spirit in power. So God is called a *trinity*; three in one, a confusing concept.

Early Christians looked long and hard at this question. The primary question was whether Jesus is God. Over a period of 350 years after the time of Jesus, scholars and leaders in the church studied all that was written by those who knew Jesus personally, or had known His apostles. They concluded that Jesus is God and that He is the Son of God and that He sent the Holy Spirit of God to the early believers. Christians agree that those conclusions do not contradict all that had been written in the Old Testament (before the birth of Jesus), because the Father, Son, and Holy Spirit are One. (The Nicene Creed was the name of the written conclusion of those scholars.)

The Old Testament (the part of the Bible written before Jesus) contained earlier revealed truth which the Christians did not contradict. They believed it to be the unquestionable word of God that there is <u>one God</u>. In the Old Testament, God states many times through His prophets that He is God and there is no other (Deuteronomy 6:4, Isaiah 45:6 & 22). This truth was already firmly understood by the early Christians, who mostly came from a Jewish (Old Testament) background.

Jesus is not seen by Christians as separate, but as one with God. Jesus Himself states repeatedly that He is One with God, in fact it was one of the reasons that He was killed, "[He] was calling God His own Father, making Himself equal with God" (John 5:18). Later, the idea of the *trinity* emerged as a term to try to make the idea understandable. It is not surprising that many have difficulty with this concept, particularly in the logically oriented western hemisphere.

Unbeliever: a person who does not believe in Jesus, and does not believe in God. When one refuses to believe in Jesus he remains an *unbeliever*. Ephesians (in the Bible) describes *unbelievers* as people who are, "dead in [their] trespasses and sins,...indulging the desires of the flesh and of the mind and...by nature children of wrath...separate from Christ...having no hope and without God in the world" (Ephesians 2:1-3 &11-12).

Then, that same passage in the Bible declares that these *unbelievers* became believers, that is, they became people who are now, "alive together with Christ, and He [God] Himself is [their] peace, and they are of God's household... being built together into a dwelling of God in the Spirit." (Ephesians 2:5-10) Believers then, have a relationship of life and security with God, and they have purpose as members of the family of God. Christians view *unbelievers* as *lost, not knowing the way to life. Long before believers were called Christians they were called "the Way" presumably because they knew the way, they were not lost.

The position of the *unbeliever* is subject to change when brought face to face with Jesus' love and forgiveness.

Unforgivable sin: the one sin (one wrong) which is not going to be forgiven, ever. In Matthew 12:32, Jesus says, "whoever speaks against the Holy Spirit, it shall not be forgiven him, either in this age, or the age to come." Jesus said this in a crowd of people, some of whom had been saying that the miracles that Jesus was doing (casting out demons) were done by the power of the ruler of the demons (Satan) instead of by the power of the Holy Spirit. Making an accusation like that is called, in Christianese, "*blasphemy of the Holy Spirit," and it is also fairly clear that it is the *unforgivable sin*.

The *unforgivable sin* has happened when a former Christian has come to a determined decision and has spoken openly in a way that denies the power or the work of the Holy Spirit. It is when a former believer has, "insulted the Spirit of grace" (Hebrews 10:29). This *unforgivable sin* is not something that can be done by accident, not just a slip of the tongue, or something said at a time when a Christian may have been mad at God. Christians who worry if they have committed the *unforgivable sin* can stop worrying because that worry itself indicates that they haven't done it. They still care about being in good favor with God, and therefore they have not turned against the Holy Spirit.

Unforgiveness: refusing to grant forgiveness, holding a grudge. Christians take the concept of *unforgiveness* very seriously. They know the words of Jesus when He instructs them to forgive completely, "from the heart" (Matthew 18:21-35). Jesus also instructs to forgive the same person up to "seventy times seven" times, not just a few times. Jesus says, "For if you forgive others for their transgressions, your heavenly Father will also forgive you. But if you do not forgive others, then your Father will not forgive your transgressions" (Matthew 6:14-15).

Furthermore, Christians believe that those who do not forgive are open and vulnerable to attack from the devil. *Unforgiveness* is a foothold for demonic influence. Christians who do the work of praying for people to be set free from demons (*deliverance) know that in order for the prayer to be effective, the one being prayed for must not be holding any *unforgiveness*, no matter how justified he or she may feel about it, or the prayers for freedom from demonic influence will be ineffective.

To Christians, the ideal is always to forgive, not to seek revenge. No matter how badly they have been wronged, Jesus taught forgiveness and He modeled forgiveness: He forgave those who nailed him to a wooden cross. Forgiveness is a decision, in obedience to Jesus' command. It has nothing to do with whether the offender has apologized or deserves forgiveness. When Christians forgive, they often discover a new way to move forward: instead of living with hatred, they can love, and instead of bitterness, they may live in peace, and instead of continuing with the broken relationship, they have the choice of mending the friendship. *Unforgiveness* makes all of that impossible.

Vanity: that which is of no purpose or value. In common English usage this word means focusing upon one's looks. But in Christianese, *vanity* has a broader meaning, more like "useless" or, "futile," producing no good results.

And when a Christian uses the term, it usually applies to things that are of no importance to God such as, fancy homes, flashy cars, fame, riches, concerns that may be important to people in the *world (people living life without the influence of God), but these things are judged to be *vanity*, useless, by most Christians.

Common use of this word in Christianese comes from a well-known book in the Bible called Ecclesiastes. In that book it says over and over, "all is *vanity* and striving after wind." It means that there are many things that one can begin to take very seriously, but they are really just *vanity*, not important, and impossible to achieve, like catching the wind. At the conclusion of Ecclesiastes there is a definition of what <u>is</u> important, since everything else is *vanity*. It says, "the conclusion, when all has been heard is: fear God and keep His commandments, because this applies to every person. For God will bring every act to judgment, everything which is hidden, whether it is good or evil." So God will eventually judge all pursuit of *vanity*.

Veil: a curtain that hides what is behind. There are two *veils* that Christians talk about. One is a very thick curtain in the *Tabernacle or the *Temple (the place of worship of God) that kept anyone from seeing into the room where the presence of God was. Only one priest, one day a year, was allowed to enter behind the *veil*. That priest went in as representative of everyone, to ask for forgiveness from God and he took the blood of a sacrificed lamb to appeal for forgiveness. The rest of the time, that place of God's dwelling, that room, called the holy of holies, behind the *veil*, was empty of people; inhabited only by God's patient presence.

On the day that Jesus was killed by nailing Him to a cross of wood, that *veil* was torn in two, from top to bottom, by an act of God (Matthew 27:50-51). God came out from behind the *veil* and is now available for anyone who believes in Jesus, to be met by the presence of God. He is not accessible only in one special place.

There is no more necessity for a representative priest with the blood of a lamb, because Jesus is now that priest having entered behind the *veil* with His own blood (Hebrews 9:11-12, Hebrews 10:19-22). It is possible for everyone to experience the presence of God if they believe in Jesus, and symbolically each believer bears the blood of the *Lamb, who was Jesus. (One of Jesus' titles is the Lamb of God.)

The other *veil* that Christians talk about is from the time of Moses, about 1500 years before Jesus. Moses went to the top of the mountain (*Sinai) to talk to God, and when he came down among the people again they noticed his face was glowing, an after-effect of being that close to God. It frightened the people, so Moses put a *veil* over his face in order to talk to the people without frightening them. That *veil* of Moses is mentioned again in parts of the Bible written after Jesus: in 2 Corinthians 3:12-18, it says that unbelievers still have that *veil* over their hearts to keep them from knowing the glory of God, but, "whenever a person turns to the Lord, [Jesus] the *veil* is taken away." Then it goes on to say that Christians, "with a <u>unveiled</u> face beholding as in a mirror the glory of the Lord, are being transformed into the same image from glory to glory."

So, for a Christian the *veil* has been removed, and it is seen as a good thing. Whether it is the *veil* that separates one from God's presence, or the *veil* that the blinds one's heart from knowing God, Jesus is always the *veil* remover, opening the way to know God.

<u>Victory</u>: a triumph, a win. Christians say things like, "I'm getting the *victory*!" which means that they believe that they are winning the fight with the devil or with their own bad habits of sin. It might be rising above temptation to do something wrong, or it might be gaining the ability to do something that they could not do before (for example, public speaking, singing, playing a musical instrument). Maybe they used to have a bad habit and they are struggling to stop. When they are succeeding, they declare *victory*.

Christians read in the Bible, "Run in such a way that you may win," and the one who wins gets a wreath or a victor's *crown (1 Corinthians 9:24-25). Christians who are getting the *victory* thank God because they know it is Jesus that gives them the *victory* (1 Corinthians 15:57). The word *victory* is used both because it is used in the Bible and because there is a battle, and someone is going to win (get the *victory*). Furthermore, the battle was decided a long time ago, when Jesus died on the cross, and Jesus got the *victory*, so Christians know the *victory* is theirs to be realized. There is a Christian song sung in Churches that says, "You [Jesus] wear the Victor's Crown!" 1 Corinthians 15:54-57 says that because of Jesus, "Death is swallowed up in *victory*...thanks be to God who gives us the *victory* through our Lord Jesus Christ."

Vine: grape-growing plants which are symbolic of people or of Jesus. *Vineyards* (farms where grapes are grown) were common throughout Bible times. Many times the Bible uses the *vine* as the symbol of God's people: *vines* planted and tended by God with the hope of getting some fruit (Isaiah 5:1-6). When there is fruit on the *vine* of God's people, it represents faithful worship of God, the observation of His commandments, and increasing numbers of people believing in God.

Then Jesus, in John 15, states that He is the *Vine* and His people are the branches. Just like branches are part of a natural *vine*, people are part of Jesus. Just like a branch by itself won't make grapes (it has to be part of a *vine*), Christians believe they won't be able to do anything of value by themselves, but must be a part of the *vine*, part of Jesus. Jesus goes on to say that branches that do not bear fruit will be cut from the *vine* (pruned). It has always been very important to God that His people bear fruit.

So the *vine*, or the *vineyard*, means the church, either locally or worldwide, empowered by God, and it is seen as the reality of what Jesus is doing in the world today. It includes all believers.

Virgin: any girl who has not had sexual relations, and specifically, Mary, the mother of Jesus. One of the important points of belief for Christians is that Jesus' mother, Mary was a *virgin*. She became pregnant miraculously by the Holy Spirit, by God. This is also known as the "immaculate conception." This is the basis of the belief that Jesus is the Son of God, because He was not the son of Joseph (Mary's husband).

The story is in some detail in Matt 1:18-25 and Luke 1:26-38. It is also the reason that Christians believe that Jesus did not have the *sin nature (bound to sin just like any other man). He did not inherit sinfulness, and He did not sin.

It is also important that Jesus was born in an entirely human way, rather than miraculously descending from heaven as an adult. As the representative of mankind, He fully experienced the human condition, but without sin. He is the model for every believer that, once forgiven of sin by faith in Jesus, one may choose to live a life totally yielded to the Holy Spirit, as Jesus lived. Such a life will bear many similarities to the life of Jesus in its influence. Others will come to know God through such a life, and many will be set free from the oppression of the devil, whether it is spiritual oppression (demonic), or physical oppression (sickness), and the kingdom of God will be expanded.

Vow: a promise, usually a promise made to God. In the part of the Bible written before Jesus (the Old Testament) the most common *vow* was the *vow* to give thanks to God. (Psalm 116:17-18) It is a promise, a commitment, to give thanks to God regularly (daily, or several times a day), and in public, so others could hear that thanksgiving being given.

Another *vow* was the Nazirite *vow* which was the promise to be dedicated to God, signified by various things like not drinking wine and not cutting one's hair. These *vows* were taken very seriously. The one who made a *vow* had to keep it. He could not forget about it, because to do so would be a serious wrong (a sin) (Deuteronomy 23:21-23).

In the parts of the Bible written after Jesus' time on earth (the New Testament) the making and keeping of *vows* is not promoted as a means of expressing faith. In the times before Jesus, one did express faith in God by <u>doing</u> certain things, and performing certain acts. Making and keeping of *vows* was one of the ways to express faith towards God. But to the Christian, faith is not usually expressed through *vows*. Even though Paul is recorded to have made and kept a *vow* (Acts 18:18), it never became a carry-over into the New Testament practice of faith. Faith does include action. Believers step out and act on whatever they are believing, but not on the basis of a *vow*. The relationship between the Christian and Jesus is through faith and love. It is an understanding, not a visible sign, so for the Christian, faith is not made more effective by making a *vow* to God.

Walk: the journey of life for the believer. Christians will ask one another, "How is your *walk*?" meaning, are you full of faith? Are you reading your Bible and staying in touch with God? Are you joyful? Are you serving others, loving the unlovable, feeding the hungry, helping the poor, and staying free from sin? *Walk* is short for all that is involved in living a life that Honors God and expands His kingdom through the joy and love and power that is typical of all who will seriously follow the way of God.

Warfare: the battle between the people of God and the devil. Christians talk about *spiritual *warfare*. They will say, "We need to do some *warfare* about that." The idea comes from a verse in 2 Corinthians 10:4 that says, "the weapons of our *warfare* are not of the flesh, but divinely powerful for the destruction of fortresses."

In the realm of spiritual powers there is a battle going on, and the fight is over the souls of men. God wants men's hearts because He loves them and will strengthen them to overthrow the devil, and the devil wants to destroy them because he hates that God is going to use men to defeat him.

Christians do not see this battle as a never-ending fight between good and evil. There will be an end to this battle, and Christians know that the outcome of the war is that God wins. They recognize when they are under attack (maybe they get depressed, sick, exhausted, etc.), but they know that Jesus won the war when He died on the cross. Satan was defeated; death was defeated; and Jesus won, was resurrected from the grave, never to die again. Furthermore, Jesus is able to grant to the believer life forever together with Him in heaven, never again to be pestered by the devil. And the devil will be thrown into the *lake of fire, according to Revelation 20:10.

A spiritual attack may take the form of apathy, temptation, fear, or even literal assault from another human being, as well as actual appearances of frightening-looking demons (evil spirits). Christians believe that if they fight back, through believing that Jesus has already won, through adoration of Jesus, through asking for God's help, and through remembering the truths of the Bible, then the attack will fail. James 4:7 says, "Resist the devil and he will flee from you." If believers do not fight back, they may succumb to the attack, and be sick, depressed, frightened, or worse, even though ultimately the war is already won on their behalf.

Christians believe that Satan cannot alter their eternal destiny, which is to eventually be in the perfect presence of God (heaven), but he can interfere with Christians' effectiveness on earth. For further instruction, Dean Sherman wrote the classic book entitled, *Spiritual Warfare*, and Roberts Liardon wrote, *How to Survive an Attack*.

Will: in man or in God, that part of the personality that sets direction. (See also *will of God.) A person's *will* is that part of the person that decides, or decides to want, or decides to act. In Christian thinking, the natural human *will* (without the influence of Jesus) typically wants to go in a direction that is not in agreement with God's principles. Central to the idea of the human *will* is that the *will* decides what is wanted, completely independent from what anyone else wants.

The human *will* can be opposed to what God wants (God's *will*). A big part of the Christian idea of the *will* is that the believer's human *will* <u>must</u> be submitted to the *will* of God. Jesus demonstrated this kind of submission to God. Jesus spoke a famous prayer as He faced death on the cross; He said, speaking to God His Father, "not My *will* but Yours be done" (Luke 22:42-44). It wasn't Jesus' human *will* to die in the cross. (He didn't want to, for obvious reasons; the thought of it was deeply distressing to Him, to the point of sweating great drops of blood.) But it was the *will* of God the Father for Jesus to accomplish this, and Jesus was completely submitted, as a man, to the Father (God) and to the Father's *will*. This is the model for the Christian's idea of *will*. God's *will* is always good in the long run, but following one's own human *will* is going to be bad. So, to a Christian, finding God's *will* and submitting one's own *will* to the *will* of God (see below) is very important.

Will of God: that which God intends (God's will). Christians assume that *God's will* for them is going to be good: "If God wants me to do this, it must be the best for me." One Christian slogan is, "God has a wonderful plan for your life." Finding *God's will* and being assured that one is living in the *will of God* is the most wonderful life one can live as a believer.

Missing the *will of God*, whether by mistake or through rebellious behavior, is a concern for many Christians, especially for those who have not come to have any assurance of what God wants them to do. There can be nagging questions: "Am I in the right job? Am I wasting my life? Am I supposed to be a missionary? Whom should I marry?" etc.

There are two basic Christian ways of thinking about *God's will* for any given individual. The first is that *God's will* very general, based on principles. The second is that *God's will* I very specific, based on details. In the first perspective, Christians just pay attention to the life principles of what God wants and trust God to use those principles to get them into *His will*.

Some Bible passages that present the principles of the *will of God* are: the believer's *sanctification (1 Thessalonians 4:3), to rejoice, pray, and give thanks all the time (1 Thessalonians 5:16-18), to do right (1Peter 2:15), to know that He desires all men to be saved (1 Timothy 2:4). Jesus also gives some general instructions to His disciples in Matthew 10:7-8 when He sent them out. He said, "as you go, preach, saying, 'The kingdom of heaven is at hand.' Heal the sick, raise the dead, cleanse the lepers, cast out demons," clearly *His will*. It is exactly what Jesus Himself did while here on earth. How that is implemented in a Christian's life is a matter of faith. Some do go through life doing these things. See Jonathan Welton's book, *Normal Christianity* for more on that view.

In the second view of the *will of God*, some believers pay attention to little details all day, every day, trying to make sure that He is directing every step. There are biblical accounts to support that approach as well: In Romans 1:10, Paul hopes that this is the *will of God* at this time for him to go to Rome. In Colossians 1:1, Paul says he is called to be an apostle by the *will of God* (not a teacher or any other career). Psalm 139:16 says that God wrote down all "the days that were ordained for me," before one is even born. Ephesians 2:10 says that God has prepared certain works for each one to do.

There are many historical accounts of well-known Christians, some of whom have seen *God's will* as a specific target which one should not miss, and others who believe God leaves much of the direction up to them as long as they are in His general will. Other biblical and historical accounts illustrate what happens when a person totally disregards *God's will*, which predictably ends in great loss. Paying attention and submitting to the *will of God* is essential.

One common misconception is that, if it is the *will of God* it will happen. That is fatalism, see *fate. God consistently gives people the choice whether to accept or refuse His will. God's will may be refused or ignored.

The other common idea is that if anything happened, it was the *will of God*. This is not biblical either (not stated in the Bible). Tragic awful things happen every day in this world that obviously are not the will of a loving powerful God. *God's will* takes place when people submit to His general principles and to any specific direction He gives. *God's will* does not happen for people who ignore Him and choose greed, pride, or selfishness.

Witness: an observer who offers proof. Someone who saw something happen is a *witness*, and the testimony of a *witness* is used as evidence in a court of law. Christians see themselves as *witnesses* of what God has done for the world because they have experienced God's goodness as individuals and they know that what God has done for them He also intends for everyone. Christians want everyone to experience God's closeness and forgiveness. They are the evidence of God's goodness, God's love, God's mercy and forgiveness. So when they go and tell someone about Jesus, they call that *witnessing*, or giving *testimony (an account of what they experienced).

Another way in which the word *witness* comes up in Christian talk is the "*witness* of the Spirit." The *witness* of the Holy Spirit shows up in the Bible in Romans 8:16 which says, "The Spirit himself testifies [bears *witness*] with our spirit that we are children of God." This means that without any visible proof, a person can know deep in his or her own spirit that he or she is certainly accepted into God's family, loved, completely accepted and forgiven.

Proof of something that remarkable and invisible can only come to the human spirit by having the very Spirit of God come in to bear *witness* to that truth. When the Holy Spirit comes in to bring spiritual proof, the believer has received the "*witness* of the Spirit" and remains <u>convinced</u> from then on. This is the Christians foremost evidence, not only of the initial experience of becoming a Christian, but also the assurance of God's daily involvement and influence in personal difficulties, challenges, joys and opportunities of life.

Word: God's word, God's written and timeless communication with mankind. When Christians talk about "the *word*" they mean the Bible; or anything stated in the Bible. They talk about reading of the *word*, getting daily nourishment from the *word*, the bread of life, going to the *word* for answers, and looking to the *word* for encouragement and strength. They call the Bible the "*Word* of life." This deep reverence for the Bible and all that is in it comes largely from what is written about the *word* in the book of John 1:1-2: "In the beginning was the *Word* and the *Word* was with God and the *Word* was God. He was in the beginning with God." So the *word* is spoken of as a "He" who was equal with God, and in fact, was God. Then it says more about the *word* as a person, and finally, in verse 14 it says, "And the *Word* became flesh and dwelt among us and we beheld His glory, glory as of the only begotten from the Father, full of grace and truth." Obviously, this Bible passage is about how Jesus is the *Word* and that the *Word* became a human being, Jesus. Jesus is the living *Word* of God. So Christians, understandably have a deep expectation that the Bible has a supernatural life to it that soothes, brings amazing wisdom and power, and is personally attentive to the Christian's needs. Christians read the Bible to encounter the Person of the *Word*, Jesus.

Christians believe that the Bible is actually "God-breathed," or inspired by God (2 Timothy 3:16). The various authors were fully human, but wrote under the inspiration of God. Christians believe that the result of that writing is an accurate message from God.

Furthermore, Christians believe the reader is helped along by the Holy Spirit (by God) as he or she reads, especially if the reader is a believer. Unbelievers often have a pretty difficult time with the Bible and it doesn't make any sense to them, but when they invite God into their hearts, then suddenly they are captivated by the *Word*, and it begins to make sense and bring understanding.

In Revelation 19:11-13, John has a vision of Jesus on a white horse; His eyes are a flame of fire; there are crowns on His head, and His name is called "the *Word* of God." Again in the Bible, Jesus is seen as the living and powerful *Word* of God.

Word of knowledge: knowledge which is supernaturally revealed by God to a believer. Sometimes Christians will be able to know something about someone, or about a situation, that they were not told about by another human. In other words, they will have knowledge which came to them from God. And if they are led to speak to the person about whom they know something, what they say is called a *word of knowledge*. It will usually be something that is helpful to that person, or that leads to God being able to bring a healing, or new understanding, or to relieve a burden.

This is one of the supernatural ways in which God uses Christians as His hands and feet and speaks His words in the world. If God gives a Christian a *word of knowledge*, it is out of God's love and His desire to relieve a burden and make His love known through that blessing. This ability that some Christians have is called a *spiritual gift. This gift is listed along with several others in 1 Corinthians 12: 4-11.

Word of wisdom: unclouded wisdom that is supernaturally given by God to a believer, either for the believer personally or for another. Sometimes God gives a particular portion of wisdom to a Christian in order that the Christian can then carefully bring that wisdom to the people who need it. This kind of word can be seen as God's instructions. (The messenger must be trustworthy.)

Wisdom is a possession of God and apparently is a part of His personality. In Proverbs 8, wisdom writes, as if she were a person, a female, and says that she has always been involved in everything God does. Consequently, any interaction with God is going to include the giving of His wisdom, sometimes through a *word of wisdom*.

God uses His servants (Christians) to show not only God's wisdom, but also His compassion and willingness to be involved in the affairs of men. This ability that some Christians have, to acquire supernatural wisdom (wisdom from God rather than from a natural source) is called a *spiritual gift and is listed along with other supernatural abilities in 1 Corinthians 12:4-11. It is one of God's ways of interacting with His people, by giving understanding of the situation, or bringing a solution to a problem.

Works: two definitions: (1) good things one might do in order to deserve the love of God, (2) assignments that God has appointed someone to do.

(1) A slogan of Christians is, "We are saved by faith not by *works*" (Ephesians 2:8-9). What that means is that one can't *work* hard enough, or do enough good things to become a person who is welcomed into God's presence (be *saved). And one cannot be made right with God on the basis of one's *works*, one's accomplishments. So *works* are those good things that people do to try to be admirable enough, kind enough, and generous enough, for God to say, "Oh, you're a good person, you can come into heaven." But Christians state that *works* alone will never accomplish that.

Most world religions have this idea as their basis: "Work hard, do the right things, and God will like you." These are *works*-based religions. Christianity stands alone in believing that *works* have nothing to do with earning favor from God. No amount of good *works* done by a person changes how God loves him. Nothing can be accomplished that will make God love him more, and no lack of good *works* will make God love him less. Christians believe that faith in Jesus is the only requirement for being accepted by God. Ephesians 2:8-9 says, "by grace you have been saved through faith; and that not of yourselves it is the gift of God; not as a result of *works*, that no one should boast."

(2) One cannot earn a ticket to heaven by *works*, however that idea is balanced by James 2:17 which says, "faith, if it has no *works*, is dead, being by itself." Christians believe that faith that does not result in doing good things (*works*) is not the kind of faith that God sees as "saving faith," (faith that can forgive all wrongs and restore relationship with God). Real faith is accompanied by *works*. Ephesians 2:10 states, "we are...created in Christ Jesus for good *works*, which God prepared beforehand so that we would walk in them." Jesus tells His disciples, "Let your light shine before men in such a way that they may see your good *works*, and glorify your Gather who is in heaven" (Matthew 5:16).

    Christians do not give up on trying to be good. Christians work hard at doing good, but not in the expectation of getting to heaven as a reward. Christians are good because they love God, God is good, and God dwells within them. The *works* are a result of faith. Things like love, joy, peace, patience, kindness, and self control are called the "fruit of the Spirit" (Galatians 5:22-23). God living within believers results in goodness and in considering the needs of others as more important than self-interests. This is why the vast majority of free medical clinics, doing good in the poorest countries of the world, are set up by Christians. No other religion comes close to providing as much merciful assistance as Christians, if just measured by the good things they do. Christians do *works*, but the reason for *working* is not to deserve God's love. Christians do *works* because they <u>have</u> God's love, not to earn it. Christians get God's love by believing that He sent Jesus, as an act of love, to give eternal life, love, and forgiveness.

<u>World</u>: the natural social system that is driven by selfishness (pride ambition or greed). Christians speak of the *world* in that manner rather than as a matter of geography. When Christians talk about the *world* they mean the way things tend to happen in this *world* where they live. In the *world* there is more deception than truth, more greed than generosity, more hate and disrespect than love, more war than real peace.

That's the *world;* things are unfair, unjust, uncaring, and the supply always falls short of the need. Christians understand that the reason things are so messed up is because the ruler of this *world* is the devil. 1 John 5:19 says, "we know that we are of God, and that the whole *world* lies in the power of the evil one [the devil]."

Christians take seriously that they are not to love the *world* nor the things in the *world*. 1 John 2:15-16 says, "all that is in the *world*, the lust of the flesh, and the lust of the eyes and the boastful pride of life, is not from the Father, but is from the *world*."

So this *world* is offering up a whole menu of things that Christians know are in opposition to the direction they want to take. Christians desire to live lives of righteousness, peace, joy, love, patience, kindness, faithfulness, and self-control. The *world* and its system presses for materialism, greed, power, fame, and everything that satisfies selfish desires. The *world* is seen by Christians as something that must be overcome, and is being overcome. 1 John 5:5 says, "... who is the one who overcomes the *world*, but he who believes that Jesus is the Son of God?" And 1 John 4:4 says, "...greater is He [Jesus] who is in you then he [Satan] who is in the *world*."

Worldly: any influence that is not directly from God. If Christians say something seems *worldly*, that means its source is not God. Its source is either the spirit of man or Satan. A *worldly* book, for example, is probably not written by a Christian, doesn't have subject matter that inspires the reader to get to know God, or behave in a manner that Jesus would have taught.

The contrast between *worldly* values and Christian values is very clear: the world promotes pride, ambition, bodily appetites, and aggression; Jesus (and Christians) promote humility, patience, self-control, and meekness. The world promotes, "go for the fun," and Jesus promotes wisdom about what is joyful. The world promotes "get all you can" (money, power, and material things).

Jesus promotes radical giving, allowing God to be the provider, and being content with what one has. The world says, "Morality is an old-fashioned idea; do whatever you want, if it feels good." Jesus says abundant life is included in a life style of keeping God's moral laws.

So, serious Christians avoid *worldly* influence. This can take many forms: church attendance, often home-schooling or enrolling children in Christian schools, and avoiding the *worldly* hotspots. Balancing that, Christians also remember Jesus' prayer for them that they would be in the *world* but not of the *world*. Jesus prays to God saying, "As You have sent Me into the *world*, I also have sent them into the *world*" (John 17:18). Christians say, "We are strangers in a strange land." They know heaven as their eventual home and feel quite out of place in this *world*, but they also know that the purpose of their being in the *world* is to bring the influence of heaven to the *world*.

Worship: the believer's response of love to the recognized presence of God. *Worship* of Jesus Christ is part of what defines Christians. *Worship*, as a practice, is not primarily a physical activity, like singing, dancing, playing music, or bowing down. It is possible to be doing all those things and not actually be *worshiping*. *Worship* is primarily a spiritual activity. It is a response of the heart in love because God first loved the believer (1 John 4:19). Jesus says that, "true *worshipers* will *worship* the Father in spirit and truth," (John 4:23).

Worship is surrender to God, adoring God, recognizing and declaring God's absolute worthiness using song, dance, shouting, lying face-down on the floor, or any other means of expressing the wonder of being with God. By *worshiping*, Christians become more like the One they worship; they find holiness.

Every individual is radically influenced by who or what he or she chooses to *worship*. *Worship* is at the center of all religions.

Cultures, languages, and laws of entire countries are shaped by what the people of those countries choose to *worship*.

Christians will ask, "Where do you *worship*?" That means, "Where do you go to church?" Or they will call a church building a "place of *worship*." Or they will call churchgoers "*worshipers*." Sunday church gatherings are called *worship* services because that is be the main thing that happens at that time, an opportunity to *worship* God together.

Wrath: the anger of God. When Christians use this word, it is usually reserved for talking about God's anger, God's *wrath*. The Bible makes clear many times that God has the capability of becoming angry. (Two examples may be found in Deuteronomy 9:18-20, and John 3:36.) It is written in the Bible that many times in the past God's *wrath* has come upon certain people. Sometimes it was expressed upon God's people, the Israelites, because they were rebellious, and sometimes upon other peoples, for various reasons, usually because they opposed God or the people of God. It is also written that there is a "*wrath* to come" (Matthew 3:7). God is not yet done with being angry, but there will be a day when it is finished. This general *wrath* of God will be poured out in what is called the *Day of God, the final judgment. Revelation 15:1 begins the explanation of how the *wrath* of God is to be finished. "Seven golden bowls full of the *wrath* of God" are to be poured out; then God's *wrath* will be finished. He will be finished with being angry, however there will be no end to His love. It is also clear that it is "Jesus who rescues us from the *wrath* to come" (1 Thessalonians 1:9-10).

Some people see God as generally angry. Others see him only as the gentle Jesus carrying a woolly little lamb on his shoulders, and never angry. Neither of these views is biblical nor what is generally believed by most Christians. There is a *wrath*, the anger of God. God's *wrath* is usually against unbelief, whether it is His people who don't trust Him, or those who have refused to believe (Romans 1:18-23).

Jesus Himself got angry. He was angry with religious people who were getting in the way of non-Jewish people who came to the temple to seek God and worship. There was an area of the Temple that God had designated as a place of worship for non-Jews. Religious authorities had taken over the area for selling animals to sacrifice, and Jesus angrily removed them because they hindered those worshipers (Mark 11:15-17).

Christians believe that they are delivered from God's *wrath* through believing in Jesus. They will not have to experience His *wrath*. Those who refuse to believe in Jesus will experience separation from God forever and torment (God's *wrath*) in hell. If Christians do have to suffer at the hands of people who kill or persecute them, that is not God's *wrath*, in fact, that kind of suffering is filled with the nearness and support of God, and much favor is given to those who are killed for the name of Jesus. See *martyr. (Revelation 6:9-11)

Yahweh: the English pronunciation of the original name of God in the Hebrew language. Christians will sometimes use this name of God. It was (and still is) the most sacred name of God to the people of God, the Jews. God first told Moses this name and it means, "I am" (Exodus 3:13-14). God's most sacred name translates to "I am." Jesus got into trouble with the religious authorities because He used the name "I am" for Himself (John 8:58). The religious authorities knew He was saying that He was God, and they did not believe in Him as the Son of God. Those who did recognize Him and receive Him as the "I am" were the first Christians.

In the original Hebrew language this name is spelled without vowels, "*yhwh*," so it is basically unpronounceable. And that was okay because it was so sacred that the Jews refused to say the name out-loud anyway. Christians do not share the Jewish idea that the name of God is too sacred to be spoken. There are no biblical grounds for fearfully avoiding speaking the name of God. Christians joyfully say this name with gladness that they know His most personal name.

Over the years it has come to be pronounced by Christians as, *yahweh*, or as "Yehovah," or as "Jehovah." Some Christians in various parts of the world call God "Yah," or, "Jah," short for "Yahweh." The point of having a name is to try to be clear who is being named as God, since there are many false gods that have names too. In Psalm 91:14, God says, "I will set him securely on high, because he has known My name." It is important to know the correct name of the One that is worshiped.

Yoke: a spiritual burden. Literally, a *yoke* is that wooden frame that is put over the heads of beasts of burden when they are pulling a plow or a wagon. The animals pull against the *yoke*, bearing the constant weight of whatever is being pulled along. To Christians, a *yoke* represents the burden of faith. Jesus teaches that the burden of faith in Him should not be heavy and unbearable. The burdens of other belief systems (*religions) can be unbearable. The burden of carrying guilt and shame can be unbearable. In Matthew 11:28 Jesus says, "Come to Me all who are weary and heavy laden, and I will give you rest. Take My *yoke* upon you and learn from Me, for I am gentle and humble in heart, and you shall find rest for your souls. For my *yoke* is easy and my burden is light." Christians believe that although the burden of faith in Jesus is real, it is much lighter than the burden of carrying on in life without God, or worshiping false gods, or living a life in guilt and shame because of doing wrong all the time.

Another *yoke* that Christians talk about is from a Bible passage about marriage, saying that a Christian should only marry a Christian because they would be "unequally *yoked*" if married to one who does not carry the same *yoke* of faith. (2 Corinthians 6:14 in the *King James Version uses the term "unequally yoked.") Many Christians will expand that to include business partners. The *yoke* of faith in Jesus changes so much about the way one walks through all of life.

Another heavy *yoke* that the Bible talks about is the *yoke* that Jesus breaks off, and that is the yoke of the guilt of Satan, the weight of oppression, the accusations, the temptations, and the condemnation. Isaiah 9:1-7 predicts (700 years before Jesus) what He would do when He came, and it says that He would "break the *yoke* of their burden" speaking of all of the burdens people might carry before taking up the *yoke* of Jesus.

Christians also usually come to understand that a *yoke* is built for two beasts to pull it, so when Jesus says, "take My *yoke* upon you," that means He is on the other side pulling with the believer, the ideal partner, helping to bear the load.

Zion: God's dwelling place. *Zion* was the original name of a rocky ridge that was a natural fortress on the hill where the city of Jerusalem stands today. Jerusalem was built on that mountain ridge and *Zion* has come to be one of the names for Jerusalem, and for the place of worship that was there because He chose it as His resting place (Psalm 132:13-14). The Bible says that *Zion* is the place the entire world will stream to in order to know God, and out of *Zion* the word of the Lord will go out to all of the world. (This is in Isaiah 2:1-3.) Christian scholars believe that the Christian church is the present day spiritual *Zion*, fulfilling those roles written about in Isaiah: out of the church flows the knowledge of God to the whole earth, and to the church all nations will come in order to learn God's ways. "Out of *Zion*, the perfection of beauty God has shone forth" (Psalm 50:2).

Another meaning of *Zion* is the heavenly Jerusalem (Hebrews 12:22-24 and Revelation 21) which will ultimately replace the earthly *Zion* when God has finished with the final judgment, and history has come to a close at the end of the age. This New Jerusalem is described as a place of splendor, and the eternal dwelling place of God and the eternal destiny of those who have believed in Jesus. God's presence will be there, and all of the inhabitants will see His face and experience His light continually; there will be no more darkness, forever.

www.ingramcontent.com/pod-product-compliance
Lightning Source LLC
Chambersburg PA
CBHW061423040426
42450CB00007B/881